HISTORY OF BROADCASTING: RADIO TO TELEVISION

HISTORY OF BROADCASTING: Radio to Television

The American Radio

A Report on the Broadcasting Industry
in the United States from
The Commission on Freedom of the Press

LLEWELLYN WHITE

ARNO PRESS and THE NEW YORK TIMES

New York • 1971

Reprint Edition 1971 by Arno Press Inc.

© 1947 by The University of Chicago Press
Reprinted by permission of The University of Chicago Press

Reprinted from a copy in The Newark Public Library

LC# 70-161177
ISBN 0-405-03583-7

HISTORY OF BROADCASTING: RADIO TO TELEVISION
ISBN for complete set: 0-405-03555-1
See last pages of this volume for titles.

Manufactured in the United States of America

THE
AMERICAN RADIO

THE COMMISSION ON FREEDOM OF THE PRESS

BY LLEWELLYN WHITE

THE
AMERICAN RADIO

*A Report on the Broadcasting Industry in the
United States from The Commission
on Freedom of the Press*

THE UNIVERSITY OF CHICAGO PRESS
CHICAGO · ILLINOIS

The Commission on Freedom of the Press was created to consider the freedom, functions, and responsibilities of the major agencies of mass communication in our time: newspapers, radio, motion pictures, news-gathering media, magazines, books.

The Commission is operating under a grant of funds made by Time, Inc., and Encyclopaedia Britannica, Inc., to the University of Chicago. The University administers the funds, but neither it nor the donors have any jurisdiction over the Commission, which is a nongovernmental, independent group containing no members of the press, radio, or motion picture industries.

In addition to its general report, the Commission has published, or will publish, a number of special studies. The present study was prepared by Mr. Llewellyn White of the Commission staff. The Commission publishes herewith its specific recommendations with reference to the radio industry. It does not undertake to pass upon the proposals or conclusions of Mr. White but presents them for public discussion and the serious consideration of the persons and agencies framing policy in this field.

The University of Chicago Press · Chicago 37
Agent: Cambridge University Press · London

STATEMENT BY THE COMMISSION

RADIO broadcasting is an essential part of the modern press. It shares the same functions and encounters the same problems as the older agencies of mass communication. On the other hand, radio exhibits significant differences. Its ability to draw millions of citizens into close and simultaneous contact with leaders and with events of the moment gives it a reach and an influence of peculiar importance in the management of public affairs.

There are also differences with regard to its support and its control. Like newspapers and magazines, broadcasting is supported by advertising; but, for broadcasting in the United States at present, advertising is practically the sole support, and advertisers play a role in determining what is furnished the public that is exceptional in other agencies of the press.

Unlike the other instruments of the press also, radio stations gain and retain their right to do business by periodic license from a federal regulatory agency. This agency is commissioned to exercise its licensing power in such a way as (1) to secure operations of broadcasting in the public interest, (2) to maintain radio broadcasting as a competitive industry, and (3) to refrain from censorship of radio programs.

The study which follows reveals that the unusual controls exercised by advertising on behalf of immediate commercial interest and at the expense of station program direction have, so far, been much more significant than the controls established by the government on behalf of the public interest. Government intervention has been carefully limited to avoid interference with free expression on public affairs; government license has not meant censorship. The power of continuous, specialized regulation has enabled the federal agency to establish and preserve a competitive structure. But public action to bring about the full employment of radio broadcasting in the interest of general enlightenment has as yet been both tentative and timid.

In such public service the radio industry itself has much accomplishment to its credit. Nevertheless, much more is required if radio is fully to meet the growing needs of the people for understanding. Three things are necessary: an effort by members of the industry itself, acting separately and collectively; appraisal of the radio by organized groups of citizens in local communities; and vigorous, but carefully limited, action by the federal administrative agency to promote the most effective service in the public interest.

To this end, we make the following recommendations:

1. We recommend that the Federal Communications Commission, in all grants of licenses—especially for the new FM, television, and broadcast facsimile services—and in its relicensing of the AM clear-channel stations capable of serving large areas, follow a policy which will extend these services, as far as is technically possible, to every village in the land.

2. We recommend that by license policy the F.C.C. provide, as far as possible, local facilities for adequate broadcasting of local news and discussion of public issues, in communities of such size as to need the radio for these purposes, and that local groups of citizens explore the possibilities of creating and supporting such a service of mass communication in communities not now separately provided with one.

3. We recommend that the F.C.C. maintain its policy of providing for diversity and competition in station ownership by prohibiting (a) dual ownership of station facilities offering the same type of service in any community, (b) dual ownership of networks, and (c) network ownership or control of individual radio stations in excess of reasonable

needs of networks for originating programs and for extension of service to remote areas; further, that the F.C.C. explore all possible means of reducing those barriers which may prevent new groups from owning stations: i.e., by inflated purchase price, by unnecessarily high line communication charges, by rules against transcriptions and recordings, and by restrictive provisions in station affiliation with networks.

4. We recommend that further diversity and expansion of radio service by the development of noncommercial or self-supporting stations under the sponsorship of educational institutions, foundations, and state and local governments be encouraged in every practicable way; that the F.C.C. continue to reserve radio frequencies for such use; and that educational institutions seek to organize their separate facilities into combined educational networks.

5. We recommend that the radio networks, radio stations, the National Association of Broadcasters, and the organizations of writers, directors, and commentators, jointly or severally, establish the practice of separation of advertising from programs (this not to prevent the selling and programming of unrelated advertising announcements preceding or following programs). If the industry or its agencies fail to assume this responsibility within a reasonable

time, we recommend that the F.C.C. set up this separation as a regulation or standard of performance to be considered in the license or relicense of stations.

6. We recommend that the industry seek effective means of improving the quality of radio programs and of achieving proper program balance. To this end it should act through its own organized associations and publications, as well as through other agencies of the press, to encourage honest, expert criticism and the publicizing and pooling of information regarding instances of good performance in the public interest. We recommend especially that efforts be made to provide, generally, programs at good listening hours dealing with public issues and prepared with the best professional skill, and local programs adequate for local needs.

7. We recommend that the radio listeners in each community, in the various regions, and in the country as a whole organize to criticize and to evaluate the specific radio services they receive, to define additional radio services they desire, and to serve as advisory aids to the official representatives of the public in their necessary judgments as between rival claimants for the use of scarce radio frequencies.

8. We recommend that, in order to establish radio, television, and facsimile broadcasting clearly

within the meaning of the term "press" as protected by the First Amendment, the industry appeal to the courts any actual cases of interference by government with freedom of expression on public affairs via radio, and that the F.C.C. co-operate in making such appeals possible.

This recommendation would give constitutional support to the prohibition against censorship in the Communications Act. It would not prevent the F.C.C. from denying a license on the ground that the applicant was unprepared to serve the public interest, convenience, and necessity. Nor would it prevent the Commission from considering, in connection with an application for renewal, whether the applicant had kept the promises he had made when the license was granted and had actually served the public interest, convenience, and necessity. This recommendation is intended to strengthen the prohibition against censorship, not to guarantee licensees a perpetual franchise regardless of their performance. The air belongs to the public, not to the radio industry.

The establishment of these various lines of responsibility and control within the framework of free expression and widely distributed initiative are the more urgent because of impending technological development in television and facsimile. Together, these newer instruments mean that radio, as much as, or more than, the printing press, may eventually become the chief medium for distributing words, images, and ideas in our society. Freedom and accountability must represent the joint achievement of the industry, of community groups, and of government, acting in proper relation to one another.

ROBERT M. HUTCHINS   ARCHIBALD MACLEISH
ZECHARIAH CHAFEE, JR. CHARLES E. MERRIAM
JOHN M. CLARK   REINHOLD NIEBUHR
JOHN DICKINSON   ROBERT REDFIELD
WILLIAM E. HOCKING   ARTHUR M. SCHLESINGER
HAROLD D. LASSWELL   GEORGE N. SHUSTER

[NOTE.—Because of his official connection with the broadcasting industry as a director of Station WOR, Beardsley Ruml is not signing this statement. His action is without prejudice to the Commission's conclusions and recommendations or to those contained in the ensuing volume by Mr. Llewellyn White.]

xi

TABLE OF CONTENTS

xiii

xvi

xvii

1

THE PROBLEM

SCIENTISTS of Renaissance Europe knew that the air was filled with waves upon which light and sound traveled. In the latter part of the nineteenth century, men discovered that deliberately planned sounds and images could be carried by these waves in such a way that they would be faithfully reproduced over distances beyond the range of the human eye and ear. It remained for the experimenters of the twentieth century to create devices to carry, first characters and then the sounds of the human voice, whole printed pages, and photographs, around the globe with the speed of light.

Today man is opening a third dimension of communication: radiation through the ether of natural motion in natural colors. Halfway through the atomic century and only a generation removed from the first crude broadcast of Marconi's "peep-peep-peep" code signals, the world citizen is physically able to drop in on any one of his two billion neighbors with less effort than that formerly required to call on the Smiths next door.

So much man has accomplished. As he faces the future, he holds in one hand the key to universal understanding, in the other a fragment of nuclear energy so awesomely destructive that none would dare to loose it, save through misunderstanding. History will record how man reacts to this providential coincidence.

Neither the opportunist, measuring radio in terms of personal profit, nor the intellectual snob, resentful of all mass communication as an invasion of his little world of literate discourse, can deny that the innocent-looking boxes in two hundred million homes have become a powerful force—for advancement or for destruction.

What began within the lifetimes of most of us as an amateur's hobby has become a cornerstone of communication in our society. It needs to be studied with the long view. The world of tomorrow will not be the world that heard Dr. Frank Conrad broadcast the Harding-Cox election returns or even the world which, in the 1940's, smiled wonderingly over reports of the first successful transmission of television in color. The context, as well as the problem, has changed.

THE CONTEXT

No study of mass communication undertaken after July, 1945, could fail to take account of the impact of the atomic bomb upon all human intercourse. In an age in which anything short of the maximum of considered, intelligent human behavior may lead to the destruction of civilization, the historic concepts of the proper functions and minimal responsibilities of all those who shape the world citizen's thinking must be sharply re-examined.

Already men are flinching from that task. Already it has become the fashion to say, "Yes, the A-bomb makes education for survival an urgent priority; but it is not *our* responsibility." Thus the motion picture producer begs off with "We are an entertainment medium; let radio educate the people." The broadcaster retorts: "We, too, are primarily an entertainment medium; let the newspapers do it." The newspaper publisher complains that "we cannot fill our columns with dull stuff; what are the magazines for?" The magazine editor asks: "What are books for?" The book publisher turns accusingly to the schools with "You don't expect us to make up for the educators' deficiencies, do you?" The college president takes refuge in "What can we do with youngsters whose parents have failed them?" Parents blame the church, and the preachers castigate the movies, thus completing the sorry circle.

What is clearly indicated is a total effort to preserve and to develop that capacity for reasoned judgment and action which has marked man apart from the lower animals and which now is his surest and perhaps his only defense against self-destruction—a total effort far beyond anything man has yet put forth, a co-ordinated campaign from which no soldier, however humble, can be excused. Least of all can any of the media of mass communication be excused; for now, more than ever, they have special responsibilities toward society.

It seems reasonable to assume that more persons read books than complete their eight years of grammar school; that more persons read magazines than read books; that more persons read newspapers than read magazines; that more persons see whole motion pictures than read whole newspapers; and that more persons listen to the radio than attend movies. Many persons have had little or no constructive parental guidance, little or no inspiring church influence, little or no direct contact with the other leaders in the community. It is apparent, therefore, that the media of mass communication can and do reach citizens who can be reached in no other way.

Moreover, less than a third of the average citizen's life is passed under the direct influence of home and school. During the adult three-quarters of his span, he must face and form judgments upon issues for which the influences of youth can only partially have prepared him. In the many complex fields outside his ken, yet directly affecting his way of life, he needs

3

the benefit of expert judgments and of that rare interpretive genius which can reduce the most abstruse technical jargon to layman's language. It is equally apparent, therefore, that the most heroic efforts of parents, teachers, preachers, and other community leaders may avail little if the media of mass communication shirk their peculiar responsibilities.

THE NEWEST SOLDIER

Must radio bear a disproportionate share of these peculiar responsibilities that cannot be delegated to any other agency in our society? Is it more—or less—responsible for educating citizens for survival than, say, the newspaper press? Before one can answer that question, he must examine carefully the significant characteristics of radio.

In varying degree all the media—newspapers, magazines, books, radio, and motion pictures—are vehicles for entertainment, information, education, and advertising. All are profit-seeking private enterprises, which, for the most part, have voluntarily assumed certain "public service" aspects. All are marked by keen competition for mass circulation, with the natural consequence that they tend to place the emphasis on entertainment and often to avoid controversy. Like book publishers, motion picture producers, and the more enlightened magazines and newspapers, broadcasters have voluntarily accepted (though by no means always discharged) a responsibility for presenting diverse viewpoints rather than the single viewpoint of the owner. As with the movies (and, to an alarmingly increasing extent, the newspapers and magazines also), radio does not differentiate between different types of audiences but is rather an omnibus medium.

It has been said that radio is unique in that it is the only medium in which the advertisers prepare the "reading matter." It is true that the advertiser has taken over the radio to

4

an extent he would scarcely dare attempt, today, with the other media. But that situation could be corrected.

The important thing is that radio has permanently and inescapably unique characteristics that cannot be changed. It cannot separate the advertising and "reading matter" of the air in such a way as to spare the consumer the necessity of listening to the former. It is obliged to employ a circulation medium which the Congress has declared belongs to the people and which is so limited physically as to introduce into the contest for the public's ear factors other than the usual economic ones. Finally, and perhaps most important, it reaches more people than does any other medium, and always will.

To state that last simple fact is to lift the whole question of the broadcasters' responsibility in the atomic age above the level of physical accident. Not as a sullen small boy fleeing the rod of government regulation but as a giant who has bested all rivals for the honor, must radio lead us to a more peaceful, orderly world.

Is radio leading? Before the author attempts to answer that question fairly and constructively, he owes it to the broadcasters to reveal the yardstick by which he has measured their effort.

THE YARDSTICK

In its general report, *A Free and Responsible Press*, the Commission on Freedom of the Press[1] undertakes to define the task for all the media of mass communication:

Today our society needs, first, a truthful, comprehensive, and intelligent account of the day's events in a context which gives them meaning; second, a forum for the exchange of comment and criticism; third, a means of projecting the opinions and attitudes

[1] The word "press" as used in all Commission documents is meant to embrace newspapers, magazines, books, radio, and movies.

of the groups in the society to one another; fourth, a method of presenting and clarifying the goals and values of the society; and, fifth, a way of reaching every member of the society by the currents of information, thought, and feeling which the press supplies.

This states the problem in very general terms. It is unlikely that one would find in the United States fifty broadcasters disposed to take exception to a single statement. Yet it is precisely this sort of sweeping "call to duty" that alarms broadcasters (and publishers and motion picture producers). For it is perfectly true, as they say, that the same phrases have been used over and over again as a springboard for the advocacy of all manner of "reforms" and pet schemes.

"Why, you could put together almost any kind of 'yardstick,' as you call it, out of that statement," a network executive who had read it commented. "Government operation. The Canadian system (which is part government, part private). The elimination of advertising altogether. An anti-monopoly witch-hunt. Government censorship of programs. The junking of everything but news, commentary, and discussion."

It should be said at once, then, that this report advocates none of these things. It should be said that the "yardstick" has been fashioned entirely out of existing parts—things American broadcasters already are doing on a commercial basis, wholly within the bounds of the free-enterprise system and the First Amendment.

What are some of these things that American broadcasters are already doing? The author does not propose either to name them all or to cite a few. To attempt the first would require several years of traveling about the country listening to some forty thousand programs broadcast in the course of a year by more than a thousand stations. Short of a veritable army of researchers, such a task could not even be completed within the lifetimes of the programs under scrutiny. On the other hand, to prepare a "selective" list would be to court the protests not only of the slighted broadcasters but of everyone else who differed with the author's judgment. One who proposed to question the validity for sixty million persons of the seven-times-one-man judgments of the Federal Communications Commission would hardly wish to commit the same error.

But there is, in the author's view, an even better reason for not citing programs and stations by name. That is that it is both unnecessary and misleading—unnecessary because the conscientious broadcaster already knows "good" from "bad" (else he would not know how to get out a promotion brochure), and misleading because one man's meat may very well be another's poison.

No two broadcasters have quite the same problem, or quite the same responsibilities. A man with a little 250-watt local station in an agricultural community may not have to worry so much about diversity of interest as a man who broadcasts from a 50-kilowatt clear-channel station to city-dwellers, miners, dairy farmers, automobile workers, and small-town folk. A network's responsibility toward residents of New York City, who can tune in the other three chains and nearly a score of independent stations, will not be the same as its responsibility toward the thousands who must depend upon it for the only radio fare they get.

It is perfectly true, as has often been remarked, that it is simple arithmetic to say that, if the hours from 6:00 to 11:00 P.M.—the only weekday hours when 75 per cent of the voters can listen to the radio—are packed night after night with one variety, comedy, popular music, and silly audience-showoff program after another, there will be no time left for anything calculated to help the citizen win his battle for survival. But

7

that is not to say that all the broadcasters' problems can be reduced to simple mathematics: so many hours of "entertainment" and so many of "education." In a medium that has learned so well how to make "entertainment" educational and "education" entertaining, the attempt to allocate hours to these two forms always seems to the author a little silly.

Nothing, perhaps, has done more to confuse the layman's (and the broadcaster's and the government official's) thinking about radio than this business of labeling and categorizing. Thus, just as all religionists are thought to be "religious," moronic daytime serials as entitled to the designation "drama" as the rare performances of the theater's truly great, and anyone with a "sweet horn" as much a "musician" as Arturo Toscanini, so all "comedy" is "comedy," and anything with a box-top is a "children's show."

No reasonable person would wish to see "popular" music displaced altogether by the symphonic classics, or the comedians engrossed in debate over the United Nations veto principle. The broadcaster's familiar plaint that his critics wish to suppress the entertainment side of radio is a red herring. What is wanted is *better* comedy, and better through-the-week, choice-listening-hour balance between comedy and certain other things.

Moreover, it must be obvious to us all that the citizen requires a somewhat larger ratio of red meat to pastry than even he realizes. This is something the listener surveys do not show but which every alert broadcaster knows, just the same. Perhaps the alert broadcaster hides behind the meaningless (except to advertisers) decimal points of these surveys because knowing carries with it a responsibility to do something about the situation—for example, to present "educational" material with all the care and expense that goes into the enter-

8

tainment shows, so that people will listen, instead of just turning a little time over to the local pastor or high-school principal.

One of the challenging things about the information business today is that what every world citizen needs to know has grown so enormously in sheer volume and in complexity that the purveyors of information are confronted with a task of condensing and simplifying and explaining never dreamed of in the days of John Peter Zenger. The print press, with its Sunday review-of-the-week sections and its news magazines, is beginning to meet the challenge. It is high time the broadcasters did, not only for the sake of their own prestige but also for the sake of the fifty million adult Americans who do not read Sunday review-of-the-week sections or news magazines.

The author's "yardstick," then, is simply this: Let the broadcasters, of their own volition, contribute more that is "plus" in terms of the five goals of the Commission on Freedom of the Press; and let them, realizing that not everything that is not "plus" is by that token "neutral," eliminate those "minuses" which have the effect of cheapening the goals and values of our society.

What does this boil down to? It may well reduce itself to nothing more complicated than for the better broadcasters to devise effective means of preventing the frustration of their purposes by any of the frustrating forces that have surrounded them for twenty years. It might involve nothing more revolutionary than the emancipation of broadcasting from the overseership of advertising, the writing of a set of standards for the industry which would reflect the practices of its best practitioners rather than some common denominator, and effective measures to insure the observance of the standards. Certain it is that, if a "yardstick" of satisfactory performance can be fashioned out of existing performance, the solution need not be sought in a drastic change of systems, or even in a bold extension of governmental authority.

In a context of democratic thought which appears to be swinging away from governmental checks, the solution may have to be worked out between the industry and the listening public. Let the broadcaster, then, since he must make the first move and since in any case his primary role is that of world citizen, consult his conscience. But let him not consult it in the complacent atmosphere of an air-conditioned office or apartment in Manhattan or Beverly Hills or Lake Forest. Let him, rather, retire for one solid week to the woods and there, locked in a cabin, without newspapers, magazines, or books, his only contact with the outside world a cheap four-tube portable radio on which he can get only one station (preferably his own), simulate the conditions under which many of his customers live, week in and week out.

2

MARCONI'S MARVEL

A NEW field of science and industry was opened in 1895 when Guglielmo Marconi succeeded in transmitting a message by wireless across his father's Bolognese estate. Two years later the enterprising young Italian organized a British company for wireless point-to-point and ship-to-shore communication. In 1899 this company, later known as the Marconi Wireless Telegraph Company, Ltd., incorporated an American subsidiary.

Meanwhile, other inventors were striving to transmit the sounds of the human voice by wireless. In the United States, where the chief rivalry was between the Navy and the American Marconi Company, the first established successes in this direction were achieved by Reginald A. Fessenden and Dr. Lee De Forest, in each case about 1906. Their experiments first attracted wide attention when, on January 20, 1910, the sound of Enrico Caruso's magnificent tenor voice was broadcast from the stage of the Metropolitan Opera in New York.

By the end of World War I, General Electric had acquired the patents on the Alexanderson alternator; American Telephone & Telegraph had bought all the De Forest rights, including his audion tube; and Westinghouse had developed important new transmission equipment, all vitally important to the future of wireless, yet none complete without the others and without devices controlled by American Marconi. The infant industry faced a wasteful patent war, in which the British might come off winners.

11

To meet this threat, Navy Secretary Daniels proposed government ownership. The Army, the Navy "brass," and a majority in the Congress opposed such a step, but they agreed that the patents should be secured to the United States. Owen D. Young, chairman of the board of General Electric, had a solution: Let the three American firms directly involved pool their resources and buy out American Marconi. Pursuant to Young's suggestion, on October 17, 1919, the Radio Corporation of America (R.C.A.) was formed.

But while the new R.C.A. set about building the world's largest and most powerful wireless station at Port Jefferson, New York, to step up American participation in the expanding point-to-point dot-dash news and private-message market then beginning to parallel that of the cables, Dr. Frank Conrad, of Westinghouse, and other quasi-amateurs[1] relentlessly pursued the elusive goal of voice broadcasting. As early as 1919, Conrad had begun amusing a few friends by playing phonograph records in his garage in East Pittsburgh, Pennsylvania, and broadcasting them from a homemade antenna. Soon a Pittsburgh department store was urging its customers to join the charmed circle by purchasing the crude Westinghouse-made crystal sets which it had in stock. To Westinghouse Vice-president H. P. Davis this was an omen: "If there is sufficient interest to justify a department store in advertising radio sets for sale on an uncertain plan of permanence, I believe there would be sufficient interest to justify the expense of rendering a regular service, looking to the sale of sets and the advertising of the Westinghouse Company for our returns."

[1] The lively and continuing controversy over who was the "first" broadcaster probably will never be definitely settled. Among KDKA rivals with equally impressive claims are WHA (Madison, Wisconsin); KQW (San Jose, California); and WWJ (Detroit).

On November 2, 1920, having sold a good many sets in anticipation of the event, Westinghouse broadcast from KDKA (Pittsburgh) the Harding-Cox election returns; and others were venturing. Commerce Secretary Hoover had designated 300 meters as the band in which anyone could try his hand at broadcasting if so licensed. By January 1, 1922, thirty licenses had been issued. Fourteen months later, no fewer than 556 broadcasting stations were making the ether crackle with strange sounds.

This tremendous expansion was due in no small part to the fact that the other members of the Big Three that had formed R.C.A. were catching the Davis fever. In 1922, R.C.A. became part owner of Westinghouse's WJZ (Newark, New Jersey), which, two years later, it took over entirely and moved to New York City. General Electric built WGY (Schenectady, New York); Westinghouse itself expanded to Chicago, Philadelphia, and Boston.

In that same year, A.T. & T. decided to withdraw from the R.C.A. consortium and erect two powerful broadcasting stations in New York, to be supported by leasing time to all who had wares to sell. On August 16, 1922, A.T. & T. opened WEAF for business as the first advertising-supported station in the world.

It soon became apparent, both to the station and to those sponsors with more than the New York metropolitan market in mind, that more outlets would bring more listeners, more sales, and higher tolls for the broadcaster. How could this be achieved? In 1921, KDKA, wishing to broadcast a church service, had called on the telephone company for a line to carry it from downtown Pittsburgh to the Westinghouse studio in East Pittsburgh. Encouraged by the results, WEAF brought the 1922 Chicago-Princeton football game from Stagg Field, Chicago, to New York. On January 4, 1923,

WEAF and WNAC (Boston) were linked for a special program lasting three and a quarter hours. During the following summer, Colonel Edward Green, who had built a station at Salter's Point, Massachusetts, but who had no programming facilities, made arrangements with A.T. & T. to connect him directly with WEAF by telephone long-lines. When A.T.&T.'s new Washington station, WCAP, was completed, it, too, was linked to WEAF. In October, 1923, WJAR (Providence) was admitted as the first "independent affiliate." By the end of 1924, A.T. & T. had added Worcester, Boston, Philadelphia, Pittsburgh, and Buffalo. Within another year, it was able to boast a chain of 26 stations, reaching as far west as Kansas City in what was to be known for many years as the "Red Network."

Unable to use its rival's telephone lines, R.C.A. countered as best it could by linking WGY, WJZ, and WRC (Washington) with Western Union and Postal Telegraph wires, which, because they had never been designed to carry the sound of the human voice or music, proved inferior. Fortunately for R.C.A., however, as we shall see in the next chapter, A.T. & T. by 1926 was eager to step out of broadcasting. In September of that year, the National Broadcasting Company was incorporated as a subsidiary of R.C.A., and two months later it acquired WEAF for $1,000,000. Thus the Red Network was added to that already launched by R.C.A., which came to be known as the "Blue Network." During the following year the Columbia chain came into being. Network broadcasting was firmly established by the turn of the depression decade.

Obliged for nearly twenty years to work within the standard broadcast band (550 to 1,500 and, after 1937, to 1,600 kilocycles), the engineers performed wonders. Range was increased by improvements in the location and structure of transmitters and by a gradual stepping-up of power from a few watts to 50,000 and more. Reception quality was raised by the substitution of vacuum-tube sets for the early crystal models and by refinements in the construction of microphones and studios. Interference was reduced by wider separation of the bands of contiguous stations and by the use of directional antennae to concentrate the impact of signals within specified arcs. A portion of the spectrum which some in the early twenties had thought would not accommodate 300 stations was made to support more than a thousand, 800 of them connected with one or another of four great national networks and/or some thirty regional chains.

SHORT-WAVE AND RADIO RELAY

For the engineers and laboratory technicians, however, standard aural broadcasting was only a beginning. A hundred times the width of the standard band lay above 1,600 kilocycles in the spectrum. They would explore it.

The basis of Marconi's work was laid by an Englishman named Clerk Maxwell, who, in 1864, formulated the mathematical equations governing all electromagnetic radiation (including light) and pointing to many then undiscovered forms of radiation. This gave rise to the modern idea of a scale or spectrum of electromagnetic radiation, ranged according to wave length, which includes radio waves, infrared and ultraviolet radiation, visible light, X-rays, gamma rays, and cosmic rays.

Radio waves, the existence of which had been postulated by Maxwell twenty years before, were first produced and detected in the laboratory by the German scientist, Heinrich Hertz, in 1888. When Marconi pioneered his application of radio for commercial purposes in 1895, he utilized frequencies in the region of 300 megacycles. These very high frequencies did not come into general use until forty years after Marconi's

15

early experiments and have been intensively developed only during the recent war. For long-distance work, Marconi and others dropped to the frequency band between 120 and 2,000 kilocycles. Indeed, in the early days of broadcasting, only the low, medium, and broadcast frequencies were considered important. (The division of the spectrum as we know it today runs roughly as follows: the portion below 100 kilocycles is referred to as "low"; 100–550 as "medium"; 550–1,600 as "broadcast"; 1,600–6,000 as "medium high"; 6,000–30,000 as "high"; 30,000–300,000 as "very high"; 300,000–3,000,000 as "ultra-high"; above 3,000,000 as "superhigh.")

When the broadcast band was fixed by law, the amateurs were pushed up into higher bands, which were thought to be valueless for commercial or government use. The "hams" proceeded to pay for what seemed at the time a discrimination by making important new discoveries, to be compared in importance with their discovery of aural broadcasting itself. Among the new vistas that they opened up during the 1920's and 1930's was short-wave international broadcasting.

After Westinghouse went into commercial broadcasting, Dr. Conrad, the "father" of KDKA, continued to experiment with his amateur station in East Pittsburgh, 8XK. After 8XK was moved into the higher bands, Conrad tinkered with the "useless" short waves and finally convinced Westinghouse that they might prove to be the answer to the problem of linking stations together for simultaneous broadcasting without benefit of the expensive telephone long-lines. In August, 1922, he built a short-wave transmitter adjoining KDKA. In March, 1923, a program was successfully transmitted from KDKA to KDPM (Cleveland). By July, Westinghouse was providing regular network broadcasts through radio relay.

As has so often been the case with radio experimentation,

altogether unlooked-for results were obtained. In August, 1923, KDKA's short-wave broadcasts were clearly received in England. London soon was rebroadcasting some of the programs over the British Broadcasting Corporation transmitters; and in February, 1924, Calcutta reported extraordinarily good reception. Searching for an explanation of the phenomenon, engineers discovered that the Heaviside layer[2] surrounding the earth apparently "reflected" the short waves, causing them to skip like flat stones on a millpond, striking the earth at certain intervals. As understanding increased of how to adjust frequencies to times of day and seasons, so as to control the interval of the arc, the band between 1,600 and 6,000 kilocycles was set aside for short-wave broadcasting, and amateurs everywhere developed the strengths and weaknesses of the marvelous new device. In the late thirties, N.B.C. and C.B.S. joined Westinghouse, General Electric, and the Crosley (now Aviation Corporation) interests in Cincinnati in experimenting with the commercial application of short-wave international broadcasting.

Meantime, attention had been diverted from Conrad's original application of short wave as a means of linking domestic stations; for, by the time the Westinghouse veteran had demonstrated that he was on the track of something promising, R.C.A. was committed to the use of A.T. & T.'s telephone long-lines for network interconnection. Moreover, the quality of the signal delivered by telephone wire could not be matched in the first fumbling experiments with radio relay. To the extent that anyone thought of the less favored areas which, for want of telephone long-lines or of a profitable advertising market or of both, were to go without adequate broadcasting service for a quarter-century, it was thought that these areas would be taken care of by "secondary" serv-

[2] So called for the Englishman of that name who discovered it.

17

ice, i.e., by being able to pick up the programs of powerful stations, 500–1,500 miles away. Hence, radio relay languished for twenty years in the laboratory.

The coming of frequency-modulation aural broadcasting, facsimile, and television has brought radio relay techniques out of the laboratory. Spurred by wartime developments, especially in the radar field, a number of companies, by the summer of 1946, were experimenting with relays in the very high frequencies.

Westinghouse had come forward with a novel principle called "stratovision," based on a number of airplanes flying continuous circle routes in the stratosphere, receiving signals from ground stations and relaying them to other pairs of planes and/or the ground, much as a tandem series of lawn sprinklers covers a large area. Press Wireless, Inc., a dot-dash and facsimile carrier limited by charter to the transmission of press intelligence to and from the North American continent, was seeking permission to transmit broadcasting programs by radio within the United States. Raytheon was developing radio relay in the "superhigh" frequencies. Du Mont was experimenting with the transmission of television programs on light beams. Nearly all the new systems being tried contemplated "multiplexing," or the simultaneous emission of aural, television, and facsimile signals.

Fully aware that their long-lines would not be adequate for television or, from a purely quantitative, geographical standpoint, for the expected increased traffic in all three types of modern broadcasting, the A.T. & T. fitted two strings to its bow. While experimenting with various types of radio relay, including an adaptation to broadcasting of its "mobile-highways" plan for telephonic service to moving vehicles, the telephone company appeared to be placing its greatest reliance on underground coaxial cables, which were capable of carrying

18

several-score telephone, aural broadcasting, television, and/or facsimile messages simultaneously. Because it required the new cables in any event for its expanding telephone traffic, the A.T. & T. was not waiting for the results of its tests to determine which of the two systems would be cheaper to instal and operate, more readily installed, and calculated to give the most reliable service: as of the close of 1946, it had put into operation a coaxial cable linking New York and Washington and was better than halfway to the Pacific Coast with the first transcontinental span. For the sixty million radio listeners standing on the threshold of FM, television, and facsimile, the answer to the question, "Which is the better system?" had perhaps a greater urgency.

Another interesting development which may enlarge the horizons of radio is called "pulse-time" modulation, or PM, a product of the Federal Laboratories, a subsidiary of the International Telephone & Telegraph Corporation. By using a "scanning" ray inside a special cathode-ray tube, which revolves much like a lighthouse beam, except that its rate is eight thousand times per second, Federal has been able to transmit up to twenty-four telephone conversations simultaneously and hopes to be able to transmit that many radio programs on a channel less than twenty-four times as wide as the normal broadcasting one, thus perhaps opening the door to more broadcasting stations in a given area.

FREQUENCY MODULATION

Radio waves, like all electromagnetic radiations, have a common speed, the speed of light—300,000,000 meters per second. However, they are distinguished by three measurements: "amplitude," the height of a wave from trough to crest; "wave length," the distance from crest to crest of successive waves; and "frequency," the number of occurrences of an entire wave in some given period of time, usually 1 second. These occurrences are called "cycles," and frequencies are therefore measured in cycles per second, often loosely referred to simply as "cycles." When the number of cycles is very large, they are reckoned in thousands, or kilocycles; when the number is even larger, they are counted in millions, or megacycles.

Since the speed of all radio waves is the same, when the rate or frequency gets higher, the wave length gets shorter; for, if more waves going at the same speed have to pass a given point in a second, they must be crowded more closely together. Once the speed of transmission (300,000,000 meters per second) is known, it is easy to convert frequency into wave length (and vice versa) by remembering that frequency in cycles *times* wave length in meters must always equal 300,000,000. Thus 30 meters equals 10,000,000 cycles (10 megacycles), and 1,500 kilocycles equals 200 meters. In short, wave length and frequency are interchangeable terms, and one is left with only two variables: amplitude and wave length/frequency.

The difference between amplitude-modulation (AM) and frequency-modulation (FM) transmission can be very simply explained, although at some expense to scientific precision. Each radio transmitter puts out what is called a "carrier wave" of the frequency listed for it in the F.C.C. allocations. (This is the frequency printed on radio-set dials and listed at the top of newspaper radio-program logs.) The carrier wave is a true carrier of information; for on it is superimposed a form of change, called "modulation," which represents the variations in the sound as it strikes the studio microphone. The type of modulation used by so-called "standard" broadcasting stations is called "amplitude modulation" because in it the amplitude, or height of the carrier waves from trough to crest, is varied.

In the late 1920's, however, engineers began to experiment with other possible variables, and they found that, by varying the frequency of the carrier to correspond with the original studio sound, while keeping the amplitude constant, they gained several significant advantages. Notable among these was the virtual elimination of "static," the random radio noise produced by thunderstorms, some home appliances, and other electrical disturbers of the peace. This unwanted noise is in itself an amplitude-modulated signal. Therefore, it passes through an ordinary AM receiver along with the wanted broadcast signal. But the FM receiver is unresponsive to amplitude-modulated signals.

Frequency modulation requires a much larger bite out of the radio spectrum to convey its intelligence than does AM, and this makes it impossible to transmit FM on the tightly packed broadcast band. But this seeming disadvantage was turned into a blessing when FM settled in the huge spaces of the frequency spectrum among the higher megacycles. Here, at least for a time, there was room for all comers, and the engineers were able to provide for the carrier wave to be modulated by a much wider range of sound frequencies than could be squeezed into the broadcast band. Thus, for the first time, the vital upper ranges of musical instruments could be faithfully reproduced on a commercial system.[3]

These striking advantages—freedom from static and faithfulness of tonal rendition—appeared to those interested in network broadcasting, and particularly to those possessing long-range clear-channel stations, to be outweighed by a cramping limitation of FM: i.e., the range of a station is limited in practice to the distance of the horizon as seen from the transmitting antenna, much as if the antenna were a light-

[3] Some engineers argue that it is the higher frequency and wider band rather than the difference in modulation that accounts for FM's superiority.

house whose rays would not carry around the curvature of the earth. This limited range of 30–40 miles seemed to spell the death of commercially sponsored network radio; and FM was therefore firmly told to stay in the laboratory and was dismissed by most radio executives as an engineer's pipe-dream.

To Major Edwin Armstrong, of Columbia University, this gloomy verdict was merely a challenge. The very weaknesses of FM, he thought, represented its real strength. If FM required wider operating bands, then, fortunately, in the unused part of the spectrum there was enough room to accommodate more FM stations than AM stations in virtually any given area. Moreover, these very wider bands made possible a tonal reproduction forever barred to AM transmitters, with their necessarily narrower bands. FM put all the stations in a given area on a footing of mechanical equality. Finally, if the range was limited, then there surely was need for more purely community stations; besides, these could be linked, as effectively if not so simply as with standard stations, into regional and national networks.

In May, 1940, the F.C.C. authorized commercial operation of FM stations as of July 1, 1940. By the end of the following year, one license had been issued, one special temporary authorization had been granted, and six construction permits were in the hands of broadcasters. By 1942, when the F.C.C., at the instance of the War Production Board, imposed a freeze on all new station construction, the number of commercial stations had increased to thirty. Meantime, set-manufacturers, led by Philco, had produced and distributed nearly 400,000 sets built to receive FM signals in the 42–50-megacycle band—a band which, as we shall see in a later chapter, was destined to be rendered obsolescent when, in 1945, the F.C.C., heeding the advice of its engineers, "kicked FM upstairs" into the 88–108 megacycle band.

There have been other setbacks, some of which will be discussed in the following chapter. Suffice it to note here that, instead of the "four to five thousand FM stations and ten or a dozen networks" envisioned in mid–1945, there actually were, as of January 10, 1947, one hundred and forty-two licensed stations, twenty-five of them still operating in the old bands; some three hundred additional construction permits and conditional grants; four-hundred-odd pending applications; and no networks.

SIGHT WITH SOUND

The concept of television is older than voice broadcasting. The first serious experiments looking toward the transmission of visual images by electromagnetic waves were initiated in 1877. In the early 1920's relatively successful tests combining radio transmission and mechanical manipulation of the images were held in this country. In 1923, President Harding's moving image was televised between Washington and Philadelphia. Three years later, the Bell System conducted successful wire television tests in black and white, and by 1929 they had added color.

The first great strides were not made, however, until after the perfection of the cathode ray, when a number of engineers attempted to devise an all-electronic, all-radio system. In 1930, N.B.C. opened an experimental television station in New York and borrowed from Westinghouse Vladimir Zworykin, who had demonstrated his kinescope or cathode-ray receiver the year before. Shortly after going to R.C.A., Zworykin perfected his iconoscope; and in 1933 both he and Philo Farnsworth, of the Farnsworth Laboratory, Ltd., produced 240-line black-and-white images over short distances which compared very favorably with the 30- and 60-line images theretofore transmitted, but which still required mechanical "scanning" at the sending end. By 1935, the standard had been raised to 343 lines, and by 1940 to 525. At this time also, C.B.S., Zenith, Du Mont, Paramount, General Electric, Westinghouse, and the Don Lee Network had become interested in the new field, and a threatened patent war between R.C.A. and Farnsworth had been settled to the advantage of all concerned.

Since with television, as with FM, transmitter height is a factor, N.B.C. in 1932 moved its experimental station to the top of the Empire State Building, the tallest building in the world. In 1936, Zworykin successfully demonstrated outdoor television, using a mobile "pickup"; and, in 1939, N.B.C. announced that it was ready to make the new art available to the public, with two hours of programming a week which would be received on R.C.A.–built sets. Soon others were ready to enter the lists on a regularly scheduled basis, and in 1940 the F.C.C. authorized N.B.C., C.B.S., Zenith, General Electric, and Philco to operate commercial stations for the benefit of the fewer than two thousand set-owners in New York, Philadelphia, Chicago, Schenectady, and Hollywood. The war, of course, shelved commercial television temporarily;[4] but, in 1941, N.B.C. completed the first television station to accept sponsored programs. This example was followed two years later by Du Mont Laboratories, and in 1944 N.B.C. and C.B.S. resumed broadcasting to the general public.

Meanwhile, a controversy of major proportions had developed between the proponents of color television "soon" and the advocates of black-and-white "right away," with the lineup, as of the close of 1946, Zenith, Bendix, Westinghouse, and Federal Telephone & Radio behind C.B.S. and color;

[4] Television was widely used, however, in hospitals and for air-raid warnings and student training.

General Electric, Philco, Du Mont, and most of the others rallying to N.B.C. and black-and-white. Amid the smoke of this battle, the Yankee Network, Philco, and some eighty other television pioneers quietly withdrew their applications for construction permits, leaving the field to six licensed commercial stations, thirty-six with construction permits and forty with applications pending.

THE RADIO NEWSPAPER

Like television, facsimile—or the transmission of characters, printing type, and pictures by radio—is older than broadcasting. The principle was established in England as early as 1850; and in 1924, facsimile (or radiophoto) pictures of President Coolidge, Prime Minister Stanley Baldwin, and the Prince of Wales were sent from London to New York in 20 minutes. Four years later, the Federal Radio Commission allocated two channels for facsimile experimentation. In 1938, an experimental facsimile network was established, based on WOR (New York), WGN (Chicago), WLW (Cincinnati), WGH (Newport News), KSTP (St. Paul), WHO (Des Moines), WSM (Nashville), and WHK (Cleveland).

That facsimile has not progressed beyond the experimental stage is probably due to a number of factors. To begin with, to be practical for home use it must be, as J. R. Poppele, vice-president and chief engineer of WOR, puts it, "97 per cent electronic," since supplementary mechanical devices located in the receiver would be continually getting out of synchronization. Sets being turned out in small volume as late as the summer of 1946 still required the threading of paper into the receiver. Until about 1944, they had to be turned on and off manually and at precisely the correct instant. By 1946, paper was available that did not soil the hands, and the quality of printing had been vastly improved. The remaining physical defects undoubtedly will be ironed out by 1950, but it is the fact that, as of the close of 1946, facsimile was not ready to begin regularly delivering a home newspaper. It is not unlikely that it will have its first commercial application as a by-product or sideline of FM. The F.C.C. has authorized commercial FM broadcasters to transmit some facsimile (provided it does not encroach on the required six hours of aural FM broadcasting) and eventually may permit the multiplexing of the two. When that time comes, the capsule newspaper may be evolved as a supplement to, and as reader-pull "come-on" for, established newspapers.

In sum, then, the story of the technological development of broadcasting is the story of all technological development: the technicians have brought forth miracles faster than men bound by economic factors could deliver them to the public. Let us examine some of these economic factors in radio.

3

RAGTIME TO RICHES

THE founders of the Radio Corporation of America consortium had been less concerned with what would come
out of the magic receiving sets than with who would sell
them. A natural division of the whole vast new equipment
market suggested itself: Westinghouse and General Electric
would manufacture sets, R.C.A. would distribute them, and
American Telephone and Telegraph would build and lease or
sell transmitters, which, thanks to the patent concentration,
all would-be broadcasters would be obliged to use.

Meantime, a public which during the earphones stage had
been delighted to hear almost any disconnected series of rec-
ognizable sounds was demanding better programs, better continuity, better signals, now that it was buying receiving sets
costing anywhere from twenty-five to several hundred dollars.
It had had a taste of grand opera, of prize fights and baseball
games, of market and weather reports. It wanted more. Where
was the money to pay for it?

David Sarnoff, onetime American Marconi engineer, who
had come over to R.C.A. and was now a vice-president, ex-
plored several avenues. He wrote in a memorandum of June
17, 1922:

The cost of broadcasting must be borne by those who derive
profits directly or indirectly from the business resulting from radio
broadcasting: manufacturer, national distributor, wholesale distributor, retail dealer, licensee. I suggest that the Radio Corpora-

tion of America pay over to the Broadcasting Company [no such company had yet been formed] 2 per cent of its gross radio sales, that General Electric and Westinghouse do likewise, and that our proposed licensees be required to do the same. We may find it practicable to require our wholesale distributors to pay over a reasonable percentage of their gross radio sales. It is conceivable that the same principle may even be extended in time to the dealers.

And, as though he divined that even this arrangement might not prove adequate for long, he added:

It is conceivable that plans may be devised whereby it will receive public support. There may even appear on the horizon a public benefactor who will be willing to contribute a large sum in the form of an endowment. I feel that with suitable publicity activities, such a company will ultimately be regarded as a public institution of great value in the same sense that a library, for example, is regarded today.

Expenses were mounting the while. If the listening public wanted more recognized stars, the recognized stars wanted something more substantial in the way of remuneration than their carfare to New Jersey and the realization that they were participating in the making of history. In the fall of 1922, the American Society of Composers, Authors, and Publishers (A.S.C.A.P.) decided that broadcasters should pay royalty fees on phonograph records. As the majority of broadcasters were on the verge of bankruptcy, this was a real blow. A number of them organized the National Association of Broadcasters (N.A.B.) to fight A.S.C.A.P. Some signed royalty contracts meekly. Others simply dropped transcribed music, falling back on news bulletins, market and weather reports, and amateur skits. Still others appealed to their listeners for contributions. Among these latter was the A.T. & T's WEAF (New York City), which returned to a handful of donors the less than $200 its pleas had brought forth.

The truth was that for some time A.T. & T. had been eyeing R.C.A.'s rich manufacturing profits with undisguised envy. The power to force broadcasters to use A.T. & T. transmitting equipment at fees ranging from $500 to $3,000, in addition to the price of the apparatus, had seemed to the telephone corporation's executives, at the time that the bargain with R.C.A., G.E., and Westinghouse had been made, to offer a fair share of the spoils. But it soon became apparent that the number of broadcasting stations could not expand so rapidly or so far as the number of listeners, who, every few years, would want new receiving sets. Moreover, A.T. & T. felt that R.C.A. and the others had got off on the wrong track: a radio broadcast, like a telephone conversation, should be paid for by the person originating it; those who were using the new medium simply to promote their own products, far from performing a public service, were "exploiting a popular craze."

Two weeks after A.T. & T. put WEAF on the air, a real estate firm on Long Island paid $100 for a 10-minute talk which resulted in the quick sale of two apartments. In September a second customer tried the new medium. By March, 1923, WEAF boasted twenty-five sponsors, including the R. H. Macy department store, the Metropolitan Life Insurance Company, the Colgate Company, and I. Miller Shoes. At first, the advertisers contented themselves with what today would be called "spot announcements." Before 1923 was many months old, however, Gimbel Brothers and Browning King were sponsoring hour-long programs of dance music.

The companies deriving their revenues from the sale of sets—R.C.A., G.E., Westinghouse, Philco, Zenith, Stromberg-Carlson, and others—protested that broadcasting was being "debased." Under the prodding of their delegates, the First Radio Conference passed resolutions denouncing "direct sales talk." Secretary of Commerce Hoover, who was responsible for radio "regulations," viewed the trend with "alarm." But the public showed itself ready to accept the "nuisance" in return for better programs and other improvements, among which were regular, scheduled broadcasting and "networks," making it possible for the listeners of one community to hear the talent of another, miles away.

The competition of advertising had been met by R.C.A. with an offer of free time to anyone who would pay for the talent and other "program charges." Even this subterfuge strained the tripartite agreement, which gave A.T. & T. the exclusive right to charge advertising tolls. Independent stations were effectively discouraged from accepting advertising by A.T. & T.'s monopoly in transmitters. As we have seen, R.C.A. countered the telephone long-lines monopoly by linking WGY (Schenectady), WJZ (New York), and WRC (Washington) by Western Union and Postal Telegraph wires. This, too, proved a feeble gesture, for A.T. & T.'s long-lines had been refined in the Bell Laboratories for the express purpose of carrying the human voice, whereas Western Union and Postal, interested only in dot-dash, were able to offer only inferior connective service.

Master of the situation, A.T. & T. should have been content, but it was not. It longed to break the tripartite agreement and start producing its own vacuum tubes. It was not popular with the independent broadcasters, who wanted to see it prosecuted as a trust. Within the corporation there were many who questioned the wisdom of staying in the radio broadcasting business: A.T. & T., they argued, was (1) a telephone company, (2) a manufacturer of electronic devices. If it contented itself with leasing telephone long-lines to, and manufacturing equipment for, the broadcasters, it could draw down a substantial income from the new industry without incurring any of its mounting risks.

Even more obvious were R.C.A.'s sources of discontent. In the summer of 1925 a committee, headed by Sarnoff, reported to the directors that (1) R.C.A. could never be assured of adequate financial underpinning unless it went into advertising, and (2) it should do this through a broadcasting subsidiary rather than directly because (*a*) listeners wanted good programs with little or no advertising and (*b*) the sponsor expected a type of program which R.C.A. would be "embarrassed" to give him.

In May, 1926, stealing Sarnoff's thunder, A.T. & T. incorporated a subsidiary, the Broadcasting Company of America. The move was designed to frighten R.C.A. into making further concessions, for A.T. & T. already had decided to get out of the broadcasting business. In July, WEAF and WJZ were united under the management of R.C.A. In September the National Broadcasting Company was incorporated as a subsidiary of R.C.A., with R.C.A., G.E., and Westinghouse holding 50, 30, and 20 per cent of the stock, respectively. In November, exercising its option, R.C.A. paid A.T. & T. $1,000,-000 for WEAF, in return for which A.T. & T. agreed not to re-enter the broadcasting field for seven years, on pain of refunding $800,000, and to lease its telephone long-lines to N.B.C. At the close of the year, N.B.C. issued advertising rate cards for the Red Network, with WEAF (since October, 1946, WNBC) as the key station, and for the Blue Network, headed by WJZ. In the network field they had, for the moment, no rival.

But broadcasting was not the only, or even the major, concern of R.C.A. Although N.B.C.'s time sales of $3,000,000 in 1928 were encouraging, they had to be compared with a traffic in receiving sets which, as early as 1924, had reached the proportions of a $50,000,000 business. Meantime, R.C.A.

31

sought new fields. In March, 1929, it acquired a majority of the stock of the Victor Talking Machine Company. In December of the same year it persuaded G.E. and Westinghouse to permit it to manufacture, as well as distribute, receiving sets and tubes and set up the R.C.A.–Victor Company to do it. Two years earlier, it had set up another subsidiary, the Radiomarine Corporation, to handle ship-to-shore and aviation traffic. In 1928 it incorporated R.C.A. Communications, Inc., to operate a world-wide point-to-point radiotelegraph system. In May, 1930, R.C.A. bought out the G.E. and Westinghouse interests in N.B.C. Previously, the corporation had acquired a toehold in the motion picture industry through the formation in 1928 of the Radio-Keith-Orpheum (RKO) Company. By 1932, R.C.A. had acquired a better than 60 per cent interest in this production-distribution firm, which also controlled more than two hundred theaters; but in 1935 it sold half its holdings to the Atlas Corporation, and, by the spring of 1943, it was out of the movie business.

Minor subsidiaries, organized or acquired by R.C.A., included the Photophone Company, organized in April, 1928, and merged with Victor in January, 1932; R.C.A.–Radiotron, formed in 1929; and the Audio Vision Appliance Company, which was incorporated into the R.C.A.–Victor Company in 1929. All these units were brought under unified management in 1934 in the R.C.A. Manufacturing Company, a wholly owned subsidiary. In December, 1942, this company was consolidated with R.C.A. and became the R.C.A. Victor Division of the company, which produces radio sets, tubes, records, Victrolas, transcriptions, and electronic and communications equipment.

On May 13, 1930, the government brought an antitrust action against R.C.A., G.E., A.T. & T., and Westinghouse, as a result of which G.E. and Westinghouse were forced to dispose of their R.C.A. stock and terminate all exclusive cross-licensing agreements; but R.C.A. continued to control the patents on tubes used in the manufacture of receiving sets, and, in 1931, this was held to be in violation of the Clayton Act. Since then, the percentage of tube business controlled by R.C.A. has declined.

Shortly after the formation of N.B.C., a rival network was organized. At the fourth annual meeting of the N.A.B. in September, 1926, a promoter, George A. Coats, incensed over the rights and royalties demanded by A.S.C.A.P., proposed setting up a great radio program bureau. The idea appealed to Arthur Judson, manager of the Philadelphia Symphony Orchestra, who was apprehensive of the threat to talent booking inherent in the vast plans of R.C.A. A corporation known as the Judson Radio Program Corporation was organized to book talent and develop radio programs. After an unsuccessful attempt to place talent on N.B.C., the two men, in January, 1927, incorporated the United Independent Broadcasters (U.I.B.), for the purpose of contracting for radio time, selling it to advertisers, and furnishing programs to broadcasters. In April, U.I.B. became affiliated with the Columbia Phonograph Company, and an operating company was formed, the Columbia Phonograph Broadcasting System, Inc. (C.P.B.S.), with U.I.B. remaining as the holding company.

The new network succeeded in signing sixteen stations, with a standard contract which obligated C.P.B.S. to pay them $500 a week for 10 specific hours. Owing to unexpected difficulties, the chain was not able to begin broadcasting until September, when the first program went out over the sixteen stations. Meantime, heavy financial losses had piled up, and the following month the Columbia Phonograph Company felt obliged to withdraw. At that time a controlling interest in

U.I.B. was acquired by three men, two of them owners of WCAU (Philadelphia), one of the contracted stations. Shortly thereafter, U.I.B. acquired all the outstanding stock of the Columbia Phonograph Company, and the name of the network was changed to the Columbia Broadcasting System, Inc.

The WCAU interests continued to lose money in the company, which was finding it hard to contract sufficient business to cover its expenses. But rich new blood was in the offing. William S. Paley, impressed with the effect on sales of his La Palina cigars of advertising over the new chain, became interested in radio. In September, 1928, he and his family bought 50.3 per cent of the stock of C.B.S. The new owner set out to turn it into a profitable business. In December, 1928, he bought WABC (New York) (since October, 1946, WCBS), one of the original outlets and still one of the key C.B.S. stations. Although at the close of the year C.B.S. still was in the red, the books showed a profit of $474,203 by December, 1929.

Like Sarnoff, Paley had expansionist ideas. In 1929 he made a deal with the Paramount Publix Corporation, whereby 58,832 shares of Paramount were traded for 50,000 shares (roughly 50 per cent of its stock) of C.B.S., with the proviso that if the latter averaged earnings of a million during each of the next two years, the motion-picture company would buy back its shares at a premium. But C.B.S. did better than the stipulated amount and bought back its shares instead, thus dissolving the short-lived merger.

In December, 1938, C.B.S. purchased from Consolidated Film Industries, Inc., the capital stock of the American Record Corporation and its subsidiaries, changing the name to the Columbia Recording Corporation, still the opposite number to R.C.A.'s Victor Division and sharing with the latter a major portion of the lucrative phonograph record and transcription market.

THE SCRAMBLE TO "AFFILIATE"

From the earliest days of broadcasting, the pull from every direction has been such as to make the rapid expansion of networks inevitable. The listeners wanted to hear the "finished" programs from New York and other talent centers. Independent broadcasters wished not only to please their listeners but also to claim a share in the national advertiser's dollar. The networks themselves naturally worked to expand that dollar by putting themselves in position to offer more and more stations.

The irresistible tide flowed swiftly. On November 1, 1926, N.B.C. had 19 stations in its Red and Blue networks. By the end of 1927, the number had increased to 48. Ten years later, it stood at 138. As of December, 1946, the chain (meantime divested of the old Blue Network) boasted 159. Meanwhile, C.B.S., from a start of 16 in 1927, had 28 within a year and 113 by 1939. At the close of 1946, it had 162. By 1938, roughly 38 per cent of the 721 standard stations were either owned by, or under contract to, one of the two big companies. As of the end of 1946, approximately 800 of the more than a thousand on the air were divided as follows:

M.B.S.	384*
A.B.C.	238*
N.B.C.	162
C.B.S.	162

*Many M.B.S. and A.B.C. affiliates also are affiliated with another network.

As network broadcasting developed, business relationships changed. In the early days, A.T. & T. had asked for no binding contracts with the member stations that formed the nucleus of its 1923–24 network. When N.B.C. was organized, it continued these informal understandings, making special contracts only with those stations that demanded them for protection. In general, it was agreed that the affiliates would receive $45 an hour for commercial programs and pay N.B.C. $45 an hour for sustaining service. No option on time was taken by the network, which had to clear on each occasion with each station before making definite arrangements with the sponsor. On the other hand, C.B.S. wrote individual contracts with its affiliates from the start, agreeing to pay $50 an hour for commercial time and charging the same rate for sustainers.

After Paley bought into C.B.S., payments for sustaining programs were eliminated, and, in return, the stations waived compensation for the first five hours a week of commercial time. In August, 1929, C.B.S. adjusted its rates according to the power, popularity, physical coverage, market, and spot rate charged national advertisers. Hourly rates ranged from $125 to $1,250 for commercial programs, which stations were required to carry, although they were free to take or refuse sustaining programs. In 1932, N.B.C. abolished hourly rates for sustainers, and the stations began paying the network a flat sum of $1,500 a month. By 1935 the older network had changed its contracts to conform to C.B.S.'s option policy.

In that year C.B.S. paid affiliates 24.09 per cent of gross network time sales, and N.B.C. paid 22.02. The stations got, for nothing, sustaining programs which cost the networks an average of $387 an hour to produce. Affiliates joining C.B.S. after 1927 were forbidden by an "exclusivity" clause to make their facilities available to any other broadcasting chain. In 1937, at the insistence of some of the stations, a clause was added to prevent C.B.S. from offering to rival stations in the affiliate's territory any network program, whether the affiliate desired to air it or not. A year earlier, N.B.C. had intro-

36

duced similar clauses, and in both instances the contracts were made binding upon the affiliates for a period of 5 years, though upon the networks for only 1 year.

Meanwhile, the networks were acquiring stations by ownership as well as by affiliation. When it was organized, N.B.C. had owned three stations: WEAF and WJZ (New York) and WRC (Washington); C.B.S. began with none but acquired WABC (New York) in December, 1928. Between 1930 and 1935, N.B.C. purchased seven more: WMAL (Washington), WTAM (Cleveland), WMAQ and WENR (Chicago), KOA (Denver), and KPO and KGO (San Francisco). By 1936, C.B.S. had picked up eight to add to WABC: WJSV (Washington) (now WTOP), WBT (Charlotte, North Carolina),[1] WEEI (Boston) (by lease), WBBM (Chicago), WKRC (Cincinnati),[1] WCCO (Minneapolis), KMOX (St. Louis), and KNX (Los Angeles). The net effect of this concentration was to give N.B.C. and C.B.S. absolute control of 14 and affiliation with 14, or the use of 28 of the 30 clear-channel stations of 50-kilowatt power then in existence. At this point the government, as we shall see in a later chapter, stepped in to stem the tide.

Many independent stations did not wish to be bound by the rigid contracts of the national networks. Others were primarily interested in coverage on less than the national scale. Still others could not get an N.B.C. or a C.B.S. affiliation. The obvious advantages of limited network operation were not lost on these. In the late 1920's, groups of two or more independent stations began to exchange programs and quote advertising rates based on the combined markets. In the thirties some of these smaller chains expanded and became quite powerful in their regions, using their dominant positions in the markets to bargain collectively with the national net-

[1] Since disposed of.

works. Others were content to go quietly along on a state-wide basis. Not a few of the earlier ones failed to survive.

Among those that prospered, the 1946 leaders would include the Don Lee Network, which, through an arrangement with the Pacific Network, covered California, Oregon, and Washington; the Yankee Network, which, by absorbing the Colonial Network, secured a dominant position in New England; the Texas Network; and the Michigan Network. Meanwhile, another type of small combination, based upon common ownership of a number of stations, had developed. Although Westinghouse was first in this field, the bulk of such chains came to be associated with newspaper combinations. (The tables in Appen. I will give some idea of the regional and common-ownership network situation as of January 1, 1947.)

It was perhaps inevitable that the radio advertising boom of the thirties should bring N.B.C. and C.B.S. face to face with controlling factors quite outside the realm of government regulation. A number of powerful stations had resisted the networks' offers of affiliation and had succeeded so well as community stations serving large market areas that they could not be ignored by the advertisers. At the same time, a number of the advertisers were beginning to complain that N.B.C. and C.B.S. charged them for more stations than they needed. In 1934 several advertising agencies offered WOR (New York) and WGN (Chicago) contracts based on the regular card rates to local advertisers charged by these two stations if they would link themselves for simultaneous broadcasting at certain hours. WOR and WGN agreed to divide the line charges involved, and soon WXYZ (Detroit) and WLW (Cincinnati) joined the "co-operative" on the same basis. In October, 1934, the Mutual Broadcasting System was incorporated, the capital stock being divided between the Bamberger Broadcasting Service, Inc., licensee of WOR, and WGN, Inc., a subsidiary of the *Chicago Tribune*, licensee of WGN. Each of the four co-operating stations originated programs and received the local card rates, less 5 per cent commission for the time salesmen and the line charges.

In September, 1935, WXYZ left M.B.S. to join N.B.C. as an affiliate and was replaced by CKLW (Windsor, Ontario), which also served the Detroit area, thus lending an international flavor to the new venture. The next year, Don Lee and Colonial joined the M.B.S. fold. By January, 1939, there were 107 "co-operating" stations, 25 of which were able, thanks to the very loose arrangements with M.B.S., to retain affiliation with N.B.C., and 5 with C.B.S. In January, 1940, the original incorporators issued stock to five additional companies: the Don Lee Broadcasting Company, the Colonial Network, Inc., the Cincinnati Times-Star Company (licensee of WKRC), the United Broadcasting Company (a subsidiary of the *Cleveland Plain Dealer* and licensee of WHK [Cleveland] and WHKC [Columbus]), and the Western Ontario Broadcasting Company, Ltd., licensee of CKLW.

It had been decided, however, that the original formula of loose, voluntary mutuality would not enable the new network to compete successfully with the older chains. In 1938, M.B.S. began to ask for options from its affiliates, although it did not, as a network, maintain a programming organization or originate programs. In 1941 the stockholders elected a paid president, who undertook to turn a necessity into a virtue: since M.B.S. had only two of the powerful 50-kilowatt clear-channel stations as full-time affiliates (WOR and WGN), he went after local stations, especially in one-station communities, and managed to convince a number of important national advertisers that such a system offered them a better total audience than those claimed for N.B.C. and C.B.S.

Though the advertising inroads made upon the older networks were not so great as to shake their hold on the cream of the business, M.B.S. did succeed in winning three types of sponsor: those who objected to the rates charged by N.B.C. or C.B.S.; those who wished to test their programs and products in a few selected markets before embarking on a nation-wide campaign; and those who desired intensive regional coverage, either in conjunction with major network advertising or independently.

M.B.S.'s intensive drive soon brought it to the top in the number of affiliations. But the figures were misleading; N.B.C. and C.B.S. at the close of the 1930's were interested not only in all but 2 of the 30 powerful 50-kilowatt clear channels but in 53.4 per cent of the regional stations as well.

Moreover, as the Federal Communications Commission was to disclose, N.B.C. and C.B.S. had what amounted almost to a stranglehold on radio talent. The former had set up an Artists' Service in 1926. In 1935 it acquired the Civic Concert Service, Inc. In 1937 the gross talent bookings of the merged unit were $6,032,274. C.B.S. presented a similar situation, having set up Columbia Artists, Inc., and having acquired 55 per cent of the stock of the Columbia Concerts Corporation in 1930.

Moves in the early forties had the effect of breaking up these talent monopolies, relaxing affiliation contracts, and limiting ownership of broadcasting stations to one to a market area, and (by gentleman's agreement) eight over-all. They also were responsible for N.B.C.'s having to dispose of one of its networks. The choice was not difficult. In 1938, N.B.C. had paid the seventeen "basic" Red Stations $2,803,839 for airing network commercial programs; Blue's eighteen "basics" got $794,186. In October, 1943, R.C.A. sold the Blue Network to Edward J. Noble, candy manufacturer and licensee of WMCA (New York), and, since the summer of 1945, the network has been officially known as the American Broadcasting Company.

Several attempts subsequently were made to launch a fifth national network. In November, 1939, Elliot Roosevelt, one-time president of Hearst Radio, Inc., announced the formation of the Transcontinental Broadcasting System. It never took the air, largely because it failed to secure in advance sufficient promises of revenue to hold in line the 100 stations involved. In July, 1945, Leonard A. Versluis, a Michigan broadcaster, managed to get the Associated Broadcasting System operating on the basis of a very loose arrangement with a dozen independent stations. Associated threw up the sponge on February 11, 1946.

CROSS-CURRENTS

With the coming of the first two big national networks, the demand for radio sets and broadcasting equipment naturally increased. Even by the end of 1927, the 5-year-old "novelty" had become a $425,000,000 business in terms of gross receipts for apparatus. By 1938 there were 40,000,000 receiving sets in use in the United States. The original cost to the public of the nearly 100,000,000 receiving sets (excluding FM, television, and facsimile receivers) turned out between 1921 and mid-1946 has been estimated at almost $5,000,000,000. For the two-dozen broadcast licensees primarily interested in radio manufacture,[2] these figures meant divided interest, if not divided allegiance. The apparent conflicts flowing out of this situation have sometimes given rise to charges that the manufacturers shaped future plans to present stock inventories.

Thus Major Armstrong, the "inventor" of FM broadcasting, accused R.C.A. and others of holding FM back for a

[2] Biggest: R.C.A., G.E., Westinghouse, Zenith, Philco, Aviation Corporation, Du Mont, Farnsworth, Stromberg-Carlson.

41

decade because of heavy inventories in AM equipment. And some observers saw in the attempts of Zenith to discredit F.C.C. engineering tests leading to the shift of FM to higher bands an undue concern for several thousand FM sets built to receive in the old band. In any event, it may be stated as a valid generalization that the equipment manufacturers have been, on the whole, less enthusiastic about FM than those broadcasters who have no interest in the lucrative apparatus market.

Even more spectacular has been the controversy between black-and-white and color television, with four important manufacturers (Zenith, Bendix, Federal, and Westinghouse) supporting C.B.S. in the campaign to wait for color and the others either on the fence or lined up behind R.C.A. for going ahead without color. C.B.S. has expressed a fear that if color television is not pushed, it may be artificially retarded for a decade or more by two factors: (1) a flooding of the market with black-and-white sets which, because television receivers are considerably more expensive than AM sets, the owners might not wish to replace very soon, and (2) a freezing of frequency allocations in the two limited bands assigned by the F.C.C. in September, 1945, one of which is designed for black-and-white and the other for color.[3] In October, 1946, N.B.C. stole a march on C.B.S. by demonstrating all-electronic color television. (C.B.S. at that time still employed mechanical color disks.)

Corollary interests in television extend far beyond the lim-

[3] C.B.S. has favored moving television all the way up into the microwave bands, arguing that release of the black-and-white band between 44 and 88 megacycles would free 220 additional FM channels; the F.C.C. and a number of set-manufacturers point out that this would create FM receiver design problems and probably involve the manufacture of two- and three-band sets, since 20–30 megacycles is the practical limit for a single-band receiver dial.

its of equipment manufacture, however. Du Mont has boasted that it is not "big business," inasmuch as the initial investment "need not run over $272,500." Other telecasters disagree, and the F.C.C., challenging Du Mont's figures, warns prospects that television is still "a rich man's game." Under the circumstances, it is scarcely surprising that some advertising agencies, long accustomed to programming standard broadcast stations, are quietly preparing to play an even more dominant role in television. It is even less surprising that the agencies plan, because of the higher costs involved, to make the new medium more, rather than less, commercial than aural broadcasting has become.

It goes without saying that the motion picture industry is interested in television, although Hollywood does not appear to have made up its collective mind whether the wireless talkie will supplant the neighborhood movie or merely serve as a means of bringing "trailers" of forthcoming films into the home and see-it-as-it-happens newsreels into the theater. Department stores, with an eye to the possibilities for fashion shows, also are active in the field. Indeed, these two groups, together with the big networks, the equipment manufacturers, and perhaps the newspapers, may have to support commercial television for several years.

Merlin H. Aylesworth, former president of N.B.C., has predicted that there will be 3,000,000 television sets in use by 1948, "at least 10,000,000 by 1950"; and that television will give movies a run for their box-office half-dollars and newspapers a run for their advertising dollars. If there is anything to what he says and to precedent, Hollywood may be expected to try to narrow, and the publishers to try to resist, the relentless flow of progress. It will be remembered that both the movies and the press fought radio in its salad days.

43

As a matter of fact, the publishers have more reason to be on their guard now than they had in the early twenties. Then radio was tolerated as something of a toy, and, although several newspapers owned stations, they did not regard them as competitors. In 1922, the Associated Press warned its members that the broadcasting of its news was contrary to A.P. by-laws; but, as the United Press and International News Service were supplying news to broadcasters, those warned felt obliged to strain the by-laws. So little did the newspaper owners fear radio that they cheerfully accorded the broadcasters a courtesy long denied (in effect) by most periodicals to motion picture exhibitors, theatrical producers, and book publishers: free announcement of scheduled attractions without the usual *quid pro quo* of paid advertisements.

With the rapid expansion of N.B.C. and C.B.S. in the early thirties, however, the picture rapidly changed. Newspaper advertising lineage fell as radio time billings soared. Radio news coverage, which had dealt a death blow to the afternoon "extra," was utilizing the press association reports—the .very raw material of newspapers—to beat the publishers at their own game, and with a decided advantage in timing. The dormant radio committee of the American Association of Newspaper Publishers sprang into action. By 1933 it had persuaded A.P., U.P., and I.N.S. to suspend the service of news to broadcasters.

The response of at least one network was immediate and initially effective. In October, C.B.S. News Chief Paul W. White, a former U.P. editor, quietly began to organize his own news-gathering staff. Newspapers in areas where C.B.S. had outlets promptly withdrew the network's program listings, and the publishers' committee urged newspapers to

44

accord like treatment to all listings, as a means of bringing concerted broadcaster pressure to bear on C.B.S.

The broadcasters lost their nerve. They had managed their relations with the press badly, especially in the matter of failing to accompany requests for free space with paid advertisements. Most of them stood in awe of the older medium, insisting that radio needed the support of the press (which, since 1933, it has never received). The network front cracked when N.B.C. decided to play both ends against the middle instead of supporting its news chief, A. A. Schechter (now news chief of M.B.S.), in his move to follow White's lead by building up N.B.C.'s own news-gathering staff.

A few days of going without printed program logs convinced all but a handful of broadcasters that they could not win in a showdown. The spirit of panic swept C.B.S. up in its tide, and in December, 1933, representatives of both networks met with spokesmen for the A.N.P.A., A.P., U.P., and I.N.S. in the Hotel Biltmore, New York, and signed a ten-point "agreement," which later, perhaps for legal reasons, became known as "the Biltmore program."

A sweeping victory for the publishers, the "agreement" provided for the setting-up of a special news bureau, to be supported wholly by the networks, which was to "edit" the files of the three press associations and release a small distillate to the broadcasters for two daily newscasts of not more than 5 minutes each, one after 9:30 A.M. and one after 9:00 P.M., and for "occasional" broadcasts of special bulletins involving news of "transcendental [sic] importance," which were to be followed by the admonition to "see your local newspaper for further details." Commentators were not to dabble in spot news, and newscasts were, under no circumstances, to be sponsored. Finally, C.B.S. was to suppress its burgeoning news service, and both networks were solemnly to promise never again to attempt anything of the sort—a promise which, fortunately, has not been kept.

Two contributing factors to this curious pact should be noted in passing. One, of particular interest in view of the 1946 newspaper campaign against "government interference" with the broadcasters (touched off by issuance of the F.C.C.'s famous "Blue Book"), was the subtle press agitation just prior to the Biltmore conference for congressional legislation more strictly regulating the radio industry, accompanied by some kind words for the British system of government ownership and operation. The other was the broadcasters' mounting coolness toward frequent interruptions of commercial programs by news bulletins, a practice which distressed the sponsors and their advertising agencies. The two time periods selected for newscasts happened fortuitously to fall in "optional" segments which normally produced little or no advertising revenue.

The new clearing house, known as the Press Radio Bureau, began operating on March 1, 1934. It never met with any great success, although the networks obligingly supported it for three years. Its failure stemmed in part from the refusal of certain stations to abide by its provisions and the ineffectiveness of measures taken by the press and the two networks to punish them for their temerity. Even more serious, however, was the rise of Trans-Radio Press, an independent news-gathering agency founded by Herbert Moore, former U.P. and C.B.S. news editor, which sold news directly to radio advertisers for sponsorship. So well did Trans-Radio succeed that U.P. and I.N.S., never very enthusiastic about the Biltmore "solution," gave way to envy, and in May, 1935, on the pretext that they were making nothing more than a temporary excursion to squelch the "upstart" news service, persuaded the die-hard A.N.P.A. radio committee to modify the agreement to the extent of permitting U.P. and I.N.S. to sell news on the side. A.P. soon liberalized its news policy for members and, in 1940, removed the no-sponsorship restriction. In the same year Press Radio passed quietly out of existence. The war appeared to be over.

The extent to which the outcome was a Pyrrhic victory for the broadcasters, as well as a missed opportunity for their listeners, may not even today be fully realized. A 1939 *Fortune* survey indicated that 70 per cent of Americans relied on the radio for news and that 58 per cent thought it more accurate than that supplied by the press. A survey by the Survey Research Center of the University of Michigan, due for publication in 1947, substantiates these findings very dramatically. On many occasions during the war, at subsequent international conferences, and in the midst of numerous strikes which kept newspapers off the stands for days and weeks, listening America might well have wished that radio's handful of reporters had been an army.

Actually, the wartime cessation of hostilities between press and radio may have marked not so much a victory, Pyrrhic or otherwise, as a long armistice. The aggressive reappearance of radio newsmen during the war, together with a succession of time-beats over the newspapers, all the more galling because they usually involved news gathered by and for the press, caused the A.P. management to "re-examine" the situation, with a view to exploring the possibility of trying to reinforce restrictions on the broadcasters' use of press-association material.

Moreover, as we have seen, facsimile offers a brand new source of possible friction. True, virtually all the pioneering in facsimile has been done by newspapers, notably the *New York Times*, the *Chicago Tribune*, the *St. Louis Post-Dispatch*, the *Louisville Courier-Journal* and *Times*, and the *Columbus Dispatch*. But this may indicate simply that certain publishers have taken steps to attain a position in which they can better control the adaptation of the new medium to news dissemination. There is also the factor of pressure from publishers not eager to see facsimile developed, which was graphically illustrated when West Coast A.P. members forced that agency to withdraw leased wire facilities over which the *New York Times* was delivering its invaluable facsimile edition to the San Francisco conference in 1945.

It is to be hoped that the publishers will find a way to avoid further squabbles in which the public would be the chief sufferer. The fact that, as of the end of 1946, nearly three hundred of them operated standard broadcasting stations and more than four hundred, including most of these three hundred, were clamoring to get into FM or television or both may be a good augury. Perhaps the "pioneers" can persuade their reluctant brethren that radio is here to stay.

"KING CANUTE" PETRILLO

It was radio's peculiar misfortune that it was obliged to rely from the first on many well-intrenched groups other than the publishers and that it developed in a period when some of these were coming to the height of their power. The first such group to waylay the hopeful youngster and levy toll was the American Society of Composers, Authors, and Publishers.

As we have seen, even in the crystal-and-headpiece days, long before the broadcasters had got an inkling of where their revenue was to come from, A.S.C.A.P., which controlled the bulk of copyrighted sheet and recorded music, saw a chance to exact tribute from a medium that could not live without copyrighted music. In 1922 stations were presented with formal demands for royalties to be paid every time a piece of

48

music was played, whether by "live" musicians operating in front of a microphone or on phonograph records. Some broadcasters promptly went out of business, others merely continued to pirate copyrighted music, but a few of the larger stations like A.T. & T.'s WEAF elected at the outset to comply with A.S.C.A.P.'s demands. After a good deal of haggling and some litigation, N.B.C. in February, 1930, signed an agreement covering WEAF, WJZ, WRC (Washington), KOA (Denver), and KGO (San Francisco), which protected the network and all its affiliates but had the effect, naturally, of discouraging the origination of musical programs by stations other than those specified.

By 1935 the sums being paid in royalties by the networks were so staggering that the National Association of Broadcasters (N.A.B.), a trade-group formed specifically to fight inroads of this sort, began looking about for ways to lower the cost. When A.S.C.A.P. in 1937 announced a rise in royalty scales, N.A.B. redoubled its efforts to line up the industry solidly behind the networks. In September, 1939, the broadcasters decided to take a step from which they had shrunk in their feud with the press: they approved a $1,500,000 N.A.B. war chest with which they set up Broadcast Music, Inc., to develop their own music. Meantime, A.S.C.A.P. became embroiled with the Department of Justice. But when the government accepted a consent decree, the broadcasters in October, 1941, signed new contracts, based on a 1940 A.S.C.A.P. offer considerably more moderate than the ultimatum of 1937: B.M.I. had done its job. Record 1940 A.S.C.A.P. royalties of $5,000,000 plummeted to $300,000 in 1941 and did not reach $3,000,000 in 1942. By 1946 the figure had climbed back to $5,000,000, but only on the basis of a much larger gross volume. For once, the industry appeared to have won a victory destined to benefit all concerned.

While they were winning that battle, however, the broadcasters were assailed from flank and rear. The spearhead of the new hosts was James Caesar Petrillo, at that time president of the Chicago local of the American Federation of Musicians (A.F.M.). To Petrillo two things were apparent: the gains registered by the authors of popular music did not benefit the men who played it; and "live" musicians would always be indispensable to the broadcasters.

Petrillo has been denounced as a "Canute" who is determined to stay the tides of technology. His critics, both in and out of Congress, where he has been made the subject of special legislation, have never bothered to suggest what better course might be followed with respect to the 100,000 artists who entertain America nightly. Buggy-makers could be taught to turn out automobiles. But, as records and transcriptions of music cannot be made without "live" talent for the initial playing, neither training pianists to weave baskets nor expecting them to eke out an existence on the wages of two or three days' employment each month appears to be the answer for radio musicians. The coming of talking motion pictures, catching less resolute A.F.M. leaders without a plan, had thrown 8,300 movie-theater musicians on the human scrap-heap. Radio would not repeat the performance if Petrillo could help it.

Moved by a sense of timing that has characterized his actions ever since, Petrillo in 1935 calmly ordered all broadcasting stations to hire "stand-by" musicians to the number of those used in the making of any recording or transcription[4] every time a "platter" was played more than once, on pain of seeing the musicians walk out of the Chicago recording studios. Early in 1936 he made good his threat. Locals in other cities promptly brought pressure on Joseph Weber, then presi-

[4] A transcription is a recording made at the time of "live" broadcast.

50

dent of the A.F.M. Weber extended the stand-by order to the entire country, advising the networks to bring pressure on their affiliates. This the networks declined to undertake. But it was apparent that they would lose, whatever they did; and so, on September 15, 1937, they formally capitulated. Affiliated and independent stations, as well as record manufacturers, had, of course, to follow suit.

Petrillo had outdone the W.P.A. in creating "make-work," but meanwhile the engineers had not been idle. The coming of the automatic record-player or "juke box" presented both a new problem and a new opportunity: the recording companies were making a mint of money, but the 1937 agreement provided no way for the musicians to tap the major portion of it, even indirectly. In June, 1942, having failed to persuade the record-makers to agree to a formula whereby the A.F.M. would receive a graduated scale of fees on all records to be played in public, the new boss threatened to forbid his musicians to make recordings. In August he carried out his threat. Congress stormed. The War Labor Board stepped into the picture, held lengthy hearings, and ordered Petrillo to end his strike. In October, 1944, President Roosevelt personally appealed to the A.F.M. chief to send his men back. But Petrillo turned a deaf ear to all. Decca and WOR had broken the united front by signing in September, 1943. In November, 1944, despairing of any help from the government, Columbia Recording and R.C.A.–Victor gave in.

In the midst of this exhilarating skirmish, Petrillo waded into two more. In 1943, professedly alarmed by the number of "amateur" musicians playing over the air, the leader blew a loud blast on his trumpet: A.F.M. members playing with nonmembers would lose their cards. Dr. Joseph E. Maddy, president of the National Music Camp for school children at Interlochen, Michigan, stuck by his youngsters and lost his card. Again Congress acted. Senator Vandenberg and Representatives Dondero and Hoffman introduced bills. Petrillo shrugged, later graciously "exempted" the Cleveland Public Schools from his ruling.

Meantime, his eagle eye had long since noted that more and more radio stations were employing staff (usually announcer) or mechanical record-changers. Having organized the manual "platter-turners" of Chicago, Petrillo moved in the spring of 1944 to require all stations to employ hand labor, thus providing work for an additional 2,000 A.F.M. scale laborers. This brought him into collision with the National Association of Broadcasting Engineers and Technicians (N.A.B.E.T.), an independent union which had organized most of the "disk-jockeys" outside Chicago. Afraid of Petrillo, N.B.C. and A.B.C. hesitated about signing new contracts with N.A.B.E.T., who in turn, took the case to the National Labor Relations Board. The latter upheld N.A.B.E.T., directing N.B.C. and A.B.C. to sign new contracts with the anti-Petrillo union. There, as of the close of 1946, the matter rested. No one supposed that Petrillo, with C.B.S. and a number of independent stations whose "platter-turners" were members of the International Brotherhood of Electrical Workers rather than N.A.B.E.T. in his pocket, would let it rest for long.

In February, 1945, "Little Caesar" forbade his musicians to appear on television programs until he had had an opportunity to examine the probable effects of the new medium on employment. In October, he set FM development back at least a year by banning dual AM-FM programming of music unless the full complement of stand-by musicians was hired. In December he proscribed the airing of foreign musical broadcasts other than those originating in Canada. In January, 1946, he ordered the networks to take the lead in forcing stations throughout the country to employ an "adequate" number of full-time musicians.

Congress whipped through a bill sponsored by Representative Lea of California to amend the Communications Act so as to outlaw "featherbedding" and virtually every type of "coercion" that Petrillo had practiced against the broadcasters. President Truman signed it in April. The A.F.M. chief promptly ordered WAAF (Chicago) to employ three additional musicians as "librarians," announcing that he would fight all the way up the line to the Supreme Court and would refuse to obey such a law even if the highest tribunal ruled it constitutional. At the A.F.M. annual convention in June, 1946, Petrillo spoke bluntly.

When I became president of the American Federation of Musicians, I made sure that the contracts with the locals in the three cities where network shows originate . . . . New York, Chicago, and Los Angeles . . . . would all expire on one day. That day is coming next January 31. If the Supreme Court rules the Lea Act constitutional, the small stations won't get any music, because the three locals will make agreements to play locally only.

And if the government attempted to prevent his collecting a fee on each record sold?

We'll just send out a little letter. We'll just say, "Gentlemen, on such and such a date, members of the A.F.M. will not be permitted to perform in the making of recordings or transcriptions."

As a thousand delegates rose to their feet cheering, James Caesar Petrillo put a flourish on his theme song:

Now, Congressmen: dream up a law to make us go to work!

At the end of the year Petrillo had his test case in the judicial wringer. Behind him stood the American Federation of Radio Artists, affiliated through the Associated Actors and Artistes of America with Actors Equity, the American Guild of Musical Artists, and the American Guild of Variety Art-

53

ists; the Radio Directors Guild; the Screen Actors Guild; the United Office and Professional Workers of America; the International Brotherhood of Electrical Workers; and half-a-dozen other unions, any one of which could disrupt the broadcasting industry on a moment's notice. In December the United States District Court in Chicago dismissed a criminal intelligence against Petrillo in the WAAF case, ruling the Lea Act unconstitutional on five counts involving the First, Fifth, and Thirteenth amendments. The federal government moved to appeal directly to the Supreme Court. Meanwhile, however, in October, the transcription manufacturers had agreed to meet the A.F.M. "czar's" 50 per cent "across-the-board" wage increase. Once again, the wall had been breached.

THE ADVERTISING MEN MOVE IN

It will be recalled that, when broadcasting took its first halting steps in the early 1920's, it was thought by R.C.A., G.E., Westinghouse, and the other manufacturers that the sale of equipment would support the new medium indefinitely; and that, when A.T. & T., which had virtually no equipment to sell, failed in its appeal to the public for contributions, it turned to the merchants. But potential advertisers were skeptical. For more than a century, they had been dealing with the written word. Those who controlled the print media were loath to see the advertiser's dollar split. Weighing the bird in hand against the rumored two in the bush, the advertising agencies that got their 15 per cent from the print media hesitated to break with old friends.

The rising generation in the advertising-agency field took the longer view. It seemed apparent to them that radio was the ideal medium for certain firms which made package sales that depended on constant iteration of their brand names and which, therefore, naturally desired maximum impact; that maximum impact meant network hookups to bring the number of those "exposed" to a single advertisement well above the top figure for any grouping of newspapers, magazines, outdoor posters, or car-cards.

They began with prospects whose sales graphs were going down despite heavy advertising in the older media: brand coffee, which was feeling the pinch of the cheaper, chain-store lines of coffee "ground before your eyes"; canned soups, which were suffering from the elimination of the soup course and, along with packaged desserts, from the growing American habit of eating out; cigarettes, which were beginning to find pretty-women symbols a drug on the market and had a story to tell about "scientific tests" of "doctors" and tobacco auctioneers which nobody would read in type; pipe tobacco, which had become a sideline because pipe smoking was on the wane; automobile fuel, which was just going into the "ethyl" and "high-test" grading phase.

Corporations in these and other lines were worried. In a nation of "experts," they took it for granted that these impetuous young advertising men knew what they were talking about. By the mid-thirties, radio shows that had creaked along on budgets of $25,000 a year were giving way to variety and comedy shows like "Maxwell House Showboat" and Ed Wynn's "Texaco Fire Chief," running to a quarter-million and employing as many as a hundred and fifty entertainers. By 1935 the net incomes of N.B.C. and C.B.S. had soared to $3,656,907 and $3,228,194, respectively; by 1940, to $5,834,-772 and $7,431,634. Meanwhile, the sponsors were making money, too. And advertising agencies dealing almost solely with the new bonanza were springing up overnight.

That this was a fateful step for the advertising industry was at once apparent. The official historian of the N. W. Ayer

Company offers some interesting testimony on what sweeping decisions had to be faced and made:

The Ayer agency . . . . believed that radio advertising was particularly open to abuse which might alienate public opinion. It therefore adopted the policy that it would maintain direct control over the arrangement and production of all programs for which it was responsible, instead of leaving program production to the stations. Gradually it developed a staff of workers especially trained and experienced in this work; and in 1928, when the possibilities of radio advertising were clearly established, this staff was separated from the firm's other publicity work and organized as an independent department. Its duties were to assemble information about all phases of broadcast advertising, build up programs, hire talent, direct production, and handle the leasing of station time and all other details connected with broadcast programs. . . . .

It was, perhaps, both natural and inevitable that the purpose of, and attitude toward, programming should change significantly. The horse, as the Ayer historian explains, had to follow the cart:

. . . . Until 1930, all agencies tended to look for attractive programs and then to seek advertisers who would take a fling at broadcasting. After 1930, much of the original glamor and mystery of radio had vanished, and men had to take a more realistic approach. The Ayer firm rapidly developed the view that an agency must start with the client's sales problems, determine whether radio can help, and then devise a program which will achieve specific ends in terms of sales. The complete reversal of the method is significant.

How significant may be gathered from the following wistful historical note in the December 8, 1945, issue of *Billboard:*

The networks have always tried to get a firmer foothold in the production field . . . . a position they lost to advertising agencies in the early days of radio.

Soon the agencies were not only building programs and hiring the talent but also choosing the times at which their shows would be broadcast and the cities in which they would be heard. How much further could they go? As Niles Trammell, president of N.B.C., told the Senate Interstate Commerce Committee in December, 1943:

The argument is now advanced that business control of broadcasting operations has nothing to do with programming control. This is to forget that he who controls the pocketbook controls the man. Business control means complete control, and there is no use arguing to the contrary.[5]

This is not to say that Trammell and all his colleagues were entirely happy about the situation. Indeed, on several occasions during the late thirties, William S. Paley, then president and now chairman of the board of C.B.S., suggested that the broadcasters ought to take steps to free themselves from advertiser domination. The reaction he got was very much the same as that which usually greets the timid householder attempting to quiet a noisy party across the hall. The feeling was general that what the advertising agencies had given, the advertising agencies could take away. "Why shoot Santa Claus?" the cynics asked.

The sponsors and agencies were building up a solidarity entirely unmatched by the broadcasters. By 1944, C.B.S. had thirteen customers who bought more than $1,000,000 worth of time each, and three who spent more than $4,000,000 each,[6] while N.B.C. had eleven million-dollar-plus clients, A.B.C. nine, and M.B.S. three. But advertising-agency concentration had become even more pronounced. J. Walter Thompson bought $13,470,003 worth of time from C.B.S., A.B.C., and M.B.S. in 1944; Young and Rubicam, $10,034,721; Dancer,

---

[5] It is perhaps only fair to say that Trammell was speaking of evils he detected in the Chain Broadcasting Regulations rather than in advertiser domination.

[6] General Foods, $5,537,409; Lever Brothers, $4,842,781; Proctor and Gamble, $4,348,795.

Fitzgerald, $7,062,811. In other words, three agencies bought nearly a fourth of the time on three of the four networks.[7] In 1945 seven sponsors and six agencies furnished almost half of C.B.S.'s $65,724,362 billings; twelve sponsors and five agencies contributed more than 40 per cent of A.B.C.'s $40,045,-966; six sponsors and five agencies accounted for a third of M.B.S.'s $20,637,363 (see Tables 1 and 2).

What this could mean in the way of "pressures" should be apparent even to the layman. It is equally apparent that the small independent stations, operating sometimes on a "shoe-string," have no effective way of resisting such pressures. But the networks are not immune, for, obviously, an advertising agency responsible for as much as 10 per cent of a chain's business can wield a good deal of influence over not only the network but also the scores of stations that rely largely on the chains for their livelihood.[8]

The merest suggestion from a courageous network executive that he might set aside a choice hour in the evening for a brave new venture in public service could bring a reminder from half-a-dozen agencies of the fact that they could easily take their business next door—and his listeners with it. What would happen if the broadcasters, or even the four networks, moved in unison is a matter for conjecture. They have never tried it.

Pending some such declaration of independence, the situation as of the close of 1946 was not without its significance for the future. Thus, as regards standard, or old-style, broadcasting, *Variety*, as early as December 8, 1945, noted a new trend which has since become more marked:

[7] N.B.C. has not released figures since 1941; they would approximate those for C.B.S.

[8] The average affiliate's revenue breaks down into about three equal parts: a third from networks, a third from local advertising, and a third from national advertisers using station-break spots.

TABLE 1

CONCENTRATION OF GROSS BILLINGS BY AGENCIES FOR A.B.C., C.B.S., AND M.B.S. IN 1945*

Network	Total Gross Billings	Total No. of Agency Accounts	No. of More than $1,000,000 Accounts	Total Billings of Top Five Agencies	Percentage of Top Five Agencies of Total Gross
A.B.C....	$40,045,966	77	14	$13,223,825	33
C.B.S....	65,724,851	78	19	30,039,399	46
M.B.S....	20,637,363	61	5	7,792,453	38

A.B.C. billings of top five agencies:

J. Walter Thompson......................	$ 4,540,394
Compton................................	2,309,467
Kenyon and Eckhardt....................	2,248,536
Batten, Barton, Durstine and Osborn.........	2,082,855
Young and Rubicam......................	2,042,573
Total................................	$13,223,825

C.B.S. billings of top six agencies:

Young and Rubicam......................	$ 9,492,434
Dancer, Fitzgerald, Sample.................	6,495,750
Biow..................................	4,976,900
J. Walter Thompson	4,648,864
Ruthrauff and Ryan, Inc..................	4,425,451
Compton................................	3,151,963
Total................................	$33,191,362

M.B.S. billings of top five agencies:

Erwin, Wasey...........................	$ 2,961,043
Hixson-O'Donnell........................	1,368,203
D'Arcy................................	1,286,571
Gardner................................	1,093,172
Kenyon and Eckhardt....................	1,083,464
Total................................	$ 7,792,453

Top agency billings for the three networks combined:†

Young and Rubicam......................	$11,945,652 or 9.45%
J. Walter Thompson......................	10,052,515 or 7.90%
Dancer, Fitzgerald, Sample.................	8,612,751 or 6.81%

* N.B.C. has not disclosed figures since 1941; but subtracting the figures for the above three networks from the estimated total for national network gross billings gives N.B.C. a gross of $64,339,448.

† The order of these agencies would probably change somewhat if N.B.C. figures were included.

59

TABLE 2

Top Advertisers for A.B.C., C.B.S., and M.B.S. for 1945*

A.B.C.:

Total gross billings..............................	$40,045,966

(This included 115 advertisers, 12 with billings of more than a million dollars each)

Proctor and Gamble†	$ 2,240,537
General Mills....................	2,159,021
Miles Laboratories................	1,956,191
Kellogg.........................	1,678,207
Coca-Cola.......................	1,493,370
Quaker Oats.....................	1,489,247
Swift and Company...............	1,483,725
Libby, McNeill and Libby.........	1,420,561
Esquire, Inc.....................	1,176,187
Westinghouse....................	1,148,557
Philco...........................	1,144,236
Ford Motor Company.............	1,055,915
Total........................	$18,445,754

46% of total gross

C.B.S.:

Total gross billings..............................	$65,724,851

(This included 127 advertisers, 16 with billings of more than a million dollars each, of which 7 had billings of more than two million dollars each)

Proctor and Gamble..............	$ 5,358,496
Lever Brothers...................	5,091,929
General Foods....................	4,164,948
American Home Products.........	2,984,922
General Electric..................	2,842,841
Sterling Drug....................	2,275,351
William Wrigley..................	2,057,578
Total........................	$24,776,065

38% of total gross

M.B.S.:

Total gross billings..............................	$20,637,363

(This included 74 advertisers, 4 with billings of more than a million dollars each)

R. B. Semler....................	$ 1,713,953
Coca-Cola.......................	1,286,571
Ralston Purina...................	1,093,172
Sinclair Refining................	1,043,899
Total........................	$ 5,137,595

25% of total gross

* N.B.C. has not disclosed figures since 1941, but subtracting the figures for the above three networks from the estimated total for national network gross billings gives N.B.C. a gross of $64,339,448; billings would approximate those of C.B.S.

† Proctor and Gamble was the top advertiser, with a total of $7,603,070 for these three networks, which includes a billing of $4,037 for M.B.S., ranking among the five lowest advertisers for that network. Proctor and Gamble is a top advertiser on N.B.C. Exact order of other top advertisers cannot be given without N.B.C. figures.

The sponsors are going to play it safe. Instead of making any definite commitments on the new shows, and plunking down a quarter or a half a million dollars for time and talent, only to find that they're saddled with a product that isn't exciting the customers, the clients are hitching the intro for the products onto their established network shows for a series of regional tests. Proctor & Gamble, for example, is getting ready to launch its new Velvet Skin Lotion. One of the P & G airers, possibly the Rudy Vallee show, will be used on an experimental basis, with a line piped into Buffalo for a strictly regional plug. Meanwhile lotion will be shuffled off to Buffalo for a super sales campaign.

As with the old-fashioned medicine show, those who do not buy a bottle of what's good for man or beast will not get to see the little lady do her dance.

"LOVE THAT SOAP!"

That this concentration of advertising power should have had its effect on programming tastes is hardly to be wondered at. Once the decision had been made, shows began to stress a more "popular" appeal. Commercial "plugs" became more frequent and more direct. The broadcasters' "rules" against direct advertising, "relaxed" as early as 1927, gradually disappeared altogether. Radio became "show business."

The new pattern formed and hardened swiftly. In 1929, Rudy Vallee, sponsored by Fleishmann's Yeast, expanded the dance-band-with-plugs formula by introducing "radio personalities." The same year saw the beginnings of the "Amos 'n Andy" and Goldberg shows, the latter among the first of the afternoon dramatic serials, forerunners of the "soap operas" of today. Housewives, the advertisers said, found such dramas a relief from "the grim reality of housework." Certain it is that the serials were easy to produce, cost little, and were found to be very successful in selling their sponsors' products. Soap companies like Proctor and Gamble and Lever Brothers flocked to the new standard, and soon this type of program had a generic name to vie with the "horse opera" of the screen.

The logbooks of WEAF and WJZ, at that time both N.B.C. stations, show no prominent commercial sponsors before 6:00 P.M. during 1932 and 1933. By 1936 the daytime hours were filled with 15-minute shows, sponsored primarily by Oxydol, Ivory, Best Foods, Chipso, and Climalene. By 1939 the serial was well established, and such clients as Kolynos, Phillips, Dr. Lyons, and Camay had mounted the bandwagon.

Costs of evening programs, paradoxically, rose steadily through the years from 1935 to 1946. At first, this trend alarmed the sponsors and advertising agencies; for, although there was no doubt about the existence of radio audiences, there was considerable about the radio market: that listeners were purchasing radio-advertised products had not yet been "conclusively" demonstrated. The sponsors, still to be introduced to corporate and income-tax schedules which were to make "good-will" advertising the cheapest commodity on the market, wanted results. Led by the American Tobacco Company's George Washington Hill, with his "unprecedented" Cremo contest and strident Lucky Strike program, they had shaken off all the old network inhibitions against "direct" advertising, except the one about specifying the price. That this taboo to which the broadcasters clung was meaningless was made clear in practice: Eno Fruit Salts described a trial bottle costing "a little less than two packs of cigarettes"; another sponsor announced that his product could be purchased for "the smallest silver coin in circulation"; Richman Brothers boasted that "men who pay $45 for their suits can now get them . . . . for half that." The dropping of such "subtleties" was only a question of time.

Even though it often seemed like sending good money after bad, the advertising agencies eventually went after Hollywood names to "hypo" fading music-and-variety shows. At first, the film capital resented this "exploitation," but the producers soon discovered that radio appearances enhanced the popularity of their stars, as well as the box-office pull of their pictures. The actors, delighted to stumble onto new sources of revenue beyond the reach of the California income-tax collectors, soon learned to demand what the market would bear. During the 1930's, Eddie Cantor, Ed Wynn, Burns and Allen, Jack Benny, Fred Allen, Stoopnagle and Bud, Jimmy Durante, and many another veteran of vaudeville strode to the microphone as the popularity of variety shows steadily increased. Rarer were those who, like Marian and Jim Jordan ("Fibber McGee and Molly"), started more modestly, since they lacked the convenient Hollywood-Broadway spring-board, but eventually got to the top.

The first strictly "dramatic" program of the type now common, "First-Nighter," was launched in 1930. It was soon followed by the "Lux Radio Theatre." From this point it was only a step to the dramatization of mystery and murder stories: "The Shadow," "Bulldog Drummond," "The Green Hornet." The Kellogg Company gave the formula a new emphasis with "The Singing Lady," a presupper-hour children's program. Soon all the breakfast-food people were combining cowboy or G-man derring-do and package-top prizes to persuade young Americans to hound their mothers into buying new "taste sensations." The "sealed-in vitamin" fillip was to come later.

By 1938, *Fortune* observed, radio entertainment was becoming "increasingly complicated." Major Bowes had pointed the way for amateur shows, which enjoyed a brief reign and then gave way to quiz and other audience-participation programs, the more extreme types of which proved so popular that thousands of citizens still clamor weekly for the chance to make themselves ridiculous.

Henry Ford and General Motors each had a symphony program. The sponsoring of "serious" music was felt to be a matter of "prestige," as well as a completely noncontroversial form of "public service"; and soon C.B.S. had the New York Philharmonic and N.B.C. its own symphony with Toscanini conducting. The public, *Fortune* feared, "still preferred swing to symphony, comedy to uplift. Program-makers had accustomed the listener to the Big and the New, and now had a self-created mandate to produce it over and over again." Unconvinced, the Blue Network (now A.B.C.) clung to the Metropolitan Opera broadcasts it had begun in December, 1931, occasionally finding a prestige-hungry (or tax-ridden) sponsor for it (American Tobacco in 1933–34, Lambert Pharmaceutical in 1934–35, Texas Company from 1941 to ·1943). Symphonies became fixtures. And many a lesser orchestra found a place on a local station.

As early as 1931, broadcasters began to experiment seriously with forum and other "discussion" programs. The oldest of the forums is the "University of Chicago Round Table," launched on N.B.C.'s WMAQ (Chicago) in February of that year and, since October, 1933, a Sunday afternoon sustaining feature of N.B.C. "America's Town Meeting of the Air" has been a Blue Network (A.B.C.) feature since May, 1935, sometimes sponsored but during 1946 sustaining. The "American Forum of the Air" was started by M.B.S. in January, 1939. C.B.S. introduced "People's Platform" in July, 1938. The latter's "American School of the Air" and N.B.C.'s "University of the Air" have been sustaining features since the early 1930's.

As with the "serious" music programs, most broadcasters have been content to let the networks hold the "forum franchise" for them with one each, and these four coming later and later in the evening or on Sunday afternoon. Unrehearsed discussion of controversial public issues by "outsiders" has been frowned on by the N.A.B., as we shall see. Such expansion as there has been under the heading of "news and discussion" since the outbreak of World War II, therefore, has been in the direction of a quantitative increase in straight news bulletins and the development of one-man commentaries. The latter device, which made its appearance shortly after Munich and probably reached a peak before V-J Day, brought to the microphone a wide variety of speakers, a handful of them well qualified by experience for the work.

Table 3 will give some indication of the trends between 1932 and 1945. The spectacular rise under the heading "Drama" should be noted with the reservation that it coincides with the development of the "soap opera" and children's serial; bona fide experimentation in the theater arts, symbolized by the "Columbia Workshop" and the outstanding contributions of such men as Orson Welles, Arch Oboler, Norman Corwin, and Archibald MacLeish, represents only a small fraction of the total and, indeed, for a time declined. In connection with the figure for "news," it should be borne in mind that interest reached a peak during the war and has since receded somewhat.

It should be noted in conclusion that the radio advertising situation was changing very rapidly during the summer and fall of 1946. Three factors were cited for a diminution of interest on the part of many wartime broadcast sponsors: (1) the easing of the newsprint shortage, which allowed them to take more space in the print media; (2) the new tax law, which, after January 1, 1946, enabled corporations to pocket profits formerly spent on advertising because 90 cents on the dollar would have gone for taxes if it had not been used in advertising; (3) the high cost of talent; (4) labor stoppages and materials shortages.[9]

This trend, in turn, affected the agencies in more ways than one. Some of them had urged their stars to incorporate them-

TABLE 3

ANALYSIS OF PROGRAM CLASSIFICATIONS (IN PERCENTAGES)

	N.B.C.*			C.B.S.†			M.B.S.‡
	1933	1939	1944	1933	1939	1944	1944
Music:							
Classical and semi-classical........	26.9	14.1	12.2	8.8	6.2	7.3	6.9
Dance and light...	40.4	43.1	20.5	45.4	30.8	25.8	32.4
Drama.............	11.2	20.1	26.7	18.1	26.6	28.6	7.2
News..............	2.0	3.8	20.4	4.7	10.9	16.5	22.5
Variety and quiz....	2.6	2.9	14.0	7.9	8.4	13.6	8.7
Talks and discussions	7.0	9.6	2.4	7.2	4.8	6.2	12.8
Sports.............	1.0	1.2	1.1	1.5	7.0	0.8	0.9
Children's§........	3.6	2.9	0.4	5.3	3.1	...	4.6
Religious..........	1.8	1.3	1.1	1.1	2.2	1.2	4.0
Physical training‖...	2.3	.....	.....	.....	.....	.....	....
Total..........	100.0	100.0	100.0	100.0	100.0	100.0	100.0
Sustaining.........	76.4	70.3	50.6	77.1	51.3	52.2	69.0
Commercial........	23.6	29.7	49.4	22.9	48.7	47.8	31.0

* The 1933 and 1939 figures for N.B.C. are the combined Red and Blue networks—1944 are the figures for N.B.C. (formerly the Red) alone.

† C.B.S. figures in 1933 and 1939 for dance music, drama, and variety were combined into one class ("Popular Entertainment"); whereas it was possible to reclassify the commercial programs, such figures on sustaining were unavailable, hence the figures in the table are an estimate.

‡ Although M.B.S. was already organized in 1934, its sustaining programs in 1939 were broadcast on a mutual basis, and no record was kept to make the figures complete.

§ These figures should be compared very approximately, since the networks differ not only on the methods of classification but in degree of change since 1933. C.B.S. no longer classifies children's programs.

‖ A program of setting-up exercises that was popular at the time and was broadcast as much as an hour a day. Such programs are no longer significant.

selves, as a device to save the agencies the few dollars for social security deductions which they would otherwise have had to pay; and the stars had found that they rather enjoyed

[9] One might add another: the American businessman's extra-sensory knowledge of the precise moment when the customers have had enough.

dealing directly with sponsors, with whom they shared the 15 per cent service charge formerly paid to the agencies. Far more serious from the agency standpoint was the trend toward "package" firms, often consisting of a writer and a salesman, who sold finished shows either to the stars or to the sponsors, in either case by-passing the agencies.

How these trends would affect the broadcasters themselves remained to be seen.[10] Having been denied the cream of the agency business and therefore obliged to scratch for new ideas long ago, A.B.C. and M.B.S. may have found a partial solution in the co-operative sponsorship idea, whereby several-score local merchants in various communities help to defray the expense of such $100,000-plus attractions as Raymond Swing and Elmer Davis. Some affiliates had built up enough local business to cushion the shock, and, of course, the independents for the most part always had been, vis-à-vis the networks, national advertisers, and agencies, just what the word implies.

So much for the historical development of a business whose gross time sales grew from a few thousand dollars in 1925 to $100,000,000 in 1935 and to more than $400,000,000 in 1945. For the most part, it has been a natural phenomenon, a case of a hidden spring producing a brook that became a stream and then a torrent, making its own bed as it swept along. Let us now examine the extent to which the torrent has been curbed and channelized, by the broadcasters themselves, by the educators, by the listening public, and by the government.

[10] Whatever happens, the broadcasters should have some "fat" to keep them warm. The sixteen heaviest advertisers in the country spent $147,741,-252 in 1945 on newspapers, magazines, and radio; $76,183,530 of it went to the four national networks and their affiliates. C.B.S. reported an increase in net income for the first half of 1946 over the first half of 1945 of nearly a million. According to an autumn survey by *Broadcasting*, billings were up all around the country.

4

TOWARD SELF-REGULATION

IT OFTEN has been remarked that the radio broadcasting industry operates under a poorly defined charter. Possibly it would be more accurate to say that it operates under no charter. A study of the public and private utterances of those most directly connected with broadcasting reveals (1) that the attitudes of individuals changed sharply as the industry developed and (2) that at no period in this quarter-century of development have the industry's spokesmen been able to agree on a precise definition of the broadcasters' responsibilities.

Probably changing attitudes were inevitable in a changing industry. Certainly, much of what was said in the 1920's was a natural expression of the groping for guidance in a new field the outlines of which were then clearly visible to no one. It will serve no useful purpose to recall here that David Sarnoff, in 1922, envisioned radio as a "public service" comparable to the free library or that delegates to Secretary Hoover's First Radio Conference in the same year voted to outlaw all direct advertising. Advertising was not at the time an issue.

Nor is it remarkable that the broadcasters should have come, in time, to depend for their revenues upon the "evil" which they had once banished by resolution; the remarkable thing is that the shift of emphasis was so thoroughgoing that twenty years later Mark Woods, president of the American

Broadcasting Company, could say unblushingly[1] that "we are selling time for one specific reason, and that is to sell goods." And what makes it remarkable is that Woods, who was not an advertising man, nonetheless spoke the vernacular of the advertising man. Like the beleaguered Czechs of ancient Bohemia, the broadcasters had cried out for succor. Like the Hapsburgs, the advertising men who came to rescue remained to rule. And, like many a philosophical Slav, the broadcasters accepted the conquerer's tongue.

The point is significant because the advertising people brought to broadcasting not only their language but also their mores and standards. One may criticize the broadcasters for accepting them, but he could hardly accuse the broadcasters of failing to live up to them. For example, there is nothing immoral in an advertising man's admission that his primary purpose is to sell goods. So that, if we weigh Woods's words as the words of an advertising practitioner and still find them shocking, then the indictment will have to cover all advertising men, as well as a majority of the broadcasters. Perhaps it should also cover those educational and eleemosynary bodies that talked a good deal about "rescuing" radio in the twenties but did very little; a Congress that did not heed the broadcasters' plea for help; and a listening public that responded to it with contributions of dimes and half-dollars.

NATIONAL ASSOCIATION OF BROADCASTERS: FIRST PHASE

As has been noted, the American Society of Composers, Authors, and Publishers was as alert to the possibilities of radio broadcasting as Westinghouse's Dr. Frank Conrad. It had long been the practice of A.S.C.A.P. to exact royalties for copyrighted music sung or played upon the stage or etched on

[1] In a colloquy with Commissioner Clifford J. Durr during F.C.C. hearings leading to separation of the National Broadcasting Company's Red and Blue networks.

phonograph records. The application of this royalty principle to broadcasting seemed altogether reasonable. To many a broadcaster struggling along on a shoestring, it was a move fraught with peril. A number of midwestern broadcasters organized an informal committee of correspondence, and on April 25, 1923, met in Chicago to form a society for mutual aid, which they styled the "National Association of Broadcasters." The idea of a trade-association to resist the inroads of well-organized groups like A.S.C.A.P. (and government, since the conscientious Secretary of Commerce was believed to be getting increasingly "stuffy" about licenses to use already overworked frequencies) gained nation-wide favor; and on October 11 a second meeting was held in New York, at which time the membership base was broadened to include broadcasters from all parts of the country.

Organized resistance to A.S.C.A.P. was less successful than organized resistance to Hoover, but for six years these two relatively specific items constituted the agenda. There is not one word in the literature of N.A.B. or in the transcripts of its proceedings from 1923 to 1929 to indicate that a yearning for self-regulation played any part in its councils until the passage of the Radio Act of 1927 made government regulation an unpleasant reality. Not until March 25, 1929, did N.A.B. get around to writing its first "Code of Ethics," an admirable, if somewhat sketchy, document which was commended to the attention of all broadcasters by the newly appointed Federal Radio Commission.

Briefly, it proscribed the broadcasting of anything which would be barred from the mails as "fraudulent, deceptive, or obscene" and of "any matter which would commonly be regarded as offensive"; warned members to be wary of the claims of advertisers and their products; forbade statements derogatory to competing broadcasters, sponsors, or products;

70

and provided for investigation of violations of these restrictions. (The essential portions of the 1929 Code will be found in Appen. II.)

The N.A.B. of this period was still essentially an association of broadcasters. Half-a-dozen advertising agencies that had begun to manifest interest in the new medium sent "observers" to the N.A.B. sessions, as did the American Association of Advertising Agencies (A.A.A.A.) and the Association of National Advertisers (A.N.A.). At the 1929 convention some of these "observers" ventured to suggest to the broadcasters that they include in their Code a set of advertising standards comparable to those which the advertisers had applied in the other media. The station-owners and managers were still concerned about how much straight commercialism the public would stand for, and they wrote provisions so much more drastic than anything the advertising men had had in mind that the latter prevailed on the broadcasters to circulate them quietly among the N.A.B. members rather than make them public along with the Code. This "Standard of Commercial Practice," which any present-day radio listener will recognize as a collector's item, provided:

1. There should be a "decided difference" between what might be broadcast before 6:00 P.M. and what might be broadcast after that hour. The time before 6:00 P.M. was declared to be included in the "business day," and it was decided that "part at least" of it might be devoted to "programs of a business nature." After 6:00 "time is for recreation and relaxation; therefore commercial programs should be of the goodwill type."

2. Commercial announcements, "as the term is generally understood," should not be broadcast between 7:00 and 11:00 P.M.

3. "The client's business and product should be mentioned

71

sufficiently to insure an adequate return on his investment, but never to the extent that it loses listeners to the station."

The 1929 Code was reviewed at the annual N.A.B. meeting in 1931, but certain changes that had been tactfully suggested by the F.R.C. were tabled. Not until 1935 did the standing Code Committee produce a new instrument, and then the clamor was for something that would subdue the "unethical" fly-by-night stations that were springing up over the land. Clause 6 of the 1929 Code, the only one referring to the functions of the government's regulatory agency, was dropped. Three new clauses sought to bulwark the positions of the "ethical" advertisers and station-owners.

The new Code lasted two years and pleased no one. Some independent broadcasters regarded it as simply a watered-down version of the 1929 instrument and blamed the networks for the watering-down. Network representatives spoke bitterly (albeit in private) of the "downward pull" of the "lowest common denominator." Members[2] of N.A.B. observed the Code to the extent that it pleased them. There were no penalties for flouting it.

Even so, many broadcasters felt that the diluted standards were too confining. In 1937 this latter element took over the direction of N.A.B., reorganized it, and publicly dedicated the industry to a simple five-point program:

1. Find a solution for the music-copyright problem.

2. Resist efforts of the International Allied Printing Trades Council to saddle a tax on radio time sales.

3. "Eliminate certain practices and policies" reflected in programs and commercial announcements which had had "an adverse effect on the industry."

[2] At no time has N.A.B. embraced all broadcasters; as of the close of 1946, some three hundred stations were not members.

4. Promote the wider use of radio as an advertising medium.

5. Prevent "unfavorable" legislation.

In February, 1938, N.A.B. installed its first full-time paid president, Neville Miller, former mayor of Louisville. But the industry needed more than a "front" and a "practical" program. The networks were in the throes of monopoly hearings before the F.C.C. In the course of these hearings, President Sarnoff had stated:

The fate of broadcasting in other nations and the attacks on democracy throughout the world clearly indicate the necessity of finding a democratic solution for the problems of the American system of broadcasting—a solution which on the one hand will enable us fully to meet the social obligations of radio and on the other will protect our traditional freedoms. I would therefore like to take this opportunity to advocate to the broadcasting industry that it establish a voluntary system of self-regulation in its field of public service, and that it take the necessary steps to make that self-regulation effective.

Miller promptly appointed a new code committee to produce the sort of charter that radio had ignored or resisted for more than fifteen years. Before the committee had finished its deliberations, however, the war had precipitated a showdown in the field of international broadcasting. World Wide, the National Broadcasting Company, the Columbia Broadcasting System, General Electric, Westinghouse, and Crosley were sending to Europe and Latin America by short wave pretty much what they pleased. In May, 1939, the Federal Communications Commission drew up a tentative statement of principles. In hearings lasting into the summer, N.A.B. successfully combated this first attempt of the government to sketch the barest outlines of program standards. This offending statement of principles, shelved in favor of laissez faire until the Coordinators of Information and Inter-American Affairs took over short-wave broadcasting early in 1942, read:

A licensee of an international broadcast station shall render only an international broadcast service which will reflect the culture of this country and which will promote international goodwill, understanding and cooperation. Any program solely intended for and directed to an audience in the continental United States does not meet the requirements for this service.

N.A.B.: SECOND PHASE

To the advertising agencies then completely dominating the industry, and especially the networks,[3] the outlook seemed unpromising, if not downright alarming. If the F.C.C. could say that domestic programs would not pass muster abroad, might it not soon conclude that they were not adequate at home either?

Moreover, there was the war. Father Coughlin had shown how explosive the isolationist-interventionist feud could be on the air. Had not the time come to call a halt to controversy altogether, to curb this violator of the first tenet of advertising: "Don't upset anybody"?

Could the broadcasters, who, after all, had offered no protest when the advertisers moved in to an extent that they had never dared to do in the press, be counted on to "take a stand"?

The answer was of course "No"; and the advertising men and their friends in the networks proceeded to write a "Code To End Codes," but only after a battle in which wiser voices,

[3] The agencies were delivering 87 per cent of the chains' business—the shows being agency-conceived, the scripts agency-written, the talent agency-picked and rehearsed, the finished "package" even accompanied by a convenient check list of the optional stations that the broadcasters were to "plug in."

including that of Edward Klauber, executive vice-president of C.B.S., were silenced. Klauber had taken a "good" code to what has ever since been referred to by those who believe in good codes as "the Atlantic City fiasco."

The "Standards of Practice of the National Association of Broadcasters," made public on July 11, 1939, is worthy of the closest scrutiny and analysis by students of mass communication, advertising, and psychology. In some two hundred words, it placed "crime-does-not-pay" and cowman breakfast-food serials for children in the context of "character development." "Education" was dismissed in five lines, "Religion" in four. "News" was to be "fair" and "accurate." "Commercial programs and length of commercial copy" came straight from the A.A.A.A. handbook; the 7:00–11:00 P.M. "recreation period" of a decade earlier was to have up to 20-odd minutes of "plugs"[4]—more if in the form of "participation programs, announcement programs, musical clocks, shoppers' guides," or "local programs." But the chef d'œuvre was the section on "Controversial Public Issues." In some three hundred and fifty of the most carefully weighed words in the history of advertising double-talk the drafters made certain that broadcasters would eschew controversy as a plague-ridden orphan, feared by all, unwanted by the makers of soap and cigarettes.

That the advertising men were not altogether undetected and unopposed in their designs is perhaps indicated by an editorial in the August–September issue of *Education by Radio*, bulletin of the National Committee on Education by Radio:

Early in 1939, the National Association of Broadcasters, trade association for the industry, appointed a committee to prepare a

[4] If the 4-hour segment were cut into 5-minute periods, the figure would be 40 minutes for "plugs."

code which would constitute at once an instrument of self-regulation for the industry and a protection to the listening public. The membership of the committee was representative and able.[5] It held numerous meetings and consulted with a wide variety of organizations and interests. It prepared a document which was printed and distributed in advance of the Atlantic City convention of the NAB and which was recognized generally as an important contribution to the development of radio broadcasting in the United States. . . . . The code actually adopted . . . . at the convention . . . . is a totally different thing. . . . . Its objectives seem to be not so much meeting the social obligations set for radio by Mr. Sarnoff as making the acceptance of a code an end in itself. . . . . The proposed code was in two sections which were printed in a pamphlet of twenty pages. . . . . The code which actually emerged . . . . was . . . . printed in eight. . . . . Self-regulation is to be encouraged, but its objective must be public service, not industrial public relations. . . . .

The reader may find profit in comparing the proposed text on "Controversial Public Issues" with what was evolved in the private rooms of the convention hotel. (Relevant sections of the Code and of the committee proposals will be found in Appen. III.)

Soon N.A.B. felt obliged to issue a *Code Manual* to "clarify" questions raised by the Code. The original, or 1939, *Manual* undertook to describe the preliminary symptoms of "controversy" in the simple terms of a first-aid warning pasted in a medicine-cabinet, so that the most guileless broadcaster might be on his guard. Specific areas of "controversy," such as foreign policy; birth control; the political views of sponsors; the rift in organized labor; "discussion (or dramatization) of labor problems on the air is almost always of a controversial nature"; the "fact that employers, as a rule, are

[5] That it was. The committee's report was emasculated in private conferences and later on the floor. The fact that advertising men deny any part in this is of no more consequence than the fact that many political bosses never hold public office.

inclined to frown on" stations that "open their facilities to labor"; the existence of "small groups" of educators who were "muddying the waters of possible cooperation" were given special and extended treatment. (Excerpts from the 1939 *Code Manual* will be found in Appen. IV.)

From time to time new problems arose and were met by special bulletins from N.A.B. Thus on June 28, 1940, the following appeared:

POLITICAL BROADCASTS

Following a thorough discussion of the subject, the Board of Directors, at a meeting in New York held last Saturday, expressed the view that political broadcasts should be limited to speakers, interviews and announcements, and to broadcasts of *bona fide* political meetings or rallies held outside the studio. It was the feeling of the Board that stations and networks will find that the best interests of the industry will be served by a broadcasting policy which would bar the following: dramatizations of political issues, either in the form of announcements or programs; studio political "rallies"; audience participation programs such as the "man in the street" type; anonymous, simulated and unidentified voices at any time.

CO-OPERATIVES AND UNIONS

In 1942 there arose a thorny problem which the 1939 Code Committee had not foreseen. The Co-operative League of the United States, a consumers' group, announced that it was inaugurating a series of programs entitled "Let's Get Together, Neighbor." Shortly before the program was to have gone on the air as a paid feature over several N.B.C. and C.B.S. stations, the networks backed out. A considerable controversy was stirred up, and the F.C.C. wrote to the networks requesting a full statement. Both replied that such programs in their opinion were controversial in nature, because they proposed a system of marketing which was different from that

77

generally followed in this country and also because the League desired to solicit memberships.[6]

The late Senator George Norris of Nebraska told the Senate that, inasmuch as the movement "represents six or eight million families in the United States," he felt that the networks' refusal of time was "a direct denial of fundamental right." The Senator thereupon introduced a resolution to determine, among other things, "whether the Communications Act of 1934 should be further amended to authorize the Federal Communications Commission to prevent such discrimination."

The instinctive reaction of N.A.B. was expressed by Neville Miller, its president, in the usual "restrained" language:

. . . . one of the gravest threats to freedom of speech in recent years. It would direct a Senate committee to determine whether a government agency should decide what the people of America should hear and what they should not hear on the radio. If the proposed investigation materializes, you may be sure that all the advocates of bureaucratic control of both radio and the press will be on hand to urge the enactment of a law which would put an end to the American System of Broadcasting.

Having said this, Miller sat down and talked the thing over with N.B.C., C.B.S., and the Co-operative League. At a conference on December 14 and 15, it was decided that the League could take to the air early in 1943. Whereupon, N.A.B. added a new section to its Code:

SOLICITATION OF MEMBERSHIPS

Solicitations of memberships in organizations, except where such memberships are incidental to the rendering of commercial services

[6] A C.B.S. press release dated October 7, 1942, put it: ". . . . The programs offered by the League were designed to promote a fundamental change in the present system of marketing and distribution. . . . . The Columbia Broadcasting System has declined the offer . . . . because of [its] long-established policy not to sell time for programs devoted to public controversial issues."

such as an insurance plan either in respect to casualty to life or property, or for membership in the American Red Cross or like organizations engaged in charitable work, are deemed to be unacceptable under the basic theory of the Code, and therefore time should be neither given nor sold for this purpose.

In a separate statement applying specifically to the Cooperative League's bid for time, N.A.B. made certain things clear:

We believe that the advertising of cooperatives is and has been acceptable under the Code when the programs offered are designed to sell goods, trademarks or services of cooperatives. It is agreed that there is no objection to commercial copy incorporated in a program sponsored by a cooperative enterprise which states that (a) any person can make purchases at cooperatives; (b) membership in cooperatives is open and voluntary; (c) cooperatives are owned by members, each of whom has one vote; (d) profits or savings are returned to member-owners. However, in making such statements no attack is to be made on any other business enterprise or system of distribution. . . . .

One thing emerged clearly from the incident: the advertising man's enemies were, *ipso facto*, the broadcaster's enemies.[7]

On May 5, 1943, *Variety*, an entertainment trade-journal that has consistently maintained an independently critical attitude toward the broadcasting industry, exploded:

PLAN FOR A STORM(Y) SHELTER

. . . . The masterminds of the NAB have, in essence and by a single rap of the gavel, served notice on the American people that our broadcasting system is no longer open to any form of commercial solicitation unless it involves something like the transfer of a can of soup or a cake of soap. . . . . Is radio to become an exclusive privilege of the merchant? Is an organization, movement or cause, re-

[7] A former advertising executive, once prominent in radio, is authority for the statement that N.B.C. and C.B.S. were specifically warned by advertising men to drop the Co-operative "hot potato."

gardless of how sound or deserving, to be barred from the ears of the American people just because the broadcaster, so unlike the newspaper publisher, prefers to slap down a blanket interdict rather than exercise his powers of discrimination? The amendment puts the thumb on organizations that have become the basic fabric of the economic and social life of the American community. To mention but one: organized labor. . . . .

However, N.A.B. did not share *Variety*'s fears about labor. In a pamphlet issued in 1941 the Association boasted: "So confident are both the AFL and the CIO in the NAB Labor Relations Department that they have agreed never to complain to the FCC about alleged grievances in the handling of labor programs on the air by any station until the NAB Labor Department has been given an opportunity of trying to adjust the difference."

In August, 1943, N.A.B.'s Labor Department apparently passed up such an opportunity. At any rate, Richard T. Frankensteen, vice-president of the United Automobile Workers, wrote in that month to F.C.C. Chairman Fly that a speech made by him over WHKC, the Columbus, Ohio, Mutual Broadcasting System outlet, had been censored and that the station was following a general policy of censorship against labor spokesmen "not in the public interest."

The U.A.W. petitioned the F.C.C. to hold up the station's renewal application, pending a hearing. This the F.C.C. declined to do, and in May, 1944, it renewed WHKC's license for the usual 3 years. However, 2 months later, it held a hearing, in the course of which the disputants were brought together. In June, 1945, the Commission finally dismissed the proceedings in a memorable order which, in effect, threw the door open to the sale of time for the discussion of public issues.

Meanwhile, the labor volcano was erupting in several other directions. In July, 1943, the U.A.W. sought to buy time over several stations for transcriptions "advocating an orderly postwar reconversion and stabilization program." This occasioned the N.A.B. to get out, on July 23, a *Special Information Bulletin*, which read in part:

Manifestly any movement to influence public opinion on the subject of the actions of Congress is not "broadcasts in connection with a political campaign in behalf of or against the candidacy of a legally qualified candidate for nomination or election to public office, or in behalf of or against a public proposal which is subject to ballot." Therefore broadcasts of this nature should be not classed as political under the Code, nor should they be presented on paid time.

The broadcasters' position was put even more succinctly by Woods of the Blue Network at an F.C.C. hearing late in 1943. As Commissioner Durr recalled his heated exchanges with Woods, the latter took the view that

"anything at all about a labor union is controversial, *prima facie*." Hence Blue felt that it could not sell time to a labor union for any purpose. Woods did not think it was "controversial" within the meaning of the NAB Code when W. J. Cameron, in his intermission commentary during the Ford Symphony Hour, assailed organized labor, the President of the United States or "anyone else Mr. Ford happened not to like." Similarly Woods felt that it was "all right" for a commentator working for a company under federal indictment for allegedly engaging in improper cartel arrangements to defend cartels and attack the Department of Justice. On the other hand, he did not see how he could let a labor union sponsor a symphony, even if the union's name was never mentioned. "Things like that get around, you know." Finally, it was proper for a company devoting its entire output to the government, and therefore having nothing at the moment to sell to the public, to point out over the air how it was helping to win the war; whereas it would be a violation of the Code to permit the men who were working for these companies to tell radio listeners what they were doing, "as that would be controversial."

"The FCC has cancelled the 'controversial issue' clause," wailed *Broadcasting*, the N.A.B.'s unacknowledged "semi-

81

official" organ. Actually, a good many broadcasters were ahead of N.A.B., and even of the F.C.C. As of the summer of 1945, more than three hundred stations, and even Woods's A.B.C., were providing time for labor discussion, both sustaining and commercial. In August the Code Committee reported out a new and somewhat abbreviated set of Standards which differed little from previous Codes, save that the effort to curb "controversy" had been abandoned—at least in writing.

Variety saw other consequences. In its issue of September 5, 1945, it noted:

Apparently taking their cue from the revision of the NAB Code permitting sale of time for controversial issues, slanted commercials that have been projected in the last couple of weeks on some of the top-budgeted nighttime network shows sponsored by top industries have created considerable eyebrow raising. Apparently the fear of abuses raised by some broadcasters who opposed revision of the Code have been justified on the basis of lobby material against pending legislation in Washington already used in commercial copy. The duPont "Cavalcade of America" show on NBC managed to get through a plug citing the advantages of international agreements (cartels), while the commercials on the "Telephone Hour" show on the same net have taken up the cudgels against pending legislation for expansion of rural telephone service.[8]

N.A.B. AT WORK

The N.A.B. has other, less flamboyant functions than the drafting of codes and the citing of instances of government attack upon free speech and "the American way." In and out of its headquarters in Washington many standing committees work ceaselessly to produce that unanimity among broadcasters which thus far has eluded them.

[8] N.B.C. is said to have protested to the advertising agencies over these two "slips," which the New York script-readers thought Hollywood would check and which Hollywood script-readers understood had been passed by New York.

One such committee handles music-copyright problems. The duty of another is to "foster" the increased use of radio as an advertising medium, to which end it maintains "close contacts with advertisers and potential advertisers, and with advertising agencies." A third attends to legal matters, "with particular reference to FCC regulations," and is further charged to "scan all legislative proposals affecting radio in state legislatures and the national Congress, and take appropriate steps with reference thereto."

The functions of various other standing committees are described in the N.A.B. prospectus as being to (1) "maintain contact with departments and schools of journalism in the universities to bring about the establishment of courses of study which will equip people to more effectively write and broadcast radio news"; (2) "encourage more and better listening"; (3) "maintain contact with organized groups who use radio or are interested in its social side, such as women's clubs, religious organizations, labor organizations, civic groups, etc."; (4) study "program trends"; (5) conduct "research in advancing the welfare of the broadcast industry"; (6) handle technical engineering matters; and (7) "study office forms and general office practices." In addition, N.A.B. employs a publicity staff and avails itself of the services of a Co-ordinator of Listener Activity, Mrs. Dorothy Lewis.

What sort of body do the members of N.A.B. want it to be? A trade-association capable of mustering a united front against A.S.C.A.P. and Petrillo? If so, it compares favorably with the American Newspaper Publishers' Association (A.N.P.A.). An agency for the "harnessing" of the energies of women's clubs and others active in listener groups? If so, it compares favorably with the Johnston (formerly Hays) Office. An enforcement arm of the A.N.A. and the A.A.A.A. to project their "moral standards" into the ether? If so, it has done well, for, like the A.N.P.A., it has embraced and virtually canonized the "Golden Rules" of advertising.

Yet to say, as some do, that N.A.B. could never be more than the sum of all these things is to ignore the presence on its membership list, and from time to time in its councils, of station-owners and network executives who believe in things and accomplish things far above the lowest common denominator of the Association. The committee report on the 1939 Code, as distinguished from the Code that was adopted, bore the unmistakable imprint of men who were trying to grapple with a problem which few newspapers and magazines in our time have even touched. These men saw the strength of a formula that sought to avoid a monopoly of the airways for those with the most money to spend on "propaganda." The weakness of their formula was deeply imbedded in the greed and cynicism of a few broadcasters and in the dependence of almost all broadcasters upon national advertising revenue.

To the advertising agencies that pulled the strings, the choice was simple. They did not want "outsiders" bidding for the already overcrowded commercial time. They could see no point in running the risk of losing big business for the sake of accepting the few dollars the unions and co-operatives had to pay, particularly as the union business did not funnel through the agencies, dropping off the usual "full 15 per cent" en route. True, the advertising men could have made these points "informally," without committing the words to paper. They undoubtedly thought exclusion would seem more palatable if they called it a "Code of Ethics."

When Justin Miller, a former justice of the Court of Appeals for the District of Columbia and no relative of his predecessor, took office as president of N.A.B. in September, 1945, he was widely acclaimed as the man to lead the broadcasters back to the concept of self-regulation outlined by

Sarnoff. To which he quite properly replied that he would need the solid backing of all broadcasters to accomplish anything, for he was fully conscious of the fact that N.A.B. is no exception to the rule that trade-associations can never be much stronger than their weakest components.

Until the broadcasters get it through their heads that the price they would have to pay for needling politicians into abolishing the very mild form of government regulation that now exists would be public revulsion and a very much more severe form of regulation ultimately; until they show some signs of recognizing that public apathy is not the same thing as public approval and that sending a very pleasant lady around the country is no substitute for prying deeply into the unrealized citizen-needs as well as the surface tastes of listeners; until the N.A.B. devises a way to write a courageous, affirmative code that cannot be nullified by advertising men or flouted with impunity by "bad" broadcasters, codes and presidents are likely to come and go without effecting much change.

Meanwhile, the monotonous references to "free speech" and "the American System" which greet each criticism of broadcasting, however valid and temperate it may be, have exposed the N.A.B. not only to public ridicule but to the very real peril of eventual government excesses, for, as the A.N.P.A. might also discover in time, the American people may react one day, when their support is really needed to defend genuine freedoms, precisely as the shepherds of the fable reacted to the ultimate cry of "Wolf! Wolf!"

OTHER INDUSTRY GROUPS

To be sure, N.A.B. is not the only radio association. Some of the others are worth noting, if only to observe how little impact they have on the medium as a whole. Of these, the most important, perhaps, is the Association of Radio News Analysts (A.R.N.A.), organized in 1942 by H. V. Kaltenborn and other veteran commentators, who had noted that the war was turning announcers, news editors, and even comely receptionists into news "experts." Kaltenborn's *corps d'élite*, which numbers thirty-one[9] of the more than six hundred self-styled "commentators" in the country, also has a set of standards:

The Association of Radio News Analysts, aware of the necessity of maintaining the independence and prestige of the profession, and of improving the standards of analytical news broadcasting, particularly in time of war, has adopted the following Code of Ethical Practice:

1. The Association expects and requires of the radio news analyst painstaking accuracy in his public statements, recognizing the difficulties attendant upon the dissemination of news during wartime.

2. The Association expects and requires of the radio news analyst the exercise of sound judgment and good taste, and the avoidance of sensationalism in both the substance of his broadcast material and the manner of its presentation.

3. The Association believes that the inclusion in any radio news analysis of commercial or "institutional" advertising material in the guise of news or personal opinion is undesirable from every point of view.

4. The Association believes the reading of commercial announcements by radio news analysts is against the best interests of broadcasting. It requires its own members to refrain from this practice. The Association deplores the interruption of a news analysis by commercial announcements.

[9] Lowell Thomas, H. V. Kaltenborn, Hamilton Combs, Jr., William S. Hillman, Quincy Howe, Cesar Saerchinger, John W. Vandercook, II, H. R. Baukhage, Max Hill, W. W. Chaplin, Johannes Steel, Cecil Brown, Raymond Clapper (deceased), Upton Close, John Daly, George Fielding Eliot, John Gunther, Bill Henry, Charles Hodges, Ernest K. Lindley, Carey Longmire, Edward R. Murrow, Robert St. John, Paul Schubert, Eric Sevareid, William L. Shirer, Leland Stowe, Raymond Swing, Robert Trout, Leigh White, and Gregor Ziemer.

5. The Association endorses the Standards of the National Association of Broadcasters restricting the time allotted to commercial announcements in connection with news broadcasts.

6. The Association opposes all censorship of broadcast material except insofar as duly required by governmental authorities in the interest of public safety during a national emergency.

The A.R.N.A. has been able to keep outside its pale any commentators who did not meet its requirements; but it is obvious that the thirty-one "elect" have not been able to impose these standards on the five hundred-odd thus excluded. Actually, its own members do not always adhere to them religiously.

Great hopes were once reposed in the Radio Directors' Guild and the Radio Writers' Guild, particularly the latter. The actual influence of these groups may perhaps be gauged by a plaint of Norman Rosten, a member of both the Screen Writers' and the Radio Writers' guilds, published in the hospitable column operated by *New York Times* Radio Editor Jack Gould on July 15, 1945:

. . . . Radio writing, as it has now developed, is simply an adjunct of advertising. The word is fitted to the Product. The Product is God. The word is the interval between the announcements of God. . . . . What can be done? Much. . . . . I submit the following conservative program . . . . 1. Get back some control over writing, which is now almost exclusively in the hands of the sponsor and advertising agency. . . . .

Other organizations within the industry are barely worth mentioning in connection with a study of self-regulation. The Sports Broadcasters' Association exists primarily to protect the level of sportscasters' fees. The Television Broadcasters' Association, like the N.A.B., is a trade-association but has no code. The Institute of Radio Engineers has done much to improve engineering standards, and the Federal Communications Bar Association has contributed a sort of codification of communications law, but neither presumes to offer comment on programs. The Radio Manufacturers' Association, as the name implies, is devoted to the interests of those firms which produce equipment rather than, or in addition to, programs.

The American Federation of Musicians, A.S.C.A.P., and the American Federation of Radio Artists (which at the close of 1946 momentarily threatened a nation-wide strike against the networks and transcription companies), the American Guild of Radio Announcers and Producers, the Associated Actors and Artistes of America,[10] the American Radio Telegraphers Association, the International Brotherhood of Electrical Workers, the International Alliance of Theatre Stage Employees and Moving Picture Machine Operators, and the National Association of Broadcasting Engineers and Technicians, all are dedicated to protecting the interests of their members rather than those of the industry as a whole.

Except for the efforts of N.A.B., therefore, self-regulation in the broadcasting industry has been a matter for the consciences of individual broadcasters.

WHO IS "BOSS"?

Anyone who has listened to the radio is aware of what the consciences of some of them have produced, not as the quixotic hobbies of rich men but as the products of enlightened businessmen operating within the framework of profit-motive free enterprise. Why are there not more of them? There may be many reasons. The author, in a diligent search for the answer to that question, has come across what he thinks are three.

For one thing, broadcasters do not seem to know what other broadcasters are doing. To be sure, they know when a

[10] Which also boasts as affiliates Actors Equity Association, the American Guild of Musical Artists, the American Guild of Variety Artists, and the Screen Actors Guild.

88

rival has signed a star or a sponsor, what the other fellow's rate card specifies, who is going into FM, who is for or against color television, and what the industry is going to do about Petrillo or the latest F.C.C. ukase. But when asked what they think of a new program, four times out of five they say (sometimes when the program is their own), "Sorry, I haven't been able to catch that one." And if the program happens to be a local one in some far-removed small town, the reaction is almost invariably a blank stare.

What seems to be needed is a clearing house for this sort of information. The N.A.B., which distributes as much as a million printed words a year to its members, does not tell them much about what some broadcasters, particularly nonmembers, are doing in the way of new program techniques.[11] The industry has a trade-magazine, *Broadcasting*, which is the unacknowledged semiofficial spokesman for N.A.B.; but, although it prints columns of industry self-praise and even all the verbatim texts of F.C.C. rules and regulations readily available at the Government Printing Office, *Broadcasting* carries far less of the sort of thing here being discussed than does *Tide*, an advertisers' trade-paper, or *Variety*, the entertainment journal.

The second reason why more broadcasters are not doing more constructive things may be simply that the "better" broadcasters have never discovered a way to improve the general level. The N.A.B. is a symbol of industry solidarity that extends to business practices, engineering standards, and strategy for meeting real or imagined threats of government encroachment and minority pressures, but stops short of pro-

[11] The N.A.B. has repeatedly shown what it could do if it extended to other program areas the interest manifested in two formal studies in the field of children's shows which unearthed many excellent programs being quietly broadcast at the local level.

gram quality. Why? Certainly not because those who control N.A.B. shrink from "persuading" reluctant brethren when the occasion demands, for there are many broadcasters who would like to exceed the N.A.B. time limits for commercial announcements but are "persuaded" that it would not be wise to do so.

This lack of a clearing house for program ideas, incidentally, has contributed to reducing the controversy over what is and what is not "public service" to an exercise in semantics. Thus a network executive submits that Bob Hope renders "public service" (because the comedian has urged people not to cash their War and Victory Bonds). The educational director of a chain insists that "Amos 'n Andy" does (because Andy, the amoral one, always "pays" for his deviousness). The words "public service" call to the minds of many broadcasters the examples of "good" music on the air; and some even go into rhapsodies over its contribution to peace, forgetting that one of the most "musical" peoples on earth has broken the peace five times in the last eighty-two years.

Still others stress the potentialities of the quiz program, skimming over the fact that a citizen might answer correctly every one of the thousands of questions hurled at him through the ether every year and still not be particularly well equipped for survival in the atomic age. Many broadcasters, swelling with pride over their women's shows, go into ecstasies over their "soap operas," although they would be scandalized if they discovered their own wives listening to such drivel. A few, extolling the "citizen-building" qualities of crime-does-not-pay programs, appear not to understand the temptation to every youth to copy the culprit's techniques, omitting his one "fatal" mistake.

So-called "children's" shows that, week after week, portray the triumph of unpunished brats over idiotic caricatures of parents are offered as "public service." Broadcasters chuckle in retrospect, remembering some bit of comedy of a sort that was once heard only in burlesque houses, and then speak of the "wholesomeness" of humor.

News, of course, any and all news—news that is integrated and evaluated to give the listener some idea of what is at stake for him, as well as news that pours out in a steady, unrelated, mind-numbing stream—automatically "rates" as "public service." So, too, does the giving of time to three or four earnest but boring antagonists in the arena of controversy by broadcasters who seem to imagine that a "letters" column is as good as a reasoned "editorial page" prepared by trained commentators.

Then there are those who tend to lump all their "public service" in the charity basket. That is one point about which the broadcasters are very virtuous indeed. It is estimated that they gave up nearly $200,000,000 worth of time in order to serve their government during the recent war (and this does not include services rendered by sponsors, advertising agencies, and actors who donated free time). Radio's memorable 3-day tribute to the late President Roosevelt cost the industry at least $5,000,000 (very little of which was borne by the sponsors and agencies, however).

To the broadcasters this is "public service" on a pretty grand scale. They point with pardonable pride to the War and Victory Bonds they sold, the service and war-work recruiting they did, the dollars and pints of blood they brought into the Red Cross banks, the kitchen fats they helped save. They argue plausibly that, no matter how many noncommercial stations and networks spring up as FM develops, the government will always have to turn to the big commercial networks which emphasize entertainment and gain high listener ratings, as to the movies with their hundreds of controlled theaters, for maximum results in minimum time.

Finally, there is an understandable tendency to confuse "public service" with public relations, as when N.B.C. officials are admonished in an interoffice memo to "take the lead in public service programming, so that, when a 'Mae West' episode[12] occurs, the public will say, 'Well, that's human error; look what N.B.C. is doing for us: Damrosch, Toscanini, great plays, important foreign broadcasts!' "

One cannot dismiss these things as insincerities. Some of them are, and some are not. The truth is that such a wide diversity of concepts of the broadcasters' social goals is inevitable in a young industry peopled by drygoods merchants, hotel managers, crooners, mechanical tinkerers, lawyers, advertising men, insurance salesmen, retired dance-band leaders, millionaire dilettantes, soldiers of fortune, absentee landlords, eccentric industrial tycoons, morticians, haberdashers, clergymen, city-hall hacks, scholarly foundation curators, labor leaders, watchmakers, bankers, vaudevillians, college professors, publishers, unemployed politicians, gossip columnists, and soap manufacturers; by owners who follow the fortunes of their stations closely and owners who do not even listen to their own programs; by neophyte station managers, earning $50 a week, and their big-city idols, earning $500; by struggling beginners with 250-watt stations and executives of mammoth networks controlling millions of watts; by the kid next door, describing his experiences on Iwo Jima, and Raymond Swing, describing a United Nations Security Council impasse. In the autumn of 1945 a prospective

[12] Appearing on a Charlie McCarthy program, Miss West gave to seemingly innocuous lines an inflection that appeared to convey a meaning which was offensive to many listeners.

broadcaster, asked what he proposed to offer his twenty thousand rural listeners, innocently replied, "Lots of barn-dance music." Surely, in such a motley collection he is not unique.

The third reason why there are not more "good" things in radio is that the broadcasters themselves do not control radio. This point has been a bone of contention between the author and the majority of the broadcasters who encountered it in successive drafts of this report.

"Why," more than one has wailed, "do you get so worked up over the advertising agencies? The theory that they run our business is a myth. [At this point the broadcaster usually cites instances where his script-readers have cut out a "damn" or made the agency drop an unpleasant reference to mothers-in-law, to "prove" that he is complete master in his own house.] Besides, what's wrong with their building shows and hiring the talent? Or, for that matter, picking the broadcast times and selecting the cities to hear the programs? [Here the broadcaster drags out a rate card to show that advertisers are required to take certain blocks of "basic" stations, "encouraged" by the "full network plan" to take them all.] Would I write any differently, think any differently, if I suddenly went to work for J. Walter Thompson?"

The questions are rhetorical. Honest broadcasters know the answers. Indeed, it was from the broadcasters that the author learned the answers—from the broadcasters rather than from the alarmist pamphleteers, whose statements he was inclined to discount, that the author first became aware of the "problem" of advertiser domination of radio; for often, in unguarded moments, broadcasters discuss their dilemma—but not for the record, at least not in the summer of 1946, which was to have gushed red ink for time salesmen but happily did not. The author stated in a second-draft manuscript of this report that only two out of forty broadcasters interviewed in the first 6 months of 1946 had challenged the thesis that the broadcasters do not run their own business. That was the fact, and none denied it at the time; but in July and August, many of the thirty-eight, regarding the fact in black type for all to see and match against the names in "Notes on Sources," recoiled with a "Do you have to leave that in?"

Still, the layman may not know what is wrong with letting advertising men run the broadcasting industry. The layman is entitled to know the answers that the broadcasters know and that the author learned from them.

The first thing that is wrong with the present system is that it enables men about whom the public knows nothing and whom the F.C.C. is not required by law to investigate to enjoy franchises which the public grants to another, or "dummy," group for the use of the public's frequencies. It is rather like a householder who carefully investigates someone to whom he proposes to sublet his home, only to discover that quite another family, about which he knows nothing and which is not bound by any lease to take care of the property, intended to occupy the premises all along. Even if the advertising men were ideal "tenants" of the airways, the situation would not be businesslike; if they are to stay, they should at least be required to sign the lease.

The second thing that is wrong with the present system is that the advertising men are not, in fact, ideal "tenants" of the airways. This is not to say that advertising men are not useful citizens and often very pleasant people to know, or to disparage the vital role that they play in the national economy. It concerns their point of view, their aim in life, their *raison d'être*, which, as Woods put it, is to sell goods and services.

Now it must be fairly obvious that not everything that the

average American requires to enable him to understand and perform his increased duties as a citizen will, in terms of radio programs, sell goods and services. The more enlightened broadcasters, realizing that this is so, pay for such programs out of the profits from programs that do sell goods and services.

True, a few sponsors are willing to spend relatively modest sums on programs that do not directly sell goods and services. But few advertising men would suggest such a thing to a sponsor-client; for, to begin with, advertising men hesitate to seem prodigal with their clients' money and, what is more to the point, the advertising man's income is 15 per cent of what his clients spend, and they spend far less, program for program as well as in sum, on "good-will" advertising than they spend on advertising that sells goods and services.

One can reduce the matter to simple arithmetic: If the advertising man's earnings are 15 per cent of X, he naturally will want to see X as large as possible; and, since the size of X is dependent on the size of the potential listening (or reading) audience, he will want large audiences; and, since readers (or listeners) are supposed to be driven away by controversy and by things that make them "think" or tax their consciences, the advertising man naturally will want as little of this sort of thing as possible.

Moreover, it is said to be harder to build an audience than to keep one going, easier just to copy a successful formula than to try a new one. (A recent cartoon which seems to the author to summarize admirably what is wrong with American radio "comedy" has a producer asking, "How do you know it's a good gag if it ain't been used?") Therefore, the advertising man will be bound to resist change and experimentation.

Finally, since the largest budgets are spent on national

network shows, the advertising man will not be overly interested in strictly local programs.

Hence, as long as the advertising men call the tunes in radio, we are certain to get an absolute minimum of "educational" programs, controversy, diversity, experimentation, local service, objectivity in the handling of basic economic cleavages in which the advertising man will aggressively defend what he believes to be his clients' "interests," and "public service" from sponsors who, left to their own devices, might go further than their "protectors" will let them go.

In sum, the ideal of any advertising man is a program made up exclusively of variety, comedy, popular music, noncontroversial news (all of it in the "formula groove"), and advertising "plugs," plus, perhaps, a law to prevent the F.C.C. from doing anything to thwart a speedy realization of the ideal. To deny that this is so is to call into question both the advertising man's good sense and his value to his clients.

Let us be frank about it: What we have here is a continuing contest between two diametrically opposed approaches to the problem of public service in radio—one based on long-range citizen need as the criterion, the other based on Hooper ratings and sales charts. The sharp distinction may not always be apparent to the uncritical listener. When, during the war, for example, the advertising men "plugged" War Bonds and urged housewives to save kitchen fats or when, with fanfare of trumpets, they surrendered time to "patriotic" programs, the average listener probably did not temper his gratitude with a realization that at the moment the sponsor-clients of the advertising men had nothing to sell to the general public but patriotism and that the income-tax schedules made it a fairly cheap gesture, at that. All this is not to say that we should be ungrateful for coincidental blessings but simply that it may be useful to keep in mind that any social blessings that flow from the advertising fraternity are bound, in the nature of things, to be coincidental.

It has been said that the issue of advertiser domination has been raised only by "highbrows" who never listen to the radio. If anyone really believes that it is either a "phony" or a minor issue, let us call to the stand several hundred witnesses better qualified to testify than anyone in America—the station-managers.

TABLE 4

	Per Cent
Advertising agencies	47
Sponsors	44
F.C.C.	23
Local stations	21
Rating services	21
Listeners	10
N.B.C.	7
Transcription services	7
M.B.S.	6
C.B.S.	6
A.B.C.	3
N.A.B.	1
Other	6*

* *Broadcasting* explained that the totals came to more than 100 per cent because the votes for first, second, and third choice were combined.

The trade-magazine *Broadcasting*, in the first of a series of frank questionnaires put to station-managers throughout the country, asked the following question, among others: "Which of the following do you feel have done the most to retard improvement in programming?" The answers, printed in the November 4, 1946, issue, are shown in Table 4.

Here, then, is the situation. The people, through their Congress, have directed the F.C.C. to require of the broadcasters that the public's airways be used in the best interests of all of us. With this in mind, the broadcasters, in seeking licenses or

97

renewals, outline to the F.C.C. what they propose to do in the way of serving all the public. But the broadcasters can be, and in many instances are, prevented from following their outlines by people who are not interested in the public except as a market for goods and who can do pretty much as they please because they are not in any way beholden to the people, the Congress, or the F.C.C. The system, as it stands, is a grim farce.

The broadcasters could, if they wished, break out of this "prison," precisely as the newspaper publishers of America broke out of it less than half a century ago. Confident, as were the publishers at the turn of the century, that they have become an indispensable part of the economic machinery, they could say to the advertising men: "In future, we are going to build all our own shows, hire all our own talent, and broadcast to maximum audiences. We will have only one thing to sell to you: brief station-break time periods at the beginning and end (never in the middle) of programs. We feel that this is the only way we can honorably discharge our responsibility to the American people, who not only own our means of transportation but look to us for leadership."

Such a move would take courage. The industry would have to present a united front, aggressively led by an N.A.B. prepared to deal with those broadcasters who decline to join the united front. The step would require the support and assistance of all in a position to assist. The Department of Justice and the F.C.C. would need to assure the N.A.B. that it would not be prosecuted under the antitrust acts for setting high standards and disciplining broadcasters who failed to live up to them. The F.C.C. might, in recognition of any tangible indication that the broadcasters meant to place themselves in a position to shoulder responsibility, clarify the current situation by formally renouncing any intention of attempting to judge programs. Failing that, the Congress might give the broadcasters this assurance. If there are advertisers or potential advertisers who feel that American free enterprise should go further in meeting the social challenge than their advertising and public relations counsel seem willing to let them go, they might step forward with enough new sponsored public service programs to cushion the shock of any advertiser boycott of radio that might ensue. If there is such a thing as an advertising man who understands the moral of the fool who killed the goose that laid the golden egg, he might well ease his conscience by crying out a warning to his fellows.

Actually, it is highly unlikely that an advertiser boycott would assume serious proportions—if, indeed, it materialized at all. One might suppose that the easing of the paper shortage and other controls by the end of 1946 had already removed from the air all save those who regard radio as an absolutely indispensable and highly profitable medium. This inalienable residue has raised gross billings to the highest point in history. It might be a very good thing for us all if the broadcasters were to discover, as the publishers long since discovered, that a resolutely independent editorial policy does not drive away advertisers who have nowhere to go. Possibly it would prove a good thing even for the sponsors, for it is conceivable that the broadcasters would turn out better, fresher, more varied programs, calculated to reach even bigger audiences. And if it is true, as the rating-takers insist, that no one bothers to turn off his radio during the 60–240 seconds of closing commercial, "hitchhiker," "cowcatcher," and opening commercial between programs, better shows and larger audiences would mean more sales, even without the middle commercial and the product-related gag.

One must not suppose that this is the whole story. A free radio would not necessarily become a "good" radio overnight.

An industry delivered from the advertising man's gun-in-the-back and the F.C.C.'s handcuffs would still have to show that it knew how to deal with the substandard broadcaster who shackles its feet. A medium that has produced fewer new art forms than the movies needs brains and imagination quite as much as it needs courage. It needs new materials. It needs to make itself attractive to the vast writing, directing, and acting talent in America, most of whom now regard it as beneath their notice. It needs to produce more than two new program formats, three outstanding writers, and three or four first-rate comedians in a decade.

On the corrective side, radio needs to devise criteria for the evaluation of children's shows other than the numbers of box-tops mailed in, criteria for the evaluation of women's shows other than the packages of soap chips sold. Indeed, the broadcasters need to simplify their standards. It should be enough to know that any given program is the best of its kind that human ingenuity and hard work can devise; that, if it does not actually elevate public tastes, it will at least not degrade them; and that it is being broadcast at a time when those who need to hear it can conveniently do so. These questions do not require the services of a roomful of learned psychiatrists; any fledgling producer ought to be able to answer them.

But these are steps which cannot be taken until the first big step is taken. What the broadcasters appear to forget in appealing to the publishers for aid in their "fight for freedom" is that their causes cannot be identical so long as their attitudes toward the advertising man are not identical. No one deserves to be free unless his ultimate goal is complete freedom.

5

THE LIGHT THAT FAILED

IN THE early days of radio the newspapers were full of the ambitious plans of schools and colleges to employ the wonderful new medium. Many institutions announced that they were going to start regular extension courses over the air waves. Indeed, in 1922 such classes were being scheduled by New York University, Columbia University, and Tufts College. In the Middle West the University of Wisconsin and Michigan State College were developing programs for farmers and other groups neglected by the early commercial stations. Soon market and weather reports were being broadcast regularly by the Universities of Wisconsin, Nebraska, Illinois, Michigan, and Minnesota and by Nebraska Wesleyan, St. Louis University, and Cornell University. All in all, school-owned or -sponsored stations, reaching a high-water mark of more than a hundred, formed a very respectable segment of the total in the 1920's; but not many survived.

From 1921 through 1936, no fewer than 202 educational station licenses were granted, the majority of them before 1927. During the same period, 164 licenses were permitted to expire or were transferred to commercial interests, most of them prior to 1930. It is significant to note here that 50 of the 164, or 30.5 per cent, were held for a period of less than one year; 85, or 51.8 per cent, for less than two years; 109, or 66.46 per cent, for less than three years; and only 55, or 33.54 per cent, for three years or more.

101

By the time the national commercial networks were well launched, eight out of ten educational stations were wilting on the vine. Easily persuaded (a) that only classroom techniques could be used by educators and (b) that these could not be adapted to radio; that forum programs could never hope to attract large audiences (the American Broadcasting Company's "Town Meeting of the Air" has drawn up to four million listeners); and that the average lecturer was a poor radio speaker, the academicians abandoned the field to the networks and the advertising men. School boards, regents, legislatures, listeners, and the Federal Radio Commission apparently agreed that this was "nature" taking her "inevitable" course.

Seldom have the fruits of apathy and indifference been less surprising. At the end of 1946, 29 standard (AM) broadcasting stations were licensed to educational institutions; of these, 9 were commercial, 5 of them affiliated with networks. Thirteen, 10 of them noncommercial, were permitted to use 5,000 watts or more power; but, of these, only 2 could broadcast between sunset and sunrise, local time. What are the reasons for this amazing mortality rate? The following case histories tell much of the story:

1. *University of Colorado.*—Licensed in 1922. Deleted in 1926. No faculty interest. No funds. Too much interference with the National Broadcasting Company's KOA (Denver).

2. *School District of Boise, Idaho.*—Began broadcasting in 1922. Discontinued in 1928 when the only interested member of the faculty left. No funds.

3. *University of California.*—Licensed in 1922. On the air only one evening. No faculty interest.

4. *University of Michigan.*—Licensed in 1924. Lapsed in the same year. Faculty felt better results could be obtained more cheaply through co-operation with commercial stations.

5. *Carleton College.*—Licensed in 1923. Spent considerable money on thoroughly modern plant, which served as important training center for other institutions. Because of constant shift in frequencies, which eventually left station in an impossible position on the dial, limitation of hours for broadcasting, and time-sharing situation with two other schools and commercial station, ultimately rendered unendurable by court action of commercial station seeking full-time operation, let license expire in 1933.

6. *Ashland College.*—Refused a renewal because it could not afford to purchase equipment meeting high standard set by federal regulatory body.

7. *Antioch College.*—Licensed in 1923 to operate full time. Failed to apply for renewal in 1927 because it was being forced to share time in such a way that its early effectiveness had been lost.

8. *University of Arizona.*—Licensed in 1922 with student-built station. Faculty decided in 1925 that local commercial station could do a better job.

9. *University of Arkansas.*—Left the air after one year. No faculty interest. No funds. Continually shifted to weaker spots on the dial.

10. *University of Rochester.*—Licensed in 1922. Originally programmed by Eastman School of Music. Sold to Stromberg-Carlson in 1927 on assurance that university would have ample access to station.

11. *Alabama Polytechnic Institute.*—Licensed in 1922. Power and frequency continually shifted until Secretary of Commerce deleted station in 1925. Resumed in the fall of that year with new equipment. After June 1, 1927, again subjected to continual shifts in power and wave length. Removed from Auburn to Birmingham in 1928, where it operated in co-operation with state government and Protective Life In-

103

surance Company, additional funds being supplied by city of Birmingham. In 1929 sold stock to University of Alabama and Alabama College for Women. When city withdrew financial support in 1931, station was leased to WAPI Broadcasting Corporation, with the understanding that stockholding institutions be granted 6 hours daytime and 1 hour nighttime weekly, free of charge. Was unable to make use of this free time because of high cost of telephone long-lines connecting schools with Birmingham. In 1936 signed with a new lessee for 15 years. Subsequent experience equally unhappy for institutions involved. Three schools, together with Tuskegee Institute and other "participating" institutions, were persuaded by the Federal Communications Commission in 1946 to withdraw from field and lay plans for FM network.

That some educational pioneers managed to surmount difficulties is apparent from their case histories:

1. *University of Wisconsin.*—Began regular broadcasts on January 3, 1920. Licensed in 1922. Power increased from 750 to 1,000 watts in 1932; to 2,500 in 1934; and to 5,000 in 1936. Lost privilege of sharing evening hours with a commercial station in the Federal Radio Commission's reallocation of 1928, hence unable to broadcast adult-education programs after sundown, Madison time, when jobholders are able to listen, because of possible interference with stations in Fargo, North Dakota, and Louisville, Kentucky. Program policy initiated by alert, aggressive faculty group in co-operation with well-organized listener groups throughout state stresses appeal to groups and interests neglected by commercial stations. Despite time restrictions, station has wider geographical coverage and more regular listeners than any other serving Wisconsin.

2. *Michigan State College.*—Operated as regular department of college, directly answerable to president. Programming

policy designed to reach all Michigan with adult-education material. Well-rehearsed forums in which both sides of controversial public issues have opportunity to speak help to interest people in their local, state, and federal government, as well as in the United Nations. Twelve and a half hours a week are devoted to agricultural and home economics programs. Station is used by University of Michigan and many other colleges, as well as by public school systems. Three-point policy based on (*a*) no advertising, (*b*) no political affiliations, and (*c*) no religious programs. Station will serve as nucleus for ambitious FM network, embracing all schools and colleges in state.

3. *Cornell University.*—Its station said to be a model for part-commercial, part-noncommercial operation. Profits from sponsored programs spent on sustaining features.

4. *Benson Polytechnique School.*—This Portland, Oregon, institution's station has excellent night-and-day local coverage, despite constant shifts in power and frequency. Used by numerous local groups and by Oregon State College to relay programs not heard formerly in that part of the state.

5. *University of Florida.*—Authorized in 1927 by state legislature to erect high-power station for educational purposes. Location made assigned frequency unsuitable, hence was authorized by F.R.C. to share wave length of KOA (Denver) until sunset, Gainsville time. Now commercial, station offers service to large part of state not reached by any other.

6. *Other survivors.*—Universities of Illinois, Iowa, Kansas, North Dakota, Oklahoma, South Dakota; Ohio State, Purdue, Baylor, St. Louis, and Loyola (New Orleans) universities; Oregon State College, Luther College, Washington State College, St. Olaf College, Port Arthur College, Kansas State College, Rensselaer Polytechnic Institute, Grove City

College, South Dakota State College, and Texas Agricultural and Mechanical College.

In a somewhat different category is Syracuse University, which does not operate its own station but which maintains the Radio Workshop. Supported jointly by the university (which contributes the major share) and WSYR and WFBL —N.B.C. and C.B.S. affiliates, respectively—the Workshop not only builds outstanding programs like "Syracuse on Trial" for broadcast over the commercial stations but also advises civic groups of all kinds and from all over the United States on how to build audience-winning programs.

Outstanding in the field of FM is the Cleveland Board of Education, whose WBOE is on the air Mondays through Fridays from 8:00 A.M. to 4:00 P.M. with an in-school training program, for which regular schedules are prepared in advance. The Cleveland program features rebroadcasts of such commercial educational fixtures as C.B.S.'s "School of the Air," offered by WJAR; the weekly commentaries of Sumner Welles, from WJW, the A.B.C. affiliate; and N.B.C.'s "University of the Air," supplied by WTAM. With the co-operation of these stations and WHK, the *Plain Dealer* station, WBOE has private lines linking it with all four major networks. It goes without saying that the Cleveland system will be one of the important nuclei for the proposed Ohio FM network, which, alone of all the state projects, had passed, by the close of 1946, entirely from the blueprint to the action stage.

The University of Michigan, which, as we have seen, operated its own station during most of 1924 and which has since drawn on commercial facilities in Detroit and the Michigan State College station in East Lansing, is active in a move to realize a state-wide FM network to which, as of January, 1947, some forty colleges and public school systems had signified

106

their intention to adhere. Six applications had been filed with the F.C.C. as of that month, and the university had secured a construction permit to build a 50-kilowatt station at Ann Arbor.

As of July 1, 1946, six noncommercial educational FM stations were operating: WBEZ (Chicago Board of Education); WNYE (New York Board of Education); KALW (San Francisco Unified School District); WBOE (Cleveland Board of Education); WIUC (University of Illinois); and WBKY (University of Kentucky). In addition, twenty-one had construction permits, including the following: University of Iowa, University of California at Los Angeles, Buffalo Board of Education, Kansas City School District, University of Michigan, Newark Board of Education, Columbia University, University of Oklahoma, Oklahoma Agricultural and Mechanical College, Louisiana State University, Detroit Board of Education, and Wisconsin Radio Council (two stations, one at Madison and one at Delafield). There were pending twenty-three applications from fourteen states.

As for television as of the same date, the University of Iowa had an experimental station. Purdue had a station under construction. Western Reserve University, Kansas State College, and Johns Hopkins were among a score of noncommercial applicants. The first-named was a member of the Television Broadcasters Association, as were the Department of Drama at Yale College, the New School for Social Research in New York, Rutgers University, and Syracuse University; and C.B.S. and N.B.C. were co-operating with the New York Board of Education in experimental work. N.B.C. was also working with the William Howard Taft High School, and the University of California at Los Angeles was receiving help from the Don Lee Network.

Who was at fault for the insignificant part in AM broadcasting played by noncommercial stations? Will the same persons or factors write the same sorry story in FM, television, and facsimile? The answers to these questions are important only if one is prepared now, as neither the government nor the educators were in the thirties, to accept the thesis that commercial broadcasters alone cannot and will not realize radio's full potentialities as a medium for citizen education in a democracy.

The commercial broadcasters are fond of patting educational broadcasting on its figurative head. In theory, it is the "good little boy" who will do things they do not wish to do. In practice, it has been a competitor for scarce frequencies. The instance of the commercial broadcaster who drove Carleton College from the air because it could not contest the suit he threatened to bring is by no means unique. The threat of lengthy, expensive litigation has always been the last resort in those rare instances in which the commercial broadcasters have not been able to brow-beat the federal regulatory body into squeezing the "long-hairs" out of the picture.

FM frequencies are more plentiful, and the initial cost of getting into FM is lower. Presumably, the commercial broadcasters will gradually abandon their dog-in-the-manger attitude toward the educators. But they must do much more than that if educational broadcasting is to turn the corner and become a dominant force in the land, for the finest FM station, if it is to be heard more than 40 or 50 miles away, will require means of linking itself with other educational FM stations which are scarce, expensive, and now wholly in the hands of the powerful networks. (Transcriptions can do a large part of the job; but, if transcriptions are not quite so good as live broadcasts for the commercial people, they are not quite so good for anyone.) Television is just over the horizon, and television is a thing of expensive plant and equipment, also now wholly in the hands of the big broadcasters.

If the commercial interests want the educators to carry the wet end of the log, they must shoulder the heavy end. Perhaps that means financial assistance. It certainly does not mean mere lip service. Surely, it is time the broadcasters realized that they cannot have it both ways.

Nor can the federal regulatory authority be given a clean bill of health. Time and again, in the late twenties and early thirties, the F.R.C. made room for more (or louder) commercial broadcasting by squeezing educational stations down, and sometimes out. Often the regulators cited as an excuse the obvious fact that the educational stations thus squeezed had been no great shakes (although the criterion was seldom applied to commercial stations). Stepping into this inheritance, the F.C.C. found itself caught in the spiral of precedent: in the beginning the commercial people had got the best frequencies, the most power; ever since, when a noncommercial station had applied for a share of favors thus pre-empted, the pre-emptors could cite not only the law of possession but also the inevitable fact that they "served a wider area." Having for so long tolerated the situation, the educators discovered belatedly that the F.C.C. was bound to accept them at their own estimate.

On January 22, 1935, as we shall see in a later chapter, the Commission sought to cover its past sins of omission by reporting to the Congress that "it would appear that the interests of the nonprofit organizations may be better served by the use of existing facilities." Pontius Pilate could not have done better.

As a palliative to the death sentence they thus passed on the educators, the F.C.C. added that "it is our firm intention to assist the nonprofit organizations to obtain the fullest opportunities for expression." Not until 1945, when it set aside twenty FM channels for educational broadcasting, did the F.C.C. lift more than an occasional hesitant finger to implement that pledge. True, in 1938, the Commission did increase the power of the Michigan State College and University of Illinois stations, the latter at the price of some interference with minor commercial stations. But ten times that many similar requests have been turned down since 1935, and dozens are always pending.

The F.C.C., too, must give more than lip service to the educators; it must be prepared to fight for them. Since the courts have relieved it of any concern for the broadcaster's chances for economic survival, the Commission must judge contests for frequencies, power authorizations, and time periods not only on the merits of the two services being offered but also on the merits of the two services that might be offered if the physical advantage and disadvantage were reversed. Finally, the F.C.C. might have a look at the present costs of linking stations together. As the basis for fundamental policy, such an examination deserves a high priority on the crowded Commission docket.

So much for the educator's betrayers. The reader must not suppose that the educators have been guiltless. The commercial broadcasters and their F.C.C. apologists have been all too right in saying that most educational programs have been dull and even stupid. To a student of educational radio, prowling through yellowed scripts, it seems almost incredible that teachers who presumably hoped to reach men's minds elected to attempt it with anesthetics. Surely, secrets of audience psychology readily mastered by semiliterate movie stars and dance-band leaders are not hidden from the academicians.

But those who failed at least tried. Let the reader glance

again at the list of educational stations that went off the air, in part at least because of "no faculty interest." Let him search the lists of all the educational stations that have ever existed for the names of colleges long famed for their contributions to the dramatic arts: Harvard, Yale, and North Carolina. Let him hunt two of the wealthiest and, as they like to think, "best": Harvard and Chicago. Let him find, if he can, out of the scores of institutions that have pledged themselves to find a peaceful solution for atomic energy, "by whatever means possible," two that have thought of radio as one possible means.

The leaders have not led. This is hardly a task for a handful of land-grant colleges alone. It is not a job for the United States Office of Education, with its stream of happy little pamphlets. It is not a job for the dormant Federal Radio Education Committee, the Association for Education by Radio, the Institute for Education by Radio, the National Association of Educational Broadcasters, or the School Broadcast Conference.

It is an assignment also and especially for a few powerful, wealthy institutions of the order of Harvard, Yale, Columbia, Chicago, Duke, and Stanford—universities not bound by lean purses or niggardly state legislatures; for California, Illinois, Minnesota, Wisconsin, and Michigan—seats of learning whose active, aggressive leadership would insure the success of any educational venture. Let such as these—some of them long identified with the most hopeful trends in adult education, some of them already spending millions on research aimed at the shoring-up of a tottering civilization—step forward to show the way. And if they do not, let us hear no more from them about the "hopelessness" of American radio.

6

WHAT DO THE LISTENERS SAY?

I T HAS often been remarked that, in addition to owning the air which the broadcasters use, radio listeners in the United States have invested nearly five billion dollars in receiving sets, tubes, aerials, and other apparatus necessary to its enjoyment. The author is less impressed with these statistics than with the simple fact that the chances of Americans' being able to go on indefinitely enjoying radio under the shadow of the A-bomb may depend in large part on what comes out of the receiving sets.

What do the American people think of what comes out of their 45,000,000 sets? No one knows. The sponsors and advertising agencies know approximately how many persons listen to their programs every week. An occasional scientific door-to-door survey has produced masses of confusing and often contradictory figures covering limited population, geographical, income-group, age-group, sex-group, and education-level areas. Thanks to the business initiative of the Columbia Broadcasting System, that network and the National Broadcasting Company have known for some time what the county-by-county listening pattern was as regards chain programs in the thirties. Postwar developments in listener-survey techniques had reached a point by late 1945 where they promised to give a more exact picture; but a year later the outlines were still somewhat hazy.

The Federal Communications Commission, every broadcaster, and a good many members of Congress always keep at hand a few letters from the not very considerable number written every year.[1] A handful of organized listener groups undertakes to represent public tastes in a few communities. Now and then a newspaper radio editor or magazine writer tells us what sixty million listeners are thinking. Educational and church groups periodically publish what are described as "national surveys." Here and there, pressure groups spring up and become vocal. And all sorts of individuals, institutions, foundations, and corporations offer annual awards for the best this-and-that type of program, thus insuring that the listeners will get more of the same.

Let us examine these various techniques for probing the citizen's mind. From the earliest days of broadcasting, loosely organized listener groups have clustered around local service and women's clubs, parent-teacher associations, and energetic educators and clergymen. Few of them have had clearly defined programs or goals; and those that have, have been fairly limited and specific about them: more "wholesome" children's programs, more "good" music, more in-school training, more Sunday morning time for sermons, and so on. As with most voluntary and quasi-social groups, the majority have found it difficult to sustain interest or even attendance at meetings.

Notwithstanding, their existence as a potential problem came early to the attention of the National Association of Broadcasters and the networks, and for a variety of reasons. Harried broadcasters, some of whom were in those days extremely sensitive to the likes and dislikes of their listeners, turned to the "big fellows" for guidance. Although the impact was usually local, many of the things most complained of were

---

[1] Thirty times as many persons solicit "advice to the lovelorn" every year as commit their opinions about radio to paper.

network concerns, conducive to friction between the chains and their affiliates.

After some pressure on the broadcasters, the Radio Council on Children's Programs (R.C.C.P.) was formed. Out of it grew a number of community radio councils, the Minnesota, Cedar Rapids (Iowa), Cleveland, and Nashville councils, being among the pioneers. To Mrs. Dorothy Lewis, longtime woman's club leader, first vice-president of the R.C.C.P., and now Co-ordinator of Listener Activity of N.A.B., this was at once a challenge and an opportunity. Mindful of Will H. Hays's success in holding early film councils "in line," the N.A.B. set Mrs. Lewis to touring the country. In half a decade she helped to bring forty-five radio councils to life. As of late 1946, there were more than fifty active councils, their average membership including such groups as the parent-teacher associations, librarians, school boards, service clubs, women's clubs, church bodies, and an occasional labor union. Typical projects include improvement of children's programs, allocation and production of public service programs by central committees, distribution of material, program promotion, and periodic conferences.

Two outstanding councils are the Better Radio Listening Council of Wisconsin and the Greater Cleveland Listening Council. The former covers every community in the state, publishes monthly lists of "meritorious" programs, and stimulates discussion of radio problems, particularly among high-school students. Ready access to the University of Wisconsin's WHA (Madison) assures it a sympathetic platform which is audible throughout the state. The Cleveland group, which received its original impetus from Robert Stephan, radio editor of the *Plain Dealer*, confines its efforts to greater Cleveland; claims to speak for 155,000 women; conducts occasional door-to-door, mail, and telephone surveys; and pub-

114

lishes periodic "evaluative" program lists. Like the Wisconsin group, it bars anyone connected with the industry from membership or active participation.

The haphazard methods of the broadcasters and the inclination of the sponsors to judge programs by what their families and friends thought of them convinced the advertising-agency people that they would have to invent something more reliable than fan mail, which had proved notoriously unreliable. They needed to know what percentage of the potential listeners listened to what programs, on what days, and over what stations.

In 1929 a statistical researcher, Archibald Crossley, had conducted some tests by the "recall" method, with interrogators asking listeners to remember what they had heard one or several days previously. The American Association of Advertising Agencies and the Association of National Advertisers saw merit in his method, promptly organized the Cooperative Analysis of Broadcasters (C.A.B.), with Crossley as chief, and by 1945 had built up the service to a point where it covered eighty-one cities weekly. In 1934, Clark-Hooper, Inc., newspaper and magazine advertising analysts, entered the radio field with the "coincidental" telephone-query system, which soon was adopted by C.A.B. The Hooper ratings are currently conducted in thirty-two cities and, unlike the C.A.B.'s, are released for publication by the trade-press. By 1945 the two systems had become so much alike that broadcasters, particularly the networks, began to grumble about the expense of "duplicate" services, and C.A.B. was suppressed by the end of 1946.

A new rating method was introduced in 1942, when A. C. Nielsen perfected what he calls an "audimeter," a mechanical device which, attached to the receiving set, records on a strip of paper the exact lengths of time various stations are tuned in and out. As of July 1, 1946, more than three thousand "audimeters" had been distributed in twenty states, and Nielsen claimed for his sample a 60 per cent "coverage" of the country. The Nielsen Radio Index method has the obvious advantage over C.A.B.'s and Hooper's that it can reach the 16,000,000 nontelephone homes with radios. However, it is appreciably more expensive to operate and, of course, is not capable of differentiating between the careless leaving-on of sets and actual listening.

Other rating and survey methods in use include that of Dr. F. L. Whan, who covers Iowa and Kansas through a combination of door-to-door surveys and mailed questionnaires; Industrial Surveys, Inc., which checks weekly food and drug consumption of some thirty-five hundred families; and "Pulse," a door-to-door survey based on 4-hour "recall" and, as of 1946, confined to greater New York and Philadelphia. On a somewhat different level are studies made by Dr. Frank Stanton, of C.B.S., and Dr. Paul Lazarsfeld, of Columbia University, which for the most part have been of an intensive, though quantitative, nature.

Obviously, all these methods leave a great deal to be desired if one wishes to know what radio listeners really think. The limitations of the telephone method have been stressed. (There is here also the matter of "no answers," which Hooper neatly gets around by lumping them in as "weighted percentages" to produce what *Variety* calls "guesstimates.") Experience has shown that high-income families frequently decline to be "interviewed." A serious difficulty is presented by the simple fact that no one can listen to two programs on the air at the same time. The common technique is a little like asking someone whether he prefers vanilla ice cream to chocolate ice cream, when perhaps what he would really like is some beefsteak, which happens not to be on the bill of fare. But, as long as all the methods here described continue to show higher ratings for commercial than for sustaining programs, it seems hardly likely that some broadcasters and advertising men will want to change the diet drastically.

Serious qualitative analyses of listener reaction on a limited scale were made during the ten years after 1936. Among the first was a series begun for *Fortune* by Elmo Roper, who more recently began another for the New York Tribune Syndicate. These have developed such data as that the public relies most on radio and believes radio abuses its power less than the other media and that the more formal education a person has had, the more likely he is to want news, commentary, and discussion of topical value. An October, 1945, Roper poll of type preferences, covering both sexes and various age and education levels, showed music first, news a close second (first for males), variety a poor fourth, and quiz shows at the very bottom.

In the summer of 1945, faced with the problem of what to do about rural listeners in connection with its projected clear-channel hearings, the F.C.C. asked Rensis Likert's survey organization in the Department of Agriculture's Bureau of Agricultural Economics to conduct the first intensive nation-wide listener survey ever undertaken from the standpoint of public interest only.

The results of this survey, to which the Bureau of the Census also contributed certain rather sketchy data, were cited by the broadcasters as "conclusive proof" that no general dissatisfaction existed among rural listeners. Nevertheless, the order of program preferences developed by the Likert survey scarcely indicated that the farmers were getting what they wanted in the proportions they specified. News

117

ranked first, followed by religious music and other religious programs, "old-time" music, and market reports, in that order. Dance music, serials, and "dramatic" programs were well down the list, with classical music at the very bottom.

Meantime, the industry had decided to defend itself with facts rather than with slogans. Even before the government surveys were launched, the N.A.B. retained the National Opinion Research Center (N.O.R.C.) at the University of Denver to canvass listeners. A few weeks after the release of the last of the Likert data and almost on the heels of publication of the F.C.C.'s report on *Public Service Responsibility of Broadcast Licensees* (the "Blue Book"), N.O.R.C. issued its preliminary report. Some highlights: 23 per cent said: "I am in favor of advertising on the radio"; 41 per cent said: "I don't particularly mind advertising on the radio"; 26 per cent said: "I don't like advertising on the radio, but I'll put up with it"; only 7 per cent insisted on its being banned. In midsummer, N.A.B. authorized publication of a thoughtful 150-page analysis of its survey by Dr. Lazarsfeld.

Lazarsfeld did not attempt to soften the stinging rebukes and the clear calls for improvement with which the data themselves bristled at certain points; for, although the head of Columbia University's Bureau of Applied Social Research may have occasionally overestimated the size of the silver lining in relation to that of the cloud—as when he says, "the findings show that only a third of the people interviewed have an unfavorable attitude toward advertising," which severely strains the phrase "I don't particularly mind advertising" used by 41 per cent not included in the "unfavorable third"— he is careful to underline the "areas of potential improvement." And he concludes a Preface with: "But radio must not and cannot become self-complacent. For the radio of tomorrow will be the radio of today's critics."

Moreover, Lazarsfeld stresses the weaknesses inherent in any such survey. Thus he says:

It must be admitted, however, that a direct inquiry into people's dissatisfactions may not yield the most valid results. It is widely recognized in many fields of social research that, psychologically speaking, supply creates demand. . . . . Within certain limits, it is a recognized fact that people like what they get. It is also a fact that nobody knows whether or not a different program fare would be equally, or even more, acceptable to average listeners than the present program structure. And few would gainsay that the man in the street lacks the ability to envisage what he would like to hear that is different from what he can listen to now. . . . .

In other words, a survey like the present one cannot tell what people would like if they had the opportunity to listen to different radio fare. The desire for more knowledge on this problem is not the idle call for more research; it has eminently practical implications. The request for more serious broadcasts expressed in some quarters is now being countered by other groups with the following argument: all experience shows that the large majority of people don't like to listen to these serious programs; the American system of broadcasting is economically based on advertising revenues and, therefore, the bulk of the radio schedule has to consist of programs which reach large audiences.

But suppose that the basic assumptions were not quite so true as we take them to be at the moment. Perhaps the tastes of the listeners would be "elevated" and larger audiences obtained if there was a larger supply of more serious broadcasts with a great deal of promotion put behind them. This would certainly change the situation.

The data showed an amazingly even division, as Lazarsfeld notes: 46 per cent said: "I may get the news from the radio, but otherwise I use it only for entertainment"; and precisely the same number put it thus: "Besides the news and entertainment, I like to listen to some serious or educational programs once in a while." Moreover, an additional 6 per cent insisted: "I listen mostly to serious programs or educational

119

programs and wish there were more of them." And, as the analyst is quick to remark, the figure might have been higher had the question not been somewhat "loaded"—it might have been begun with "I am very much interested in" instead of "I listen mostly to"; obviously, few Americans would want nothing but "serious" programs.

The bare figures of the N.O.R.C. survey appear to refute the broadcasters' contention that "no one listens to discussions of public issues." They show the percentages for those professing to like such discussions varying from a low of 20 for women under forty who have not completed high school to 59 for men over forty who have. In a rather pointed aside, Lazarsfeld underscores the implications for educators of this variation. Then, noting the growing popularity of the quiz show, he drops a hint to the broadcasters: "Would it be possible to turn this effective technique to good account for more educational purposes?"

The section on the government's role is among the most interesting. Asked what specific powers the federal authority ought to have, 66 per cent said: "See to it that news broadcasts are truthful"; 53 said: "See that radio stations regularly carry programs giving both sides of public issues"; 45 said: "Give each station a regular place on the dial"; 40 said: "Make sure that each station broadcasts a certain number of educational programs"; 35 said: "Tell each station how much power it can use"; 27 said: "Decide how much time may be used for advertising"; 23 said: "Limit the profits of radio stations"; and 21 said: "Approve changes in ownership of stations." In short, more persons favored giving the F.C.C. powers which it was only just beginning to use timidly and which the broadcasters insisted were "unconstitutional" than were concerned with the "traffic-policeman" functions long since hallowed by time.

Lest the F.C.C. draw too much comfort from the figures, or the industry from its legalistic position, Lazarsfeld warns that the whole problem is

complicated by the unanticipated consequences which each move of the three parties could have. Private citizens might set in motion government interference directed towards the industry, which later on might boomerang against themselves. The industry might defend its commercial interest under the formula of freedom of speech to a point where the ideals of the First Amendment became discredited in the minds of the citizens and a vital tenet of democracy would lose its popular support . . . . the present survey contains some material which shows the extent to which the majority of the people are *not* aware of the problems involved.

In conclusion the analyst says:

There is still a considerable range within which the broadcaster can operate. And he will be expected to operate on the upper limits of this range. The situation can be summed up as follows: few people want to learn by way of the radio, but most critics agree that they should. Therefore the best thing for the broadcaster to do is to keep the volume of educational broadcasts slightly above what the masses want. In this way, he may contribute to a systematic rise in the general cultural level without defeating the educational goal by driving the audience away. This policy will disappoint some educators and bore some listeners, but it is precisely the kind of compromise solution which must be found.

For an industry that had been slow to get at the facts, it was a good beginning. It is to be hoped that it was only the beginning.

Numerous annual awards are given for "outstanding" endeavors in radio. They range all the way from a New York University citation for the "best sales promotion campaign of the year" to the George Foster Peabody Awards. Among the better known, in addition to the Peabody, are the Ohio State Institute for Education Radio Awards, the *Cleveland Plain*

Dealer Popularity Poll, the Radio Editor's Poll, the duPont Awards, and the *Variety* awards.

The Peabody and Ohio State awards, which make a faithful effort to examine all types of programs without reference to over-all listener "ratings" and to select the best of each, share the disadvantage that they do not confer local "firsts" for community merit and, indeed, lack the machinery to dig deeply at the community level. The *Cleveland Plain Dealer* citations are attracting national attention, although they are for programs heard locally. None of the three has as much serious impact on those who control the industry as the Radio Editors' and duPont bouquets, which are on the order of Hollywood "Oscars." *Time* commented in March, 1946, that not even the Peabody prizes were to be classed with newspaper honors like the Pulitzer Prize or the Raymond Clapper Award. The Women's National Radio Committee recently indicated what may perhaps be a new trend when it announced its 1946 awards for "programs of social significance only."

Far more remarkable than the meagerness of awards, however, is the dearth of praise and constructive criticism in the other media. A handful of doughty critics like Bernard Smith, a New York lawyer who acts as a legal adviser for the British Broadcasting Corporation, and Dixon Wecter, of the University of California, has plugged away doggedly at abuses in broadcasting. But these critics soon discovered, as did F.C.C. Chairmen Fly and Porter, that all newspapers and magazines except a half-dozen on the order of *Harper's*, the *Atlantic*, the *New Republic*, and the *Nation* were "not interested." Large-circulation "slick-paper" magazines occasionally accept articles on radio, but these are usually on the technical engineering aspects of the industry, with particular reference to future developments; and they are likely to be, as was the case with

Alva Johnston's 1946 series on television in the *Saturday Evening Post*, more amusing than instructive. A curious veil, half bitter jealousy and half studied indifference, separates the general press from the newest medium of information and entertainment. More newspaper space is devoted to the interests of bridge players and stamp collectors than to radio in all its aspects.

Variety in January, 1946, took account of this phenomenon in releasing the results of an intensive nation-wide survey. Some of the conclusions are worth noting:

1. Of the 1,700 daily newspapers in the country, only 324 pretend to employ radio editors. *Variety* qualified only 45–50 for the title, "by the farthest stretch," and noted that three of these represented press associations, two national magazines, and a dozen the trade-press.

2. The others, "mostly office boys or old men," simply print the daily radio logs, now and then "highlighting" a few programs in boxes, and for the rest rely on the broadcasters' "handouts" for "filler."

3. Newspapers in San Francisco and Los Angeles have agreements forbidding them to use radio columns.

4. Only thirteen radio editors who offered constructive criticism of radio with any regularity could be found: three in New York, two in Cleveland, one each in Cincinnati, Milwaukee, Portland (Oregon), St. Louis, Des Moines, Detroit, and Pittsburgh, and one in *Woman's Day*, a chain-store publication.[2]

Deprived of the normal avenues of criticism, various minority groups have turned from time to time to more direct methods. In December, 1945, the *Michigan Catholic* suggested

[2] Two of the most competent radio editors, in the author's view, are Jack Gould of the *New York Times* and John Crosby of the *New York Herald Tribune*. The New York Tribune Syndicate makes Crosby available to other papers throughout the country.

that the Legion of Decency, which has had a considerable impact on the motion picture industry, extend its attention to radio. On other occasions the National Youth Conference and the Society for Ethical Culture have threatened to intervene. By far the most aggressive move in this direction to date, however, was the National Citizens' Political Action Committee's campaign in the fall of 1945 to force the F.C.C. to adopt the following pattern for FM broadcasting: (1) grant no more than 25 per cent of available channels to AM owners plus newspapers, and these "only upon proof of exceptional public service and guarantees that they will perform a new and wholly different service on FM"; (2) prescribe standards of public service "in terms of hours and expenditures"; (3) withhold renewal of any license until the application had been advertised in a newspaper of general circulation in the community involved and the opportunity afforded to others to apply; and (4) arrange to hold public hearings wherever possible in the communities involved.

So much for the story of the curious partnership in which the listeners play the role of silent partner. Where has it brought radio? Perhaps the best possible witness would be a returning veteran who has devoted his life to broadcasting and who spent most of his time in the army abroad as manager and master of ceremonies of the Special Services Show on the Armed Forces Network. The reactions of this friendly critic, Preston L. Taplin, who has since returned to his old post at WHCU (Ithaca, New York), were printed in the March 25, 1946, issue of *Broadcasting:*

.... Most GI's would take the AFN in preference to American radio simply because they are fed up with commercials. .... When I returned .... I was shocked at the poor taste. .... My standard defensive argument had always been that radio methods could never remain distasteful long. The public, by turning the dials, would force a change. . . . . Where have they to turn? It was the same everywhere. Program production also seems to show no improvement in my four years' absence. . . . . It seems that radio, which prides itself upon being a fast-moving industry, has become bogged down. . . . .

Or this, from the same magazine and from another A.F.N. veteran, Sid Bard:

. . . . Radio is twenty-five years old, they tell us. But if radio is to contribute to the maintaining of a secure peace, if it is to take its place in the forging of an educated and enlightened public, it will have to reorient itself. . . . . Its core must be a chain of programs that cause men to think, that educate them in new approaches and appreciations. This core must not be presented to the listeners as a "public service apology." It should take its place as a characteristic of an industry that has achieved its maturity and is utilizing all its powers. . . . .

Thus speak two qualified critics, radio men who for a brief moment found themselves cast in the role of listener. How many of the sixty million full-time listeners agreed with them? If one waited for them to speak voluntarily, he might never know. Perhaps it was true, as Philip Wylie had said, that the advertising men had dulled America's traditional faculty for critical judgment.

7

THE GOVERNMENT'S ROLE

ALTHOUGH all the major concerns of government regulation were present from the first, it was never possible,
given the limited funds and manpower of the regulatory
agency and the arbitrary priorities which necessity (and now
and then the Congress) laid down, to tackle them simultaneously. From the standpoint of emphasis, therefore, the
history of government[1] regulation of radio broadcasting may
be divided roughly into five periods.

The laissez faire period.—From 1922 to 1927, Hoover operated hopefully on the theory that the greatest good for the
greatest number will somehow spring inevitably from the
natural coincidence of personal goods—a faith to which the
courts clung long after the Secretary became skeptical of it.

The traffic-control period.—From 1927 to 1932, the Federal
Radio Commission laid the groundwork for a system of
orderly sharing of frequencies designed to secure the maxi-

[1] Federal regulation. Unlike the railways in their early days, radio broadcasting from the first has been treated as an interstate matter, because of the
indisputable reach of any and all radio signals and because of the effect upon
any orderly national pattern of the emissions of any station, however small.
The states have, for the most part, refrained from interfering, although,
as of the close of 1946, Illinois was weighing a libel bill sponsored by the
Chicago Tribune and aimed at radio commentators; a New Mexico 2 per
cent gross sales tax on time sales was before the United States Supreme
Court; and Ohio was considering subjecting all television broadcasts to approval by the Educational Department, which now censors motion pictures
in that state.

mum benefits from them, for the broadcasters and their commercial backers, if not always for the public.

The cleanup period.—From 1932 to 1937, the F.R.C. and its successor, the Federal Communications Commission, turned their attention to quacks, cranks, and swindlers, driving the worst of them from the airways.

The trust-busting period.—From 1937 to 1944, the F.C.C. enlarged the scope of federal regulation to include stricter accountability for financial soundness and corporate honesty and sought to arrest certain monopoly trends related to network broadcasting.

The public service era.—From 1944 on, the Commission set out to make the broadcasters accountable for specific standards of social usefulness, as well as for telling the truth about ownership; producing evidence of financial responsibility; staying within their assigned channel, power, and time limits; giving political candidates equal treatment; refraining from profanity and obscenity; and abiding by the Chain Broadcasting Regulations and other specific F.C.C. rulings.

Setting aside the time factor, it is clear that radio under the American system of private competition has, from the first, presented a half-dozen major problems for which laissez faire offered no adequate solution and which therefore appear to require some degree and kind of regulation, governmental or other. The F.R.C. and the F.C.C. have attempted to provide a structure and policy for such regulation. The policy has often been timid and tentative and unsure of its direction. Often it has been diverted by equally unsure congressional statutory definition and direction. In some of the problems the line of direction is now clear. In others, policy is still being evolved by trial and error. In still others, policy is not yet defined or acceptable. In the main, however, the major concerns of the regulators have always been:

127

To maintain an orderly traffic, based on sound engineering principles;

To extend the physical range of broadcasting to the whole country;

To encourage healthy competition;

To protect the local interests of communities;

To provide a forum for the expression of antagonistic and minority views;

To establish standards of professional competence for broadcasters.

Let us see how they fared with these major concerns.

TRAFFIC CONTROL

The Radio Act of 1912 required the issuance of a license by the Secretary of Commerce and Labor as a condition to engaging in "commercial intercourse beyond the borders of a state or territory," such license to be issued only to a United States citizen and to be "revocable for cause." Each station was "required to designate a certain definite wave length" which "shall not exceed 600 meters or it shall exceed 1600 meters." Finally, each station was to "use the minimum amount of energy necessary."

In 1919, when the government relinquished private facilities to their owners, the radio division of the Department of Commerce designated 485 meters as the wave length for all government broadcasting, and 360 meters as the one for all private broadcasting, which meant that no single community could accommodate more than one station unless rival stations were willing to share time. In the summer of 1921, Hoover, assuming that he, too, was acting under authority of the Act of 1912, designated two wave lengths, 360 and 400 meters (750 and 833 kilocycles), and licensed all stations to operate on whichever they pleased, thus raising the community potential to two full-time stations.

Almost immediately, however, the demand in New York City exceeded the supply, as it has ever since. Consequently, when the license of the Intercity Radio Company expired in November, 1921, the Secretary declined to grant a new one, on the ground that he could not assign to the applicant a wave length that would not interfere with government and private stations near by. On November 19, 1921, the Supreme Court of the District of Columbia directed the issuance of a writ of mandamus requiring the Secretary to issue a license to Intercity. On February 5, 1922, the Court of Appeals for the District of Columbia denied the Secretary's appeal from the Intercity decision, affirming the judgment of the lower court that "the language of the Act [of 1912], the nature of the subject matter regulated, as well as the general scope of the statute, negative the idea that Congress intended to repose any such discretion in you."

Hoover was rapidly coming to the end of his regulatory rope. By November, 1925, the number of broadcasting stations had risen to 578, 197 of them using 500 watts or more power, with 175 applications on file. Every one of the ninety channels in the broadcasting band was occupied by at least two stations, many by three or more. In the congested urban areas competitors had been compelled to follow the example of R.C.A.'s WJZ and A.T. & T.'s WEAF in New York in setting up complicated time-sharing arrangements. Now they were growing restive under expedients which they had hoped would be temporary. And Hoover was pointing out the obvious fact that the numerous new applicants could be accommodated only at the expense of other radio services or by even more stringent limitations on time and power. What was needed was legislation. And the dogged efforts of Congressman (now Senator) White and others at every successive session of the Congress since 1922 had failed to produce it.

When the Fourth Radio Conference convened in Washington, November 9–11, 1925, the Secretary in his opening address spoke the minds of many of his listeners:

> I can see no alternative to abandonment of the present system, which gives the broadcasting privilege to everyone who can raise the funds necessary to erect a station, irrespective of his motive, the service he proposes to render, or the number of others already serving his community. Moreover, we should not freeze the present users of wave lengths permanently in their favored positions, irrespective of their service. . . . .
>
> It seems to me we have in this development of governmental relations two distinct problems. . . . . The ideal situation, as I view it, would be traffic regulation by federal government to the the extent of the allotment of wave lengths and control of power and the policing of interference, leaving to each community a large voice in determining who are to occupy the wave lengths assigned to that community. . . . .

January, 1926, found the indefatigable Maine congressman back before the Merchant Marine and Fisheries Committee with another version of his bill, and by March he had got it to the floor again. But Hoover once more had discovered that he could not wait for Congress.

In February, the Secretary had declined to give the Zenith Radio Corporation authority to operate WJAZ (Chicago) more than the 2 hours a week allotted to it on a frequency shared with General Electric. Zenith promptly appropriated a wave length reserved by international agreement for Canadian broadcasters. Hoover brought criminal action in the District Court of the United States for the Northern District of Illinois. On April 16, Judge Wilkerson handed down a long and labored decision, declaring, in effect, that, owing to the ambiguity of the Act of 1912 and to the necessity of construing a statute literally in criminal action, the defendant company must be found not guilty. Buried in the decision was an extremely significant intimation that, if the Secretary had power to impose restrictions as to frequency and hours of operation, the statute might have to be construed as unconstitutional, since it failed to provide a standard of control for his discretion.

On July 8, Acting Attorney-General Donovan submitted an opinion that the Secretary of Commerce had no authority under the Act of 1912 to regulate the power, frequency, or hours of operation of broadcasting stations. The next day Hoover announced that he was abandoning all efforts to regulate radio and urged the stations to undertake self-regulation. But the Secretary's plea went unheeded. From July, 1926, to February, 1927, when the Congress finally enacted the Radio Act of 1927, 194 new stations went on the air, using any frequencies that pleased them, regardless of the interference thus caused to Canadian, as well as United States, stations. Previously existing stations hopped from wave length to wave length and increased their power and hours of operation at will. When the sale of radio sets dropped $12\frac{1}{2}$ per cent, the setmakers begged the Congress for speed in enacting the long-awaited law.

The much-debated Radio Act of 1927 had the following provisions. It

1. Undertook to regulate all forms of radio communication within the United States, its territories and possessions; to maintain control of the United States over all channels; to provide for their "use, but not ownership," by individuals, firms, or corporations, for limited periods of time, under licenses granted by federal authority.

2. Divided the United States into five zones.

3. Created a five-man Federal Radio Commission, the members to be appointed by the President with the advice and consent of the Senate; each to be a bona fide citizen of the zone for which named and not financially interested in any phase of the telecommunications industry; no more than three members to be of the same political party.

4. Gave the Commission power to classify stations; prescribe the nature of the services to be rendered; assign frequencies; determine power, times of operation, and locations; regulate apparatus; prevent interference; establish the areas to be served by each station; make special regulations pertaining to chain broadcasting; require records of programs, transmissions of energy, communications or signals; hold hearings, summon witnesses, administer oaths, and "compel the production of books, documents or papers."

5. Provided that one year after the first meeting of the Commission the powers under the act, except that for revoking licenses, should revert to the Secretary of Commerce, who, meanwhile, was to continue to exercise certain powers not expressly delegated to the Commission, such as prescribing the qualifications of station operators, inspecting apparatus, and designating call-letters; that appeals from his rulings should be heard by the Commission; that no license could be granted until the applicant "shall have signed a waiver of any claim to the use of any . . . . frequency . . . . because of the previous use of the same, whether by license or otherwise."

6. Provided for government seizure and use, during war or other emergency, "or in order to preserve the neutrality of the United States," of any private facilities, upon payment of "just compensation."

7. Instructed the licensing authority to distribute frequencies and allocations of power in such a way as to provide "fair, efficient, and equitable radio service" to each state and community; limited the term of both original licenses and renewals to 3 years.

8. Stipulated that applications for license "set forth such facts as the licensing authority . . . . may prescribe as to the citizenship, character, and financial, technical and other qualifications"; ownership and location; frequencies, hours, and power desired; purpose for which the station was to be used; "and such other information as it may require."

9. Stipulated that "if upon examination of any application . . . . the licensing authority shall determine that public interest, convenience, or necessity would be served by the granting thereof, it shall authorize the issuance. . . . . In the event the licensing authority . . . . does not . . . . it shall notify the applicant . . . . fix and give notice of a time and place for hearing."

10. Stipulated that "the station license required hereby, the fre-

quencies . . . . authorized to be used . . . . and the rights therein granted shall not be transferred . . . . without the consent in writing of the licensing authority."

11. Directed the licensing authority to refuse a license to any applicant found guilty by a federal court of unlawfully monopolizing "or attempting unlawfully to monopolize" radio communications.

12. Provided that licenses would be revocable for false statements or because of conditions "which would warrant the licensing authority in refusing to grant a license on an original application, or for failure to operate substantially as set forth in the license, for violation of or failure to observe any of the restrictions and conditions of this Act, or by any regulation of the licensing authority authorized by this Act or by a treaty ratified by the United States, or whenever the Interstate Commerce Commission, or any other federal body in the exercise of authority conferred upon it by law, shall find and shall certify to the Commission that any licensee bound so to do has failed to provide reasonable facilities . . . . or . . . . has made any unjust and unreasonable charge, or has been guilty of any discrimination. . . . ."

13. Stipulated that "all laws of the United States relating to unlawful restraints and monopolies and to combinations, contracts, or agreements in restraint of trade, are hereby declared to be applicable to the manufacture and sale of and to trade in radio apparatus and devices entering into or affecting interstate or foreign commerce. . . . . Whenever in any suit, action, or proceeding, civil or criminal, brought under the provisions of any of said laws or in any proceedings brought to enforce or to review findings and orders of the Federal Trade Commission, or other governmental agency in respect of any matters as to which said Commission or other governmental agency is by law authorized to act, any licensee shall be found guilty of the violation of the provisions of such laws or any of them, the court, in addition to the penalties imposed by said laws, may adjudge, order, and/or decree that the license of such licensee shall, as of the date the decree or judgment becomes finally effective, or as of such other date as the said decree shall fix, be revoked and that all rights under such license shall thereupon cease. . . . ."

14. Designated the Court of Appeals for the District of Columbia to hear appeals from the decisions of the licensing authority.

15. Stipulated that "if any licensee shall permit any person who is a legally qualified candidate for any public office to use a broadcasting station, he shall afford equal opportunities to all other such candidates for that office in the use of such broadcasting station, and the licensing authority shall make rules and regulations to carry this provision into effect: *Provided*, That such licensee shall have no power of censorship over the material broadcast. . . . . No obligation is hereby imposed upon any licensee to allow the use of its station by any such candidate."

16. Stipulated that commercially sponsored broadcasts be so identified.

17. Stipulated that "nothing in this Act shall be understood or construed to give the licensing authority the power of censorship over the radio communications . . . . transmitted by any radio station, and no regulation or condition shall be promulgated or fixed by the licensing authority which shall interfere with the right of free speech. . . . ."

The five-man F.R.C. tackled its staggering task without further delay. On April 5, 1927, a month after taking office, it established the broadcast band as extending from 550 to 1,500 kilocycles. On May 5 it ordered the announcement of station call-letters at 15-minute intervals. A week later it initiated a study of action to prevent speculation in frequencies. By June it was facing up squarely to its most urgent assignment: the ending of bedlam on the air.

The situation beggared description. Of the 733 stations attempting to operate on ninety channels, 129 were off their assigned channels through failure to observe Secretary Hoover's 10-kilocycle separation, 41 were operating on or overlapping the six channels reserved for Canada, and virtually all were ignoring restrictions as to power and hours of operation which they had voluntarily accepted. To make matters worse, in the congested urban areas where a 50-kilocycle separation was desirable to avoid "cross-talk" interference, stations were attempting to operate with 20-, 5-, and

134

even 2-kilocycle spacing. And a score of portable stations, plus hundreds of utterly unregulated amateurs, were adding to the confusion.

On June 15, the F.R.C. issued General Order 11, which, together with General Order 13, directed all stations to return to channels of even multiples of 10 kilocycles; cleared the Canadian exclusive channels; limited the power to be used on the eleven channels shared with Canadian broadcasters; and set up wherever possible in the urban areas 50-kilocycle separations. Unfortunately for those listeners at some distance from broadcasting facilities, General Orders 11 and 13 did nothing to correct the interference resulting from the simultaneous operation of two high-powered stations on the same frequency, a sharing device which usually rendered both programs unintelligible.

What was obviously needed was a setting-aside of certain high-powered channels to be used by only one station at a time. Toward the end of the year the commissioners came to this conclusion; and on November 14 they issued General Order 19, which designated a band of channels from 600 to 1,000 kilocycles as exclusive clear channels on which only one station could operate at night.[2] This called for the transfer, effective December 1, of 25 stations to other channels. An additional 10, too powerfully represented in congressional lobbies to be treated in the same manner, were requested to get off by December 31, through voluntary division of time, reduction of power, synchronized operation, or transfer to other channels. The threat of F.R.C. action if they failed to comply was implicit in the order.

On November 11, 1928, the Commission set aside forty of the ninety channels as "clear" channels upon each of which

[2] "Night" and "day" in broadcasting parlance mean sunset and sunrise, local time.

only one station could operate at night, with minimum power of 5 kilowatts and maximum power to be fixed by the Commission; allocated four frequencies each for use by not fewer than two, or more than three, zones, with stations permitted to operate simultaneously, with power not to exceed 1 kilowatt; and allocated six frequencies for simultaneous use in all five zones, with power not to exceed 100 watts. Subsequently, the power maximum on clear channels was set at 25 kilowatts for regular service and an additional 25 kilowatts for experimental broadcasting. Provision was also made for a number of daytime and limited-service stations which might share the clear channels under conditions where the time-zone differential and the peculiar characteristics of radio signals in certain areas warranted such sharing.

This general pattern has been preserved to the present, with slight modifications. In 1945 and 1946 the F.C.C. reexamined the clear-channel situation; and in the same period, as the cessation of hostilities permitted the opening-up of the new fields of frequency modulation, television, and facsimile, it applied similar principles in allocating different types of channels for them.

Pre-war and wartime FM had operated in the band between 42 and 50 megacycles. After a considerable study by engineers, the Commission offered 50–68 and 92–106 as possible alternatives. Major Armstrong—sometimes called the "inventor" of FM—the Radio Corporation of America, the Radio Technical Planning Board, the Television Broadcasters Association, FM Broadcasters, Inc., Zenith, the Electronics Manufacturers Association, and Pioneer FM Radio Manufacturers favored the first alternative. After further study, the F.C.C. elected to swim against the tide. On June 27, 1945, it released allocations between 44 and 108 megacycles, as shown in Table 5.

Of some twenty manufacturers of receiving sets, only Philco, Motorola, and Halicrafters applauded "kicking FM upstairs." The others complained that several thousand sets based on the old band were already in the hands of listeners or on the assembly lines. The F.C.C. replied that, for an estimated cost of $10 a set, adjustment could be made which would render them capable of receiving in the new band. There were, of course, other complaints; and, determined to work out a policy, the Commission in July, 1945, issued a set of proposals for public discussion at hearings scheduled for

TABLE 5

No. of Channels	Band	Type of Service
1............	44– 50	Television
1............	50– 54	Amateurs
3............	54– 72	Television
1............	72– 76	Nongovernment fixed and mobile
2............	76– 88	Television
20............	88– 92	Educational FM
70.............	92–106	Commercial FM
1............	106–108	Facsimile

that month. These provided: (1) all stations to be licensed for unlimited time operation, with an initial required minimum of 6 hours a day; (2) no person to own more than one station in one area or more than six over-all; (3) AM licensees to be eligible, for the time being, to apply for FM, but comment was solicited on whether there ought not eventually be a rule barring ownership of an AM and an FM station in the same area; (4) the Chain Broadcasting Regulations to apply equally to FM; (5) a licensee with the only good antenna site in the area might be required to share it; (6) twenty channels to be set aside for returning veterans and other latecomers; (7) simplexing (one at a time) of FM and facsimile to be permitted, multiplexing (both simultaneously) on an experimental basis only; (8) fifty of the seventy "upstairs" commercial channels (94.1–103.9) to be reserved for "metropolitan" stations designed to serve urban areas and surrounding market areas, ten (92.1–93.9) for "community" stations designed to serve smaller cities or compact communities within or adjacent to large cities, and ten (104.1–105.9) for "rural" stations; (9) a minimum of 2 hours' programming a day to be made up of material not also broadcast over AM stations.

In the light of the criticism which it had invited, the F.C.C. subsequently made the following changes: (1) extended the FM band for the northeast from 106 to 108 megacycles; (2) designated this area "Area I," the balance of the country "Area II"; (3) barred rural FM stations in Area I and combined them into metropolitan stations in Area II; (4) dropped the reference to duplication of AM and FM programs; (5) threw the twenty "reserved" channels into the common pot; (6) dropped talk of eventually barring dual AM-FM ownership; (7) fixed 20 kilowatts as the desired power (in Area I) and 500 feet as the desired antenna height of "metropolitan" stations (in Area II), 250 watts and 250 feet as the measurements for "community" ones. In September, 1946, the Commission rejuggled Class B (metropolitan-rural) FM allocations so as to provide for 56 more stations, or 1,600-plus for the whole country.

In the thickest of the FM battle, the F.C.C. turned its attention to television. With its eye on approximately 400 stations covering 140 market areas, the Commission in September, 1945, issued a set of proposed rules and regulations substantially the same as those for FM, with these exceptions: (1) a single-ownership limit of five instead of six; (2) 6-hour daily program minimum changed to 2; (3) compulsory sharing of facilities dropped; (4) ten channels earmarked for "metropolitan" stations, three for "community."

The F.R.C. had pinned its hopes for the widest possible physical coverage of the country on the formula calling for low-power local, medium-power regional, and high-power clear channels. In arriving at this formula, it had taken into account economic and population factors which States'-rights members of Congress were unwilling to recognize. Early in 1928, the so-called Davis Amendment to the Act of 1927 became law. This amendment, a substitute for Section 9 of the act, made mandatory upon the F.R.C. an "equitable distribution" of licenses, frequencies, times of operation, and power among the five zones and, so far as possible, among the states and territories within the zones.

The first step in carrying out this mandate was to determine by rule of thumb how many stations could be supported in any area. The Commission promptly threw thirteen portable stations off the air, thus fractionally simplifying the problem. Then it promulgated, on May 25, 1928, General Order 32 requiring 164 of the less important standard broadcasting stations to show wherein their continued operation would serve the "public interest, convenience, or necessity." As a result of the ensuing hearings, 12 stations were reduced in power, 4 were placed on probation, and 5 were permitted to continue as a result of consolidations with other stations. All told, 62 stations disappeared, 32 of them by default, since they did not appear to contest their cases.

As of June 30, 1928, there were in operation in the United States, including the 13 portable stations and a few others that had been served notice to discontinue operations by July 1, 696 stations: 128 in Zone 1, 112 in Zone 2, 116 in Zone 3, 206 in Zone 4, and 134 in Zone 5.

On August 8, the Commission sought through the issuance

139

of General Order 43 to limit the use of clear channels for chain broadcasting by requiring a geographical separation of 300 miles. Designed to benefit listeners, it brought such a storm of protest from listeners that the effective date was postponed from November 11 to February 1, 1929, and later postponed again. On December 20, 1929, the order was rescinded altogether.

Meanwhile, it was clear that such piecemeal methods were not going to satisfy the Congress. The goal of maximum coverage with minimum interference and duplication would have to be approached, not through a forest of individual hearings but across the shimmering desert outlined by the Davis Amendment, with its tempting mirage of "equality" for all: listeners, broadcasters, would-be broadcasters, and political candidates. What was wanted was a plan.

The F.R.C. turned for guidance to the experts: the broadcasting committee of the Institute of Radio Engineers, the National Association of Broadcasters, the Federated Radio Trades Association, the Radio Manufacturers Association, and the Interdepartmental Radio Advisory Committee[3] of government engineers set up by Hoover.

The consensus was that compliance with the Davis Amendment, as well as further steps to bring order out of ethereal chaos, would have to conform to sound engineering principles and that economic considerations indicated as little disturbance of the existing pattern as possible. The experts' advice boiled down to three points: (1) about 700 stations could be provided for, (2) the average power ought to be maintained

[3] The Interdepartmental Radio Advisory Committee (I.R.A.C.) still survives as an important governmental agency complementing the work of F.C.C. It is composed of representatives of all federal government agencies, military and civil, which use radio frequencies, and it exists to allocate frequencies for governmental purposes. F.C.C. is represented as the agency allocating all frequencies for nongovernmental uses.

at existing levels, and (3) changes necessitated by new allocations should be held to a minimum.

Early in 1929, the F.R.C. worked out a quota system guaranteeing each zone and state absolute mathematical equality according to population figures, then a decade out of date. The quota plan had two rather obvious defects: it made every state's share come out in fractions of stations, and it ignored the painful fact that "squatter sovereignty," under a sort of "Missouri Compromise" which the Congress had tacitly condoned, made it difficult, if not impossible, to oust broadcasters in zones and states that were already overquota.

Accordingly, in June, 1930, the Commission produced a modified quota system that has guided the government licensing authority ever since. General Order 92 declared that a full-time 1-kilowatt station operating on a regional channel would be given the value of 1 unit. The spread among existing types of stations would thus range from 0.2 for a local station with 100 watts or less power to 5 for a clear-channel station with 5 kilowatts or more power. The United States was to have 400 units, each zone was to have precisely 80, and each state was to have, in so far as possible, an "equitable" share.

As only one station (Westinghouse's KYW, which moved from Chicago to Philadelphia) left the airways because it found itself operating in an overquota zone, the situation was not materially improved by the issuance of General Order 92. As of January 8, 1931, Zones 1 and 2 were underquota; Zones 3, 4, and 5 were overquota; and forty-six of the forty-eight states, plus the District of Columbia, were either over or under. Meanwhile, the pile of applications from would-be broadcasters in underquota states or zones who had taken the Commission seriously was growing higher.

In self-defense the F.R.C. promulgated General Order 102, which provided that (1) no more licenses would be given to

141

overquota zones, (2) applications from underquota states in overquota zones would have to be for facilities already in use in some overquota state in the applicant's zone, (3) no more licenses would be given to overquota states, (4) applications from overquota states would have to be for facilities already in use in those states, and (5) applications from underquota states in underquota zones could be for anything.

The courts upheld the Commission's right to apply a unit system, but not always the manner in which this was attempted. Dissatisfaction was widespread. Litigation threatened to bog down the F.R.C.'s tiny legal staff. Late in 1931, the Commission issued a new and, if possible, even more confusing set of instructions:

1. When the application is from an underquota state and is for facilities which, if granted, would not cause additional interference with any station, or stations, now licensed, then the above paragraphs may be disregarded.

2. Since the Act provides for the equalizing of radio facilities among zones and among states "as nearly as possible," the Commission may allow a slight departure, plus or minus, from an exact mathematical estimate.

The following year, still under constant pressure from Congress to "do something" about the unit system, the F.R.C. took a bold step. Illinois was 55 per cent overquota. Indiana was 22 per cent underquota. A broadcaster in Gary, Indiana, wanted a better channel. The F.R.C. took one that was being shared by two Chicago stations and gave it to the Gary applicant. The District Court of Appeals reversed the Commission, holding that it had acted both arbitrarily and capriciously. On May 8, the Supreme Court in *Federal Radio Commission* vs. *Nelson Bros. Bond & Mortgage Co.*, reversed the District Court, holding that the standard of public interest, convenience, or necessity was not so vague as to render

142

the Radio Act of 1927 unconstitutional and that the Commission had not acted arbitrarily or capriciously in deleting a station in an overquota state and assigning the channel to an underquota state.

Meantime, the Commission's sporadic efforts to improve coverage through the juggling of the clear channels continued into 1930, when it increased the mileage separation between stations operating on adjacent clear channels from 522 to 1,117 miles and authorized twenty of the forty clear-channel stations to operate with 50-kilowatts power. The attempt at geographical separation was held up by the Court of Appeals for the District of Columbia on the ground that the parties affected had not had an opportunity to be heard officially— this although the Commission's order was a direct outgrowth of recommendations submitted by the industry's various trade-associations.

As the industry recovered from the severe shocks of the depression and applicants for new stations became as numerous as they had been in the late twenties, the F.C.C.'s engineers sweated over further sharing devices and channel separations, until, by the end of 1939, more than eight hundred broadcasters had been accommodated. In part this was accomplished by wider sharing of the clear channels. But the F.C.C. had to be ever mindful of the fact that these channels had been established in the first place to serve remote rural areas wholly without primary, or local-regional, service. The constant warring of interests as between the metropolitan centers, where the clear-channel transmitters were located, and the rural areas, which, by that very token, already had lost the first round, has inhibited many Commission decisions.

In 1941 the Commission established a precedent that has plagued it ever since. In June of that year, WHDH (Boston) applied for and got permission to operate on an unlimited-

143

time basis on 830 kilocycles, a frequency previously assigned for exclusive nighttime operation to N.B.C.'s KOA (Denver), which supplied virtually the only broadcasting service (and much of that, of course, secondary) to a wide Rocky Mountain–Great Plains area. In a vigorous dissent Commissioners Craven and Case pointed out that this area, which has never had either primary nighttime or daytime service and which, at best, had a choice of two network programs at night, was being robbed so that Boston, already saturated with service from four national and two regional networks and half-a-dozen local stations, could have 4 more hours' service a day on one channel; that the Commission was thus turning its collective back on one of its most fundamental principles, formulated only after long consultation with representatives of the industry, including WHDH, which had not protested the ruling at the time; that such apparent indifference to the sanctity of an established clear channel would encourage Canadian and Latin-American stations to become equally indifferent; and, finally, that so basic an exception would hound the Commission to the end of its days. In September, 1942, the Court of Appeals for the District of Columbia reversed the F.C.C., and the following January the Supreme Court sustained the lower tribunal. But that did not end the matter, as we shall presently see.

True, the trouble had started long before, when the F.R.C. had let the situation get out of hand by leaving the clear channels clustered in the urban centers which first applied for them. But, however the blame is apportioned, the result is the same. As of January, 1947, fifty-seven 50-kilowatt stations were operating on clear channels, twenty-two of them having exclusive nighttime channels and four dividing time on two exclusive nighttime channels. Of these twenty-two three were owned by, and ten affiliated with, N.B.C.; four were owned by, and five affiliated with, C.B.S.; two were owned by, and one affiliated with, A.B.C.; and one was affiliated with M.B.S. Of the shared thirty-six, two were owned by, and ten affiliated with, N.B.C.; two were owned by, and nine affiliated with, C.B.S.; five were affiliated with A.B.C.; one was affiliated with M.B.S.; and only two were completely independent. Thus, of the fifty-seven 50-kilowatt clear-channel stations, fifty-five were in the hands of the networks (see Tables 6 and 7). Even more significant, perhaps, twenty-nine were located within 100 miles of the outer borders of the United States, twenty-two of them on the Atlantic and Pacific seaboards; whereas the 2,000,000 square miles lying between St. Louis and San Francisco and between the Canadian border and a line from Albuquerque and Oklahoma City to Nashville had only one 1-A clear channel—KSL (Salt Lake City).

Among the questions to which, as 1947 opened, the F.C.C. still was trying to find answers were: (1) Are the clear-channel stations covering as much territory as they could? (2) Are they getting the best possible signal into the areas they do reach? (3) Are they giving the people dependent on them, especially the farmers, the sort of programming fare they want? (4) If the answers to (1) and (2) are negative, does improvement lie in the direction of better spacing through reallocation along geographical, rather than primary advertising market, lines? (5) Or does it lie in the direction of encouraging the regional stations to do a better coverage job by breaking down the remaining unlimited clear channels for multistation use and reducing (or at any rate not increasing) the 50-kilowatt power limit (since this would involve the use of directional antennae, limiting the signal to a portion of the full circle, the question naturally arises as to whether x times as many part circles would equal the present number of full and part circles)? (6) Or in the direction of increasing the

TABLE 6

CLEAR-CHANNEL STATIONS IN UNITED STATES: CLASS I-A
CLEAR-CHANNEL STATIONS

Channel	Call Letters	City	Licensee	Network Affiliation
640....	KFI	Los Angeles	Earle C. Anthony	N.B.C.
650....	WSM	Nashville	National Life & Accident	N.B.C.
660....	WEAF	New York	N.B.C.	N.B.C.
670....	WMAQ	Chicago	N.B.C.	N.B.C.
700....	WLW	Cincinnati	Crosley Corp. (a subsidiary of Aviation Corp.)	N.B.C.
720....	WGN	Chicago	WGN, Inc.	M.B.S.
750....	WSB	Atlanta	Atlanta Journal Co.	N.B.C.
760....	WJR	Detroit	WJR	C.B.S.
770....	WJZ	New York	A.B.C.	A.B.C.
780....	WBBM	Chicago	C.B.S.	C.B.S.
820....	WBAP	Fort Worth	Carter Publications, Inc.	N.B.C.
	WFAA	Dallas	A. H. Belo Corp.	N.B.C.
830....	WCCO	Minneapolis	C.B.S.	C.B.S.
840....	WHAS	Louisville	*Courier-Journal* & *Times*	C.B.S.
870....	WWL	New Orleans	Loyola University	C.B.S.
880....	WABC	New York	C.B.S.	C.B.S.
890....	WENR	Chicago	A.B.C.	A.B.C.
	WLS	Chicago	Agricultural Broadcasting Co.	A.B.C.
1020....	KDKA	Pittsburgh	Westinghouse	N.B.C.
1040....	WHO	Des Moines	Central Broadcasting Co.	N.B.C.
1100....	WTAM	Cleveland	N.B.C.	N.B.C.
1120....	KMOX	St. Louis	C.B.S.	C.B.S.
1160....	KSL	Salt Lake City	Radio Service Corp.	C.B.S.
1180....	WHAM	Rochester	Stromberg-Carlson	N.B.C.
1200....	WOAI	San Antonio	Southland Industries, Inc.	N.B.C.
1210....	WCAU	Philadelphia	WCAU	C.B.S.

Network	Owned	Affiliated
N.B.C............	3	10
C.B.S.............	4	5
A.B.C............	2	1
M.B.S............		1
Total.........	9	17

TABLE 7
CLASS I-B OR II CLEAR-CHANNEL STATIONS
(50,000 Watts Only)

Channel	Call Letters	City	Licensee	Network Affiliation
680....	KPO	San Francisco	N.B.C.	N.B.C.
	WPTF	Raleigh	WPTF	N.B.C.
	KABC	San Antonio	Alamo Broadcasting Co.	A.B.C.
710....	WOR	New York	Bamberger Broadcasting Service	M.B.S.
	KIRO	Seattle	Queen City Broadcasting Co.	C.B.S.
740....	KTRH	Houston	KTRH	C.B.S.
770....	KOB*	Albuquerque	Albuquerque Broadcasting Co.	N.B.C.
810....	WGY	Schenectady	General Electric	N.B.C.
850....	KOA	Denver	N.B.C.	N.B.C.
1010....	WINS	New York	Crosley Corp. (a subsidiary of Aviation Corp.)	....
	KWBU†	Corpus Christi	Century Broadcasting Co.	A.B.C., N.B.C.
1030....	WBZ	Boston	Westinghouse	N.B.C.
	KWBU	Corpus Christi	Century Broadcasting Co.	A.B.C.
1050....	WHN	New York	Marcus Loew Booking Agency	....
1060....	KYW	Philadelphia	Westinghouse	N.B.C.
1070....	KNX	Los Angeles	C.B.S.	C.B.S.
1080....	WTIC	Hartford	Travelers Broadcasting Service	N.B.C.
	KRLD	Dallas	KRLD	C.B.S.
1090....	WBAL	Baltimore	Hearst	N.B.C.
1110....	KFAB	Omaha	KFAB	C.B.S.
	WBT	Charlotte	Southeastern Broadcasting Co.	C.B.S.
1130....	KWKH	Shreveport	International Broadcasting Corp.	C.B.S.
1140....	WRVA	Richmond	Larus & Brother Co.	C.B.S.
1170....	KVOO	Tulsa	Southwestern Sales Corp.	N.B.C.
	WWVA	Wheeling	W. Va. Broadcasting Corp.	A.B.C.
1500....	WTOP	Washington	C.B.S.	C.B.S.
	KSTP	St. Paul	KSTP	N.B.C.
1510....	WLAC	Nashville	WLAC	C.B.S.
1520....	WKBW	Buffalo	Buffalo Broadcasting Corp.	A.B.C.
	KOMA	Oklahoma City	KOMA	C.B.S.
1530....	WCKY	Cincinnati	L. B. Wilson	....
1540....	KXEL	Waterloo	John Higgins	A.B.C.

* Unlimited time (special authorization).

† Daytime only (special authorization).

147

TABLE 7—*Continued*

Network	Class I		Class I-B or II		Total
	Owned	Affiliated	Owned	Affiliated	
N.B.C.......	3	10	2	10	25
C.B.S.......	4	5	2	9	20
A.B.C.......	2	1	0	5	8
M.B.S	....	1	....	1	2
Independent.	....	....	....	....	2

power of existing licensees? (7) Or, finally, in the direction of turning the clear channels over to noncommercial broadcasters?

All during 1946, the F.C.C. canvassed interested parties. The Radio Technical Planning Board recommended the opening-up of two channels in the government band (520 kilocycles and 530 kilocycles) to add to the 540-kilocycle channel being turned over to the broadcasters by the Navy. N.B.C. wanted superpower up to 1,000 kilowatts for KOA (Denver) and possibly for some other clear-channel stations. C.B.S. came forward with an offer to operate, in connection with a nation-wide FM network based on 200 stations, two high-power satellite or relay stations, one in northern Kentucky and one in eastern Colorado. The Clear Channel Broadcasting Service (C.C.B.S.)[4] fought for superpower and against further sharing of clear channels. The Regional Broadcasters' Committee fought superpower and submitted a plan for further sharing of clear channels which its spokesmen said would

[4] The C.C.B.S., made up of twenty-six of the most powerful stations in the country, each of which contributes $10,000 annually to a "war chest," is ably represented in Washington by Louis G. Caldwell, onetime F.R.C. general counsel, who also looks after the interests of WGN, Inc., the *Chicago Tribune*, and Press Wireless, Inc. The most powerful radio lobby in the capital, C.C.B.S. has done more than all other groups combined to maintain the *status quo* among clear-channel plum-holders.

148

guarantee three secondary services to all parts of the country, four to most. WLW (Cincinnati) asked for 500-kilowatt power, which it had developed experimentally from 1934 to 1939. A.B.C. let it be known that it would do a better job than N.B.C. and C.B.S. were doing, if only it could get its hands on a few N.B.C. and/or C.B.S. clear channels; and it was no secret that M.B.S. also was eying some of the older networks' stations. Representatives of farm organizations, minority groups, women's clubs, and small-town civic and commercial bodies from the neglected areas trouped into the open hearings to tell their stories.

Meantime, the Commission itself had not been idle. In the fall of 1945, it had put its engineers to work helping industry engineers chart noise levels from coast to coast and from Canada to the Gulf, with a view to finding out who heard what, at what times, and how well. At the same time, it called on the Department of Agriculture and the Bureau of the Census to conduct intensive surveys of all the rural and certain selected small-town areas in the country. By the time of the July, 1946, hearings, it was mulling over several tentative plans. The nub of one: to designate three or four frequencies suitable for clear-channel broadcasting in and to "blank" areas shown on the engineers' map; announce that anyone using those frequencies would have to share them; choose the areas in which the new stations ought for sound engineering reasons to be located, draw circles around them on the map, and notify all comers that certain frequencies were available in certain areas for such-and-such types of service.

While all hands waited for the resumption of hearings, postponed well into the first quarter of 1947, the C.C.B.S. concocted a revolutionary scheme, the salient feature of which was said to be allocation of power on the order of 750 kilowatts to 20 stations, to be divided equally among the four networks, each of which would undertake to supply four totally different nation-wide program services.

No less important to the extension of broadcasting service was the many-sided quest for cheaper, quicker ways of linking stations together for network broadcasting and for devices designed to make a single channel do the work of many.

As we have seen, A.T. & T. very early in the game obtained a virtual monopoly of the station interconnection business, thanks to the fact that the telephone long-lines at that time appeared to offer the only practical solution. At the beginning of 1947, this situation remained virtually unchanged, and A.T. & T. was busy laying coaxial cable to carry a traffic load which was taxing the long-lines and at the same time accommodate television signals, for which the long-lines were not suited.

Meantime, however, the advocates of Dr. Conrad's radio relay principle have not been idle. Westinghouse in 1946 conducted repeated tests of its airplane "stratocasting" plan and announced that it was ready to "saturate" the country with FM, television, and facsimile signals as soon as the F.C.C. and the broadcasters gave the word. In September, the Raytheon Manufacturing Company and Radio Inventions, Inc., conducted tests on a "microwave" system linking Boston and New York which its backers insisted demonstrated not only the practical advantages of radio relay over either telephone long-lines or coaxial cables but also the possibility of utilizing a single frequency for the simultaneous transmission of multiple signals or programs, and the paving of the way for facsimile transmission with automatic synchronization at 2,000 words a minute on the 15-kilocycle band that Raytheon would make available if it moved into the region of 4,000 megacycles for relay. Also experimenting in the ultra-high frequencies was DuMont, which in November, 1946, demonstrated a new, cheap method of transmitting television images on light beams. Called "photovision," the DuMont principle may, if successful, render both cables and ordinary radio relays obsolescent. A.T. & T. likewise was reported to be going ahead with its "mobile highways" plan, though with the emphasis still on telephonic rather than on broadcast communication.

The failure of these projects to develop more rapidly has given rise to charges from their backers, and especially from laymen unfamiliar with the engineering factors involved, that the F.C.C. has been indifferent to the situation or even out to "protect" A.T. & T.'s "stranglehold" on the network interconnection business. Such charges have been based on the F.C.C.'s policy of authorizing extensions of the A.T. & T.'s coaxial system; on the Commission's denial in September, 1946, of Press Wireless, Inc.'s, application to furnish a program transmission service to broadcasting stations; and on a statement in July, 1946, by a former F.C.C. employee to the effect that A.T. & T. was overcharging the broadcasters by some $4,000,000 a year.

Actually, it would appear that the Commission has been more than alert to the burden placed upon small stations, especially those known as "bonus" stations (because, although they get network programs for nothing, they receive nothing for airing them and must pay all or a substantial share of the line charges). The fact is that the networks themselves have shown no disposition to break away from the A.T. & T. stranglehold. On the contrary, they have been cool to radio relay because of the fear that programs carried on it might be pirated. After more than a year's intensive study, the F.C.C.'s engineers are far from convinced that radio relay in any of the forms thus far put forward would prove cheaper than the coaxials. Meanwhile, the fact that A.T. & T., Westinghouse, Raytheon, Press Wireless, and a number of other firms have been going ahead with tests on ill-spared temporary frequencies granted by the Commission ought to speak for itself. The Press Wireless denial explained that "the lack of quality and reliability are such as not to justify the use of frequencies urgently needed by the other radio services using the 1.6–25 mc bands." The truth is that these bands, in which Westinghouse also seeks to operate, are not the Commission's to give away. That portion between 1.6 (the upper limit of the standard broadcast band) and 2 megacycles is occupied by the amateurs. That from 2 to 10 megacycles is being used for short-wave broadcasting and for government (principally Army and Navy) and aviation. From 10 to 25 megacycles is all government and aviation. These bands are jealously guarded by the Board of War Communications and I.R.A.C. International agreements frown on their use for domestic point-to-point communication. Almost alone of all the experimenters in radio relay, Raytheon is concentrating on a portion of the spectrum not so encumbered. And the F.C.C., under its able engineer-commissioner, Ewell K. Jett, is encouraging them all to keep trying until the solution is found.

Development of means to get more work out of both overworked and underdeveloped bands has been equally encouraging. In September, 1946, Federal Telecommunications Laboratories transmitted simultaneously eight radio programs over a single frequency (930 megacycles, far above the experimental color-television bands), in a successful demonstration of its pulse-time modulation principle. One of the salient features of this system is that any number of satellite receivers can be connected to the same antenna, so that the listener, merely by manipulating a row of buttons, can have his choice of the eight programs coming from a single station. In the same month the Bell Telephone Laboratories, a subsidiary of A.T. & T., demonstrated a new vacuum tube which it claimed would make possible a "wave-guide" network of coast-to-coast proportions capable of accommodating all the television programs that the country is likely to have for many years to come.

It was a beginning. No one pretended that any one plan would solve the whole problem for all time. The truth is that the task that Congress assigned to the F.R.C. in 1928 was impossible of complete and literal achievement. The Commission was asked to form a smooth national engineering picture out of jigsaw pieces that happened already to exist, that had come into being because of purely economic factors which completely ignored the engineering factor, and that tended consequently to overlap in certain areas more than they stretched contiguously and continuously from coast to coast and from the Canadian border to the Gulf of Mexico. Had the F.R.C. been empowered to call in all the licenses held at the time it took over and to redistribute frequencies and power with a view solely to blanketing the country, using sound engineering knowledge as the only criterion and prepared to be deaf to the anguished outcries of broadcasters thus deprived of their frequencies, it might have achieved saturation coverage within two or three years.

But one must not forget that the F.R.C. was obliged to tackle the complicated puzzle with the Congress kibitzing over its collective shoulder. The Davis Amendment was a masterpiece of mixed motives in which misguided idealism, States'-rightism, pork barrelism, and rabid antimonopolism joined forces to defeat the expressed aims of the Act of 1927.

The Congress chose (thereby obliging the F.R.C. and later the F.C.C. to follow suit) to ignore the plain fact that the only hope of extending uniformly first-class broadcasting service to communities able to support only small stations producing marginal programs was to make the larger and wealthier stations take care of them, and that the only hope of extending service to communities unable to support any local stations was to reach them by automatic relay—in either case, clearly a job for networks.

But "monopoly" was a fright-word to a generation of public men who felt that they had "invented" the Clayton and Sherman acts and who proclaimed with an excess of zeal matched only by that which greeted the discovery of the "sulfa" drugs that "trust-busting" was a sure, quick cure for all that ailed the economy. The analogy they saw was not that between radio and magazines, books, and movies, produced in their physical entirety in half-a-dozen cities, but that between radio and the newspaper press, with its supposed high degree of local autonomy. What they forgot was that from 75 to 90 per cent of what appears in local papers is "network" material (from press associations, picture agencies, and feature syndicates) and that even the humblest newspaperless hamlet has access to city newspapers on a regular daily basis.

THE FIGHT FOR FREE ENTERPRISE

Fear of monopoly manifested itself in congressional councils in the earliest days of broadcasting and has never been wholly absent from them since. Thus in January, 1923, we find Congressman White of Maine submitting a resolution, unanimously adopted by the House, which directed the Federal Trade Commission to investigate and report "the facts as they found them with respect to the alleged radio monopoly." The F.T.C. submitted a report of 347 pages, showing "conclusively" that certain companies were violating the Clayton and Sherman acts. When the House took no action on these findings, the F.T.C. on its own motion filed a complaint against the members of this alleged monopoly (the Radio Corporation). This the Department of Justice ignored until 1930.

Another aspect of "monopoly" which disturbed the Congress had been brought to its attention by noncommercial broadcasters and would-be broadcasters, prominent among whom were representatives of various religious sects, claiming that the commercial interests were getting the best of things. In January, 1932, the Senate passed a resolution requiring the F.R.C. to investigate and report on this alleged squeezing-out of noncommercial or "educational" stations in favor of commercial ones, particularly those with network ownership or affiliation. Then, as now, it was felt by many that the complete answer to bad practices among the advertising-supported broadcasters was a large number of "educational" stations.

The Commission reported that, as of the first of that year, it had licensed 95 educational institutions to operate broadcasting stations, of which only 44 had survived; that 95 per cent of the commercial stations had made it a practice to offer free or cost-of-operation time to educational institutions, of which none at all had been claimed in 32 per cent of the cases cited, and not more than a fraction of that offered in 95 per cent of the cases. The Commission felt that, in the circumstances, "educational" programming could safely be left in the hands of the commercial broadcasters, whose capacity and willingness to provide for it, the Commissioners were persuaded, far exceeded the demand, both of the educators and of the listening public.

Senators Wagner of New York and Hatfield of West Virginia thought they had the answer in an amendment introduced in May, 1934:

155

e) To eliminate monopoly and to insure equality of opportunity. and consideration for educational, religious, agricultural, labor, cooperative and similar nonprofit-making associations seeking the opportunity of adding to the cultural and scientific knowledge of those who listen in on radio broadcasts, all existing radio broadcasting licenses issued by the Federal Radio Commission, and any and all rights of any nature contained therein, are declared null and void ninety days following the effective date of this Act, anything contained in this Act to the contrary notwithstanding.

. *f*) The Commission shall, prior to ninety days following the effective date of this Act, reallocate all frequencies, power and time assignments within its jurisdiction among the five zones herein referred to.

g) The Commission shall reserve and allocate only to educational, religious, agricultural, labor, cooperative and similar nonprofit-making associations one-fourth of all the radio broadcasting facilities within its jurisdiction. The facilities reserved for, or allocated to, educational, religious, agricultural, labor, cooperative and similar nonprofit-making persons, firms or corporations shall be equally as desirable as those assigned to profit-making persons, firms or corporations. In the distribution of facilities to the associations referred to in this section, the Commission shall reserve for and allocate to such associations such radio broadcasting facilities as will reasonably make possible the operation of such stations on a self-sustaining basis, and to that end the licensee may sell such part of the allotted time as will make the station self-supporting.

The Wagner-Hatfield Amendment was defeated, 42 to 23. But on June 19, the Communications Act became law. It embraced the Radio Act of 1927, as amended, and extended the regulatory scope of the new F.C.C. to all forms of interstate and international telecommunication.

The new commission, four members of which carried over from the F.R.C., faced a staggering load. To begin with, a staff that had not been adequate to deal promptly with radio broadcasting matters now had to spread itself out to cover all other forms of telecommunication. To facilitate this, the

F.C.C. divided itself into three divisions, Broadcast, Telephone, and Telegraph, two members and the chairman serving on each. This necessary distribution of labors was to reveal a fundamental weakness in many subsequent radio cases, since, except in the rare instances where the full Commission sat *en banc* for rehearings, the Broadcast Division lacked the benefit of the judgment of four of the seven members.

No less urgent than this reorganization was the specific task assigned in Section 307(c) of the new act:

The Commission shall study the proposal that Congress by statute allocate fixed percentages of radio broadcasting facilities to particular types or kinds of nonprofit radio programs or to persons identified with particular types or kinds of nonprofit activities, and shall report to the Congress, not later than February 1, 1935, its recommendations together with reasons for the same.

During October and November, the Broadcast Division heard 135 witnesses, who testified as follows: during the first half of 1934 commercial stations broadcast 77,542 hours, or 11.3 per cent of their total day operating time, and 14,873 hours, or 8 per cent of their total night operating time, of "educational" material in co-operation with or on behalf of such groups. (Including programs initiated by the stations, the grand totals were 114,159 hours, or 16.7 per cent for daytime, and 24,582 hours, or 13.3 per cent for night.) In general, the Broadcast Division concluded, the networks were most co-operative, large independent stations almost as much so, small independents least of all.

On January 22, 1935, the Commission reported to the Congress in the negative, stating:

It would appear that the interests of the nonprofit organizations may be better served by the use of the existing facilities, thus giving them access to costly and efficient equipment and to established

157

audiences. Cooperation in good faith by the broadcasters is required. Such cooperation should, therefore, be under the direction and supervision of the Commission. It is our firm intention to assist the nonprofit organizations to obtain the fullest opportunities for expression.

Whereupon the F.C.C. sought help from the United States Office of Education in setting up the Federal Radio Education Committee, a body which, as we have seen, was destined to play a somewhat minor role in broadcasting.

Newspaper ownership of broadcasting stations had been an early concern of the regulators. They had not always known how to reconcile what seemed, on the one hand, to be a distinct monopolistic trend and, on the other hand, sometimes the only way to insure good service to certain communities. Thus in the thirties, an application for a new station in Madison, Wisconsin, was turned down on the ground that the community was well served and that, although both newspapers and the only existing commercial broadcasting station were owned by the same man, they were operated "separately." The same thing occurred in Lincoln, Nebraska, where the unsuccessful applicant was able to show that the principal owners of the only two newspapers held a substantial interest in both the existing radio stations and another in Omaha.

Apparently, the newspapers had some trouble, notwithstanding, in trying to outguess the Commission. The *Kansas City Star* and *Times*, licensee of WDAF, were turned down on the purchase of WREN, on the ground that this would have left the third station, KMBC, at "a competitive disadvantage." The *Port Huron* (Michigan) *Times Herald* and the *Fall River* (Massachusetts) *Herald News* were refused applications for new stations in favor of nonnewspaper applicants. But the Commission approved the transfer of WNAX (Yankton, South Dakota) to the South Dakota Broadcasting Company, whose president, Gardner Cowles, Jr., also was connected with the Iowa Broadcasting Company, licensee of KSO and KRNT (Des Moines) and WMT (Cedar Rapids), as well as the *Des Moines Register* and *Tribune*, the *Minneapolis Star-Journal* and *Tribune*, and the picture magazine, *Look*.

It was generally recognized that some of the best broadcasting stations in the country were operated by publishers of the printed word. The F.C.C. itself frequently took occasion to pat them on the back, as when, in renewing the license of KSD (St. Louis), owned by the *Post-Dispatch*, it commented:

> It is the policy of station KSD to reject advertising which in the judgment of the station appears likely to injure health or to cause financial loss. The advertiser who desires to use the station must be able to make good his claims and promises and all statements of fact must be fair to the public and to competitors. A list of commercial accounts refused or the continuity of proposed programs which were revised reveals a large number of such instances.

Ultimately, the Commission was to examine the congressional theory that newspaper ownership was an epidemic evil about which one could generalize, but not until it had got a new chairman.

On March 20, 1941, Chairman Fly announced a comprehensive study of the problem of newspaper ownership. On April 26 he served notice that all future applications from publishers would go in the "pending" file. Subsequently, the Commission had some studies made and held hearings. The general policy was discussed in executive session several times in 1943 and 1944, and, finally, in the spring of 1944, a short statement of policy was made to the effect that there would be no general rule against newspaper ownership of radio stations but that the factor of creating a monopoly would be taken into account in specific cases of applications for new licenses or transfers of license.

Shortly after Porter succeeded Fly in 1945, the new chairman told a House Appropriations group that "it seems to me that when a radio station in a community of say 25,000 or less has to split the advertising revenue with the independent newspaper, you are going to have a very mediocre radio station in that community." Four Commissioners (one was absent) went along with him in approving, in December, 1945, the voluntary assignment of WSRR, the only broadcasting station in Stamford, Connecticut, to the owner of the *Stamford Advocate*, the town's lone newspaper.

To many a nonradio-minded newspaperman it seemed that the print media were locked in a life-and-death struggle for advertising dollars with the upstart medium and that this fact was at the heart of the problem of newspaper ownership of broadcasting stations. Now and then this alleged survival factor came to the surface in F.C.C. rulings. In 1938, an El Paso, Texas, case came up for rehearing. The year before, Commissioner Stewart had argued against granting the publisher a license to erect a new station, pointing out that the applicant had submitted no evidence of need other than statements that he attributed to advertisers to the effect that they would patronize his station, if he got one, and that, if this were so, the existing station might be driven to the wall. The Commission again, and this time without a dissent, approved the authorization, citing the existing station's 6-year profits as evidence that it was ruin-proof. Of the fact that the only newspaper and the new station would be under common ownership the Commissioners took the customary passing notice that they had "assurances" that the two enterprises would be operated "independently."

Stewart's point was precisely the point that the Commission had made in denying the Port Huron and Fall River applications. But the El Paso decision was not the only one that contradicted the thesis. By 1940 the majority was ready to favor a newspaper over a rival applicant for a new station in Martinsville, Virginia, precisely on the ground that the newspaper might be financially ruined if it did not get the license.

Was it properly the concern of the F.C.C. whether the granting of a new station might embarrass an existing one? When, in 1941, an Erie, Pennsylvania, licensee protested the licensing of a competitor and referred the F.C.C. to what it thought were valid grounds in a previous Supreme Court decision (*Federal Communications Commission* vs. *Sanders Brothers*), the Commission replied: "The Supreme Court has made it perfectly clear that the Congress intended 'to leave competition in the field of broadcasting where it found it' and to permit 'a licensee to survive or succumb according to his ability to make his programs attractive to the public.' " The Commission felt, therefore, that it was under no compulsion to make a study of the probable effects of competition in the instant case, as appellant had requested. Only if "the financial qualification of the applicant depends on his ability to compete for business with the existing licensee" was the question of the probable effect of competition "an important fact to be considered by the Commission."

Lawyers were to puzzle over this reasoning for many a day. Did it mean that the second man in the field would have to prove that there was enough business for two? It certainly meant, as the F.C.C. was to make clear in a number of cases, that it would not consider advertising pledges as part of operating capital in judging an applicant's financial qualifications. Applicant had to have cash. How much cash? Enough to build his station and get it going? The answer, in the instance of an Amarillo, Texas, application, was "No, more than that." How much more? Enough to last how long without moving in on an established competitor? The Commission did not say. And prospective broadcasters learned to take their advertising pledges to the local bank, where they readily enough produced loans, which the Commission would accept as working capital, although the collateral was precisely the same as that offered without success by the Amarillo applicant.

With newspapers, as with all other applicants, the Commission's expressed philosophy in 1946 was "every case on its own merits." Thus it turned down New York chain-publisher Gannett's bid for a local channel in Binghamton which was also sought by a nonnewspaper applicant, reaffirming its "announced policy of so exercising its licensing power as to promote, where practical, diversification in the controls of the media of mass communication." But it also approved transfers of KHQ (Spokane) to the *Spokane Chronicle*, KOIN (Portland) to Marshall Field, WFIL (Philadelphia) to the *Philadelphia Inquirer*, and KMTR (Hollywood) to the owners of the *New York Post.*

The major policy developed during the stormy years from 1939 to 1945 was embodied in the Chain Broadcasting Regulations with which the broadcasting spokesmen identified Fly. Actually, of course, the Chain Regulations had a long history going back to McNinch. The Commission on March 18, 1938, issued Order 37 instituting the investigation, pursuant to specific directions from the Congress. On May 2, the *Report on Chain Broadcasting* was issued, together with Regulations 3.101–3.108 inclusive, to become effective 90 days thereafter. On July 22 the effective date was deferred to September. On August 14, M.B.S. petitioned the Commission to amend two regulations. On August 28 the effective date was again postponed. On October 30 and 31, N.B.C. and C.B.S. filed suit in the District Court for the Southern District of New York.

On February 21, 1942, the District Court dismissed the suits, denying jurisdiction, and the networks appealed. On April 30 and May 1, oral argument was heard by the Supreme Court, which held, on June 1, that the District Court did have jurisdiction and remanded the case to it.

What were the abuses discovered by the F.C.C. and the steps taken by it to correct them? As Fly told it to the House Committee on Foreign and Interstate Commerce while the courts sparred back and forth, there were eight of each:

1. *Exclusivity of affiliation.*—In order to get programs from one network, stations were frequently required to contract not to carry a single program from any other. Thus when, during the baseball World Series of 1939, M.B.S. offered the play-by-play broadcast to N.B.C. and C.B.S. stations, N.B.C. and C.B.S. said "No," and many communities went without. Regulation 3.101 provided that network affiliation contracts might not be so drawn as to prevent a station, if it so desired, from carrying programs of another network.

2. *Territorial exclusivity.*—Frequently, certain stations decided not to carry a particular network program, but in that event the network could not offer it to any other station in the area. Thus the contract between WRVA and C.B.S. provided not only that C.B.S. might not offer a program to any other station in Richmond, Virginia, but that it could not take on as a regular affiliate any other station within 80 miles. Thus M.B.S. had a contract with Don Lee and through that California network with the Pacific Broadcasting Company in Oregon and Washington, giving Lee territorial exclusivity for the whole Pacific coast. (M.B.S. had, however, agreed to ʑ̣ ve these up the moment that N.B.C. and C.B.S., voluntarily or on order from the F.C.C., gave up theirs.) Regulation 3.102 provided that the regular affiliate might not prevent some

163

other station from carrying a network program in case the regular affiliate rejected it.

3. *Duration of affiliation contracts.*—Stations were bound for five years, the networks for only one. Regulation 3.103 provided that both should be bound for no more than two.

4. *Option time.*—By taking an option on all the hours of its affiliates, C.B.S. had been able to discourage non-network programs, as the latter could be "bumped" on 28 days' notice. "The result has been that stations have been cramped in their efforts to produce worthwhile local programs and to procure high-quality transcriptions." Regulation 3.104 provided that (*a*) a station might not contract with one network that it would not option time to another; (*b*) a network could not use its option to oust another from time already bought and scheduled; (*c*) certain hours of the day were to be excluded from network options and left free for sale on a first-come, first-served basis; and (*d*) notice for the ousting of local programs was to be extended from 28 to 56 days.

5. *Station rejection of network programs.*—"There is reason to believe that under some affiliation contracts the licensee gives up his right to reject improper network programs." Regulation 3.105 provided that a station might not contract away its right to reject unsuitable network programs.

6. *Network ownership of stations.*—At the time that the F.C.C.'s *Report on Chain Broadcasting* was issued, N.B.C. had owned nine stations, of which eight were clear channels, including two each in New York, Chicago, and San Francisco; C.B.S. had owned eight, of which seven were also high-power clear channels. Since that time, N.B.C. has transferred three to the Blue Network, Inc. But the situation remained bad in Charlotte, North Carolina, for example, where C.B.S.'s ownership of the one 50-kilowatt station, WBT (which it subsequently disposed of), left a 1,000-watter and a 250-watter

164

to be shared by N.B.C., M.B.S., and the Blue Network. Regulation 3.106 provided that no network could own more than one station in any locality, or any in a locality where the existing stations were so few, or of such unequal desirability, that competition would be substantially restrained thereby.[5]

7. *Separation of the Red and Blue networks.*—Everyone— N.B.C., Blue, the Commission majority, the Commission minority—agreed that the separation of Red and Blue networks was a wise step. Fly even complimented N.B.C. and R.C.A. on "the businesslike and wholly cooperative way" in which the interested parties had proceeded immediately after the Chain Regulations were announced to effectuate the division, without waiting for the court test. Regulation 3.107 formally blessed the separation of Red and Blue.

8. *Network control of station rates.*—N.B.C.'s standard affiliation contract provided that if a station sold time to a national advertiser for less than that which N.B.C. charged, N.B.C. could lower the network rate accordingly. Regulation 3.108 provided, in effect, simply that stations might fix their rates without reference to the networks.

These regulations, Fly told the representatives, would do a good deal for broadcasting. Would they give the Commission a backdoor entree to program censorship? On the contrary, the regulations "do not either directly or indirectly give the Commission any power or control over program content." Was he trying to suggest that the network programs were inferior? No, "it is perfectly true that on the whole the average network program is superior to the average local program." But that was perhaps because the latter had not had a proper chance to develop. Would this ruin the networks, as

[5] An unwritten "gentleman's agreement" effectively limits the over-all ownership of AM stations to eight; F.C.C .regulations limit over-all ownership of FM stations to six, of television stations to five.

they said? Why, he thought, the regulations would open the way for new networks and brisker competition among networks.

Commissioners Craven and Case were not so sure. They felt that the Commission was exceeding its authority under the act in undertaking to deal directly with alleged monopolistic practices.

Congress provided not only for a diversification of control of radio broadcasting among licensees, but also for diversification of jurisdiction among various regulatory agencies. It was not intended that any licensee merely because he was a radio broadcaster should be exempt from the application of laws directed to business enterprise generally. The Commission does not have responsibility to determine the guilt of licensees for violations of law the administration of which is not under the direct jurisdiction of the Commission.

Such matters as the manufacture and sale of radio equipment and transcriptions by licensed broadcasters, if indicative of "at least an opportunity to engage in unfair trade practices," might better be directed to the attention of the F.T.C. The Department of Justice had always been regarded as competent to deal with antitrust matters in general.

The scope of the Chain Regulations seemed to Craven and Case too broad. "There is a temptation to overemphasize local interest to the detriment of national interest, and vice versa. The real goal should be efficiency of service from a national standpoint rather than a vague objective which fosters a conglomeration of local units uncoordinated for rendering a truly national service." The two things were not mutually exclusive, but

a policy of unlimited competition is in conflict with the legal mandate to distribute facilities fairly, efficiently, and equitably throughout the nation. This dilemma becomes even more difficult to resolve because allocation of facilities to any area is dependent upon voluntary applications. It is obvious that unlimited competition among

166

stations in any community is impractical when the total number of facilities available for the entire nation is limited. Emphasis, therefore, should be placed upon an equitable distribution of facilities to the various communities, rather than upon unlimited competition which can never be wholly achieved.

Meantime the Supreme Court had got the case, dismissed by the District Court on its merits. On May 10, 1943, the high tribunal, by a vote of five to two, upheld the Chain Broadcasting Regulations (Black and Rutledge not participating). Of far more lasting significance than this fact was an excursion by Mr. Justice Frankfurter, who drafted the majority opinion, into matters not germane to the instant pleading, to produce a statement which, though it lacked the force of law, or perhaps because it did lack the force of law, has confused everyone connected with broadcasting ever since: "But the Act does not restrict the Commission merely to supervision of the traffic. It puts upon the Commission the burden of determining the composition of that traffic."

In a dissent to which Mr. Justice Roberts subscribed, Mr. Justice Murphy felt that the court was

gratuitously bestowing upon an agency power which the Congress has not granted. We have held [*Federal Communications Commission* vs. *Sanders Brothers*] that "the Act does not essay to regulate the business of the licensee. The Commission is given no supervisory control of the programs, of business management or of policy." It is evident from the record that the Commission is making its determination of whether the public interest would be served by renewal of an existing license or licenses, not upon an examination of written applications presented to it, as required by Sections 308 and 309, but upon an investigation of the broadcasting industry as a whole, and general findings made in pursuance thereof which relate to the business methods of the network companies. If it had been the intention of the Congress to invest the Commission with the responsibility over the business operations of radio networks, it is not likely that the Congress would have neglected to include it among the considerations expressly made relevant to license applications by Section 308 (b).

For the broadcasters, the occasion was a solemn one indeed. In a May 25 brochure distributed by the N.A.B. it was stated: "Overnight American radio, under the law as interpreted by the court, has lost all the characteristics of freedom. Lawyers for the radio industry, reading and rereading the decision, can find no limits placed on the Commission's power." In a word, radio was through, ruined, finished, washed up. "This," a network vice-president solemnly assured the New York Radio Executives' Club, "is the end."

In a sense, the broadcasters had only themselves to blame. N.B.C. and C.B.S. had overreached themselves in exploiting the competitive positions which seniority had given them. M.B.S. had started the whole investigation by appealing for government aid in blasting the other two networks loose from their favored positions. Still, little as Colonel McCormick and his friends had reckoned the final cost, the debacle which they now bewailed (with tongue in cheek) never materialized. On the contrary, profits soared. Indeed, the real defect of the Chain Regulations may have been that they accomplished so little of tangible good. The mountain had labored for more than five years.

The Chain Regulations had been aimed primarily at the national networks. Toward the end of 1946 the Commission decided to check some of the regional chains. It was particularly interested to know whether the Don Lee system on the Pacific Coast was observing the 56-day notice requirement for the exercise of options and also whether it was compelling its affiliates to option more time than the Chain Regulations allowed. KGB (San Diego), KDB (Santa Barbara), KFRC (San Francisco), and KHJ and KHJ-FM (Los Angeles) were up for renewals. On February 18, 1946, all five were set down for hearings on October 7. They were still on the docket on December 31.

The matter of speculating in frequencies (i.e., selling stations for sums so far in excess of the value of the physical plant as to suggest that what the purchaser was after really was the license) had come to the attention of the F.R.C. during its first month in office. In May, 1927, the Commission issued an order "inviting" broadcasters to advertise for bids when disposing of stations. It was ignored and, embarrassed by its constant reminder of unfinished business, the F.R.C. rescinded it on September 29, 1930, despite the fact that abuses of this nature became in that year more flagrant than ever before.

They were destined to get out of hand. In 1944, Commissioner Durr cited four cases which the majority agreed violated the intent of the law but which they felt could not be dealt with without a new law. Then, in January, 1946, the Crosley Corporation closed a deal with Hearst for the purchase of WINS (New York) for $2,100,000. Called upon to bless the transaction, the F.C.C. asked a number of basic questions: (1) Since the physical assets of WINS came to less than $100,000, the principal item being an antenna system valued at $57,000; and since the "going-concern" or good-will assets would not swell the figure much past the quarter-million mark, how much of the purchase price was for WINS's recently won permit to increase power from 10 to 50 kilowatts, and how much was for the license itself? (2) Had Marshall Field been given a fair chance to bid? (A Hearst executive testified that Field's bidding had stopped at $1,500,000.) (3) Did Crosley know at the time that he bid WINS in that he was shortly going to sell all his broadcasting facilities to the Aviation Corporation (A.V.C.O.)? (4) Did the ten-year "co-operation period" during which $400,000 of the purchase

169

price for WINS would be paid in time donated to the *New York Mirror* collide with public interest, convenience, or necessity? Seizing on the weakest point, the F.C.C. in April in a "proposed finding" disallowed the application. Once the payment-in-kind clause was dropped and the price adjusted to $1,700,000, the Commission in July approved the transfer, four to two, Walker and Durr dissenting.

Meanwhile, the celebrated Crosley-A.V.C.O. deal had gone through, overshadowing everything that had gone before it. A.V.C.O. was to pay $22,000,000 for all of Crosley's broadcasting and some of his manufacturing properties. At least three commissioners were not satisfied that the breakdown offered at the F.C.C. hearing put a price on Crosley's twenty-four AM, FM, television, facsimile, and international short-wave stations, licenses, and permits. A.V.C.O. looked like one of the "Wall Street speculators" whom Porter had warned to stay out of broadcasting. A.V.C.O. officials did not appear to know the difference between a soap opera and a station break. Wise broadcasters wagered that "this one will never get by." On the contrary, the transfer was approved, four to three, in record time, the majority composed of Porter, Denny, Jett, and Wills holding that, although the case revealed a "basic infirmity" in the Communications Act which the Congress would have to cure, "to deny this application would reverse seventeen years of precedent."

Durr, Walker, and Wakefield dissented, the first two writing:

No licensee or prospective licensee has any vested interest in the Commission's past mistakes or omissions, and the Commission's statutory responsibility is in no way diminished by its failure, or the failure of its predecessors in the past, to meet that responsibility. The transferee, Aviation Corporation, is a holding company. It and those now in control of its policies are engaged in activities ranging from the manufacture of kitchen sinks to the conduct of a stock brokerage business, including the manufacture of airplanes, ships and steel and the control of a large public utility holding company. This is a type of corporate structure which has long been a matter of concern to the people of this country and to Congress itself. Programming is the essence of broadcasting, and yet not a single witness for the transferee demonstrated more than the vaguest idea about the kind of program service which would be rendered, the availability of program talent and sources, the needs of the people in WLW's service area or even about the types of program service being rendered under the previous management. They did not even know how much they were paying for the broadcasting facilities being purchased. We do not agree that the conclusion reached by the majority is required by any "basic infirmity" in the Communications Act. On the contrary, it seems clear from the opinion of the majority that if there is any "basic infirmity," it lies not in the Act but in the Commission's own precedents and procedures.

The F.C.C. majority asked for new legislation, stressing (1) the propriety of a corporation with other interests owning broadcasting stations, (2) the need for some system for breaking down price structure, and (3) absentee ownership. It was said that at least one commissioner favored recommending that all stations be required by law to be completely autonomous corporate entities, although the A.V.C.O. decision had underlined the practical difficulties in the way of such a bold move. To deny the Crosley–A.V.C.O. transfer, on the ground that A.V.C.O. had other interests, the majority pointed out, "would create a chaotic situation in the broadcast industry, since doubt would be cast upon the status of scores of present radio licensees who, like A.V.C.O., have extensive nonbroadcast interests." The majority might have added that to deny A.V.C.O. on such a ground would have raised a question as to the right of Crosley to have broadcasting properties to sell, since he was in the same boat. And it might have cited "hundreds" instead of "scores" of precedents, for, in addition to more than three hundred newspapers, there were in the station-owning business a half-dozen prominent makers of radio equipment (R.C.A., G.E., Westinghouse, Philco, Stromberg-Carlson, Zenith); and an equal number of hotels, insurance companies, and amusement concerns.

Senator Wheeler said he would introduce legislation "at once." In the interim, the F.C.C. in December, 1945, issued a set of proposed rules and regulations calling for the advertisement in local newspapers of proposed station transfers, including the price offered by the original bidder, and for a 60-day waiting period, during which competitive bidding would be encouraged. Following hearings in April, this formula was promulgated in a set of proposed regulations. In July a rule offering enough loopholes to satisfy N.A.B. spokesmen was put into effect. Biggest loophole: The rule itself could be waived in special cases.

PROTECTION OF LOCAL INTERESTS

Congress has been jealous in behalf of the interests of local communities, and the regulatory body has striven to keep them uppermost. Sometimes the problem has brought out a fundamental paradox, as underlined by Senator Wheeler in a 1938 speech to the N.A.B. The Montanan told the broadcasters:

For obvious reasons, neither you nor I want to see government ownership in American radio, but we cannot ignore the signs or the tempo of the times. Only broadcasting's own folly would make the threat real. And that would evolve if we allowed any entities in the industry or outside of it beckoning for entrée to become too large. . . . . There are several species of monopoly that might get a stranglehold on radio. . . . . One is power in watts . . . . a second is power in numbers of stations concentrated in identical ownership. The third relates to the power and the status of the networks.

It was as hard for Wheeler as for any other conscientious trust-buster to be practical and consistent in a day when mass production sometimes argued for bigness. He felt that radio's first duty was "service to a particular community" and that the moment a broadcaster got more power, he forsook his community for larger "oysters." For that reason he was opposed to clear channels. Yet he could scarcely avoid admitting that "stations in smaller communities are largely dependent upon the programs which the networks furnish them."

The two goods were relative, and, in the WHDH case cited above, the Commission majority doubtless had let community service outweigh all other considerations. Once in a while, the majority leaned so far toward local interests that it allowed itself to be victimized. Such an instance involved KIEV (Glendale, California). This station had based its original application to the F.R.C. on the high ground that Glendale was filled with "promising local talent," which, in the absence of a station in that community, was denied access to the airways. The applicant had promised to devote at least a third of his time to "educational and semieducational" programs which, he said, would include: "sketches, music, duets, quartets, excerpts from operas, cuttings from great plays, literary characterizations, interpretations of great poems, readings for children and adults, the creating of continued stories culminating in a message for children, general interpretation of literary works not ordinarily acceptable to the average layman."

Eager to see how such an ambitious and public spirited man was coming along with such a program, the F.C.C. toward the end of 1938 asked its field man to monitor the station on 3 random days. Typical December day: 143 popular records, 9 semiclassical records, 264 commercial announcements, 3 minutes of announcements pertaining to lost and found pets. For more than a year, the station had not aired

173

one word of news. Its employment of the abundant talent available locally consisted, over a 5-year period, of one imported dance band that lasted a few weeks. "With some reluctance," the seven Solomons of Washington wound up the tale, "the Commission concludes that this application may be granted."

In general, however, the Commission apparently operated on the theory that, everything else being reasonably equal, local service, which presumably improved as the station became more and more independent of networks, outweighed all other considerations.

The one thing the Commission could not do was conjure up wideawake, public spirited, financially well-cushioned applicants in communities that did not produce them spontaneously. Irate preachers, teachers, and club women who frequently wrote letters to, and occasionally called upon, the Commissioners sometimes forgot that economic fact of life.

THE PEOPLE'S PLATFORM

Some members of the Congress were less concerned for the public's right to hear than for the political candidate's right to speak, as often, as long, and as loud as his opponent, as provided in Section 18 of the Act. The *Second Annual Report* of the F.R.C. noted that "it has not yet proved possible to issue definite regulations on the subject." The broadcasters' natural inclination to protect themselves from the consequences of possible political invective by blue-penciling candidates' scripts gave the lawmakers more trouble. When they came to incorporate the Radio Act of 1927 into the Communications Act of 1934, they underlined in Section 315 that the licensees should "exercise no power of censorship" over political campaign material submitted to them. Whereupon the Nebraska Supreme Court (in *Sorenson* vs. *Wood and KFAB Broadcast-*

174

ing Co.) found that the licensee as well as the speaker was liable for defamatory utterances of political candidates, and broadcasters became warier than ever of political speakers in particular and controversial issues in general.[6]

It was sometimes difficult, for broadcasters and Commissioners alike, to draw the line on public discussion. Simple enough, in the days before labor unions began clamoring for their own stations, was the 1939 ruling denying the Young People's Association for the Propagation of the Gospel a permit to erect another station in crowded Philadelphia: "Where the facilities of a station are devoted primarily to one purpose and the station serves as a mouthpiece for a definite group or organization, it cannot be said to be serving the general public."

But if it would not always encourage them to launch their own stations, the F.C.C. fought valiantly for the right of legitimate minority groups to have time on other people's stations. As we have seen, the Commission took up the cudgels for the co-operative movement and organized labor in the early forties so successfully that the N.A.B. was forced to amend its Code to permit these groups to be heard. During 1945 and 1946, the F.C.C. gave sympathetic ear to complaints by the Steel Workers against WGY (Schenectady), by the United Electrical Workers against WICC and other Bridgeport stations, by the United Automobile Workers against WHBU and other Indiana stations and against WBCM (Bay City, Michigan), and by the Cincinnati Industrial Council against WKRC (Cincinnati). Most of them were followed up and quietly settled "out of court."

Disturbed by a C.I.O.–P.A.C. pamphlet issued in the sum-

[6] In December, 1942, the New York Supreme Court ruled that a radio station is not liable for "the extemporaneous defamatory remarks of a political candidate."

mer of 1945 and calling on labor unions to be aggressive in applying for FM station licenses, as well as by the fact that four labor groups had applied for fifteen stations, antilabor congressmen talked of amending that portion of the Communications Act which forbids political organizations to own broadcasting stations, to make it clear that labor unions were, in the meaning of this section, political organizations.

Sometimes the Commission's zeal for minorities carried it to extremes of literal interpretation of the law. Thus on July 19, 1946, it issued an opinion in the case of one Robert Harold Scott, a California atheist who had been plaguing the Commission for five years to revoke the licenses of KQW, Columbia's San Francisco outlet, and other Bay area stations for refusing to grant him time to expound his views, agreeing with Scott, in effect, that he was entitled to time. Just to be on the safe side, KQW on November 17 turned over to Scott a Sunday period for many years earmarked for the Salt Lake City Tabernacle Choir, a favorite sustaining feature on C.B.S.

Of one thing the Commission made doubly certain: that in the discussion of public issues the broadcaster would be, in contrast with the newspaper publisher, a mute instrument, deprived of any voice of his own. This dictum was written into the now celebrated Mayflower Decision of 1941.

The Mayflower Broadcasting Corporation, affiliated with and owned by the Yankee Network, had applied for a renewal for WAAB (Boston). The record showed that during 1937 and 1938, this station had broadcast the frankly editorial views of the owners. The F.C.C. reminded them (and thereby the entire industry) that the practice would not be permitted. In the specific instance the step was primarily the negative one of seeing to it that broadcasters should not irresponsibly abuse anyone and anything they happened not to like, while the abused stood by helplessly, unable to make reply. But the commissioners had in mind more than the instant issue. Some of them saw a chance to further a promising social experiment which the broadcasters themselves had initiated, whether by accident or by design. Here was a fluid new medium of public information. Its practitioners had not intrenched themselves behind the First Amendment. Some of them sincerely believed with the people in government that, inasmuch as the media of mass communication seemed to be falling into the hands of fewer and fewer men and inasmuch as these few, for natural economic reasons, seemed to be drawing farther away from the masses they served on fundamental public issues, they might better withdraw from the field of advocacy altogether and make their facilities available to all shades of opinion. Why not try it, using radio as the guinea-pig?

But was it constitutional? The broadcasters were not disposed to find out. After all, WAAB had been renewed, and that was the main thing. Why risk losing your license just to get a case to the Supreme Court? Coincidence ranged the most mixed of motives on the side of those who saw the Mayflower Decision as an unmixed social blessing. For every broadcaster who honestly welcomed the "common-carrier" concept, there were ten who, since they operated more as grocers than as molders of thought, were happy to have a law that prevented their more zealous employees from driving away customers with oral editorials before the ladies could pay for their soup. If the people in Washington and over at CBS wanted to call it by some fancy name, okay. It fitted like a glove with the 1939 N.A.B. ban on selling time for controversy. And hadn't the ban, by reducing controversy to a minimum, thus leaving time open for more profitable business, been a fine thing for the cash register?

As 1947 opened, there was fair prospect that the F.C.C.

might hold extensive public hearings, with a view to possibly changing the situation produced by its Mayflower Decision. The N.A.B. had asked for review. The Commission was more than willing. The author hopes that the Commission will not be too impressed by an apparent apathy on the part of the broadcasters which may not always indicate pure devotion to its common-carrier ideal. He hopes the Commission will not accept as historically valid the attitude toward the First Amendment of men who have demonstrated that they do not understand the First Amendment. And he hopes the Commission will not fail to examine an arresting thought which may be at some variance with its thoroughly laudable common-carrier concept. That is whether, in the present bedlam of confused thinking, the first duty of all those engaged in mass communication is not, as the only citizens in our society qualified for the task, to thresh and mill and sift the rough grain of human intercourse, so that the man in the street can bake his white bread and eat it. Do we need more voices on the air—or more clear voices?

THE BROADCASTER'S QUALIFICATIONS

Questions relating to the broadcasters' competence have plagued the federal regulators from the first. Critics often wondered out loud "why they ever let So-and-so get by." Commissioner Stewart had supplied a large part of the answer: unless an applicant was vigorously opposed by a rival for the frequency, the Commission simply had to take his word, often unsupported by witnesses or even affidavits; the most routine questioning of citizens in faraway communities usually would have elicited the information that the applicant was (a) an unknown quantity thereabouts, (b) well known and thoroughly objectionable, or (c) well known and acceptable; the Commission lacked the men, the money, and the time to canvass citizens in faraway communities.

Thus it was not always easy for the F.C.C. to know when it was being spoofed about financial qualifications. Now and then it seemed satisfied with very little proof. Thus, in 1938, it granted WMEX (Boston) authority to shift from local to high-power regional, Commissioner Case writing the following dissent for himself and Chairman McNinch:

> The examiner noticed that no stockholder or other party connected with the corporation had testified. He observed that whether or not someone else had control over the construction fund was not clear. Counsel for applicant declined to furnish additional information. The great disparity between the financial showing of April 1, 1936, and that of December 1, 1936 (the applicant appears to have "found" $100,000 in that time), coupled with the apparent incompetence of both the witness and the testimony, leaves this element of the case in such doubt as not to warrant a favorable finding.

Notwithstanding, during 1940 and 1941 the Commission did refuse to renew two stations and revoked the licenses of two others for misrepresenting their financial qualifications.

Sometimes applicants deceived the Commission by setting up dummy corporations. The punishment meted out to those apprehended was not always such as to discourage the practice. Of two lawyers caught red-handed in 1938, one was let off with a letter of reprimand as having been the tool of the other, who was suspended from practicing before the F.C.C. for two months. The most spectacular instance of concealment came to light in 1940, when Commissioner Payne was sent to look into the affairs of seven Texas stations. He found that they were all controlled by one man, who had managed to keep this fact from the Commission, sometimes by getting supposedly reputable citizens to pose for him, at other times by quietly accumulating the stock of a going concern. The key to the scheme seemed to be an attorney who had been a Federal Radio Commissioner and who operated, according to Payne, on the theory that "the Communications Act can be ignored, if only the right kind of pressure can be exerted upon the Commission or its personnel."

The Commission had issued temporary revocation orders on all seven stations before the New Yorker began his trek. He naturally assumed that the revocations would be made permanent in view of his findings. On the contrary, the majority subsequently decided (with Payne, of course, dissenting) that in the instance of one of the seven the public should not be deprived of service (it was a one-station town) because of the culprit's actions and vacated the temporary revocation. On April 2, 1941, it proceeded to vacate the orders against the other six (three of which were not in one-station communities), citing its vacating of the first order as a legal precedent.

Sometime later, a case came up on which Chairman Fly proposed to give no quarter. On January 21, 1941, the Commission had revoked the licenses of WDLP (Panama City, Florida) and near-by WTMC (Ocala), on the ground that both were, in fact, owned by the same man and that this fact had been camouflaged in the applications. On December 2, 1942, the majority, with Fly, Durr, and Wakefield violently dissenting, voted to restore service because the residents of Panama City and Lynn Haven were being deprived of primary radio service—precisely the argument used in lifting the revocation against the first of the seven Texas stations.

In March, 1945, the Commission set a precedent: For the first time in its history, it refused to renew the license of a powerful station. For two years it had been investigating the charge that the owners of WOKO (Albany) had conspired to conceal the ownership of 24 per cent of the stock by a former F.R.C. Commissioner and onetime C.B.S. official, Sam Pick-

180

ard, and his wife. The evidence on that one point seemed conclusive.

But was such a charge sufficient warrant for denying a license, if everything else was in order? A majority of the Court of Appeals for the District of Columbia thought not, holding that WOKO's generally good record of satisfactory service overrode its delinquency in disclosure of true ownership. The United States Supreme Court, however, by unanimous decision, December 9, 1946, overruled the lower court and upheld the decision of the F.C.C. Mr. Justice Jackson, speaking for the Court, emphasized that the fact of concealment "may be more significant than the facts concealed." "It may very well be," the Justice wrote, "that this station has established such a standard of public service that the Commission would be justified in considering that its deception was not a matter that affected its qualifications to serve the public. But it is the Commission, not the courts, which must be satisfied that the public interest will be served by renewing the license."

Discounting the argument that the Commission had been less drastic in dealing with concealment of other stations, the Court said: "The very fact that temporizing and compromising with deception seemed not to discourage it, may have led the Commission to the drastic measures here taken to preserve the integrity of its own system of reports."

The Commission of this period seldom winked at surrender of control over programming (except the broadcasters' wholesale surrender to the advertisers), which was the cornerstone of the Chain Broadcasting Regulations then being drafted. WMGQ (Brooklyn) was denied a renewal because the owners had sold time in great blocks to "brokers," who filled it with foreign-language broadcasts of dubious value. Nor were even educational institutions exempt. The Alabama Polytechnic

Institute was frustrated in a scheme to get a license renewal on behalf of a third party to which it long since had leased the time, the Commission pointing out that if it tolerated any such precedent, the end of it might be permanent control of facilities by existing licensees who could not be held accountable for the way in which they were used.

Porter tackled the problem with no less resolution. There was a bad situation in New Jersey, where three stations were sharing one frequency. WCAM, operated by the city of Camden, had transferred 85 per cent of its time to a company which was under no obligation to render a public service, yet which could subject the licensee to court action. WTNJ (Trenton) had misrepresented its financial responsibility and had caused anonymous "poison" letters to be written to the F.C.C. about WTTM (Trenton), a competitor. WCAP (Asbury Park) had ignored a number of Commission rules and regulations but was seeking to mend its ways. WCAP was given a scolding—and the channel.

The town of Seabring, Florida, was less fortunate. Its application for a new station had been well received at the Commission until someone spotted a story in the local paper quoting an official of a new municipal administration as saying that the town had no money to operate a station and hinting that his predecessor had hoped to get a license for the purpose of "hocking" it. At the F.C.C.'s suggestion, the application was withdrawn.

THE BLUE BOOK

Paul A. Porter, who succeeded Fly as chairman at the end of 1944, was disturbed about something more fundamental. In March, 1945, in his maiden speech to the broadcasters, the Kentuckian delivered his challenge:

"The facts are these. An applicant seeks a construction permit for a new station and in his application makes the usual representations as to the type of service he proposes. These representations include specific pledges that time will be made available for civic, educational, agricultural, and other public service programs. The station is constructed and begins operations. Subsequently the licensee asks for a three-year renewal and the record clearly shows that he has not fulfilled the promises. The Commission in the past has, for a variety of reasons, including the limitations of staff, automatically renewed these licenses, even in cases where there was a vast disparity between promises and performance. We have under consideration at the present time, however, a procedure whereby promises will be compared with performance. I think the industry is entitled to know of our concern in this matter and should be informed that there are pending before the Commission staff proposals which are designed to strengthen renewal procedures and give the Commission a more definite picture of the station's overall operation when licenses come up for renewal."

In April the Commission placed twenty-two of forty renewal applicants on temporary license, pending their replies to a form letter calling attention to "discrepancies" between the figures for the ratio of commercial and sustaining programs given in their previous applications and the actual program logs. The letter also wanted to know something about the ratio between network and local programming and between live talent and other.

When, on February 18, 1946, the F.C.C. designated Hearst's WBAL (Baltimore) for a hearing, accusing it of having used its 1941 power increase and new channel assignment, not to reach outlying farmers as it had promised, but to sell more than 80 per cent of its time to sponsors interested in the Baltimore market, the industry began to think the Commission was not altogether fooling. By the following month, the

F.C.C. had put 300 stations on the anxious seat, and whispers of a "drastic" new set of rules and regulations went the rounds. On March 7, the "Blue Book" appeared.

Titled *Public Service Responsibility of Broadcast Licensees*, the Commission's 149-page report turned out to be a well-documented review of the whole history of broadcasting in the United States, a stinging indictment of certain broadcasters and trends, a confession of government's past sins of commission and omission, a rebuke to the listening public for its indifference, and a plain warning. As the most significant milestone in the entire history of radio regulation, it is worth studying in some detail.

Horrible examples.—KIEV (Glendale, California): For the week beginning April 23, 1944, KIEV offered 88 per cent transcribed music, only 3.7 per cent of that live talent whose presence in great abundance in Glendale had been the chief argument in the original application. WSNY (Schenectady, New York): For the week beginning January 18, 1945, 78 per cent transcriptions as compared with the 20 per cent maximum promised during heated competition with another applicant for an original station grant. WTOL (Toledo) got permission to expand from daytime to full time, on the ground that local organizations needed to be heard. In the week of November 13, 1944, it was devoting 13.7 per cent instead of the promised 84 after 6:00 P.M. to local live broadcasts. WBAL (Baltimore), which had won a clear channel on a good record, then passed to Hearst ownership in 1934, thereafter faithfully promising the usual things and delivering, in the week of April 23, 1944, less than 2.5 per cent local live sustaining from 8:00 A.M. to 11:00 P.M.; 50 minutes of music, no discussion programs, only five of fourteen N.B.C. sustainers. KHMO (Hannibal, Missouri): In 1936, this station and a rival applicant were turned down on the ground that Hannibal did not need a local station. District Court reversed

F.C.C. Week of April 22, 1945, 12.2 per cent live talent, 85.8 network and transcriptions, $4\frac{3}{4}$ hours to needful civic groups, none of it free.

Precedent.—The report cited instances from the long list of specific legislative, judicial, and regulatory sanctions and indorsements of the practice of weighing program performance in connection with renewals and revocations; the Congress and the courts not only permitted this, they held the Commission accountable for it as a duty to the public in whose interest the Commission had been created. The report then undertook to spell out just what the regulators meant to use as a yardstick in measuring both promise and performance.

Sustaining programs.—These were absolutely indispensable, because they performed a "balance-wheel function." The sponsors and their advertising agencies had done a good deal for radio; yet the sponsors and their advertising agencies had shown a marked preference for straight news and entertainment only. Their preoccupation with these two types of program, justified (as they apparently supposed) by Hooper and Crossley ratings which they equated with "public approval," had led them to extremes. For example, in January, 1940, out of $59\frac{1}{2}$ daytime hours of sponsored programs provided weekly by the four networks, 55 were devoted to "soap operas."

And then there were the types of programs in which sponsors were little interested because they themselves agreed that they did not lend themselves to sponsorship. The discussion of controversial public issues, for example, which the N.A.B. repeatedly had said should be sustaining. The F.C.C. had recently held that "an absolute ban on the sale of time for discussion of public issues may under certain circumstances not serve the public interest," but it still agreed with the broadcasters that "such broadcasts should be primarily of a sustaining nature." As to a more precise cataloguing of types,

185

the Commission has never set forth, and does not now propose to set forth, the particular types of program which, for one reason or another, must remain free from commercial sponsorship. Self-regulation consonant with public sentiment, and a responsible concern for the public interest, can best insure a suitable interpretation of the basic principle which the industry itself has always recognized: that some programs are by their nature unsuitable for commercial sponsorship. . . . .

And there were the minorities, who certainly would be neglected by sponsors and advertising agencies. What sustaining programs could do for minority tastes had been well put by Frank Stanton, president of C.B.S.:

There is another feature of sustaining service which differentiates it from commercial programs. It is known that the New York Philharmonic Symphony Orchestra, the Columbia Workshop, Invitation to Learning, Columbia Broadcasting Symphony and many other ambitious classical programs never reach the largest audience, but Columbia nonetheless puts them on year after year for minorities which are growing steadily. . . . .

A long-recognized component of "balanced program structure" was service to nonprofit organizations. Here the report took occasion to remind the broadcasters that in 1934 there had been considerable sentiment in Congress for setting aside a specified number of channels for the use of nonprofit groups and that the Commission had saved the broadcasters' bacon by reporting that "it would appear that the interests of the non-profit organizations may be better served by the use of the existing facilities." This had placed a responsibility on the broadcasters but not on the sponsors and their advertising agencies, who were not legally beholden to anyone. So the responsibility manifestly would have to be discharged on a sustaining basis.

Finally, there was the matter of experimentation, vital to any new art form. Here, again, the report quoted Stanton:

"It is through the sustaining or noncommercial service that Columbia has developed its greatest contributions to network broadcasting."

The industry had done some experimenting with "packaged" programs produced by the broadcasters themselves and sold to sponsors on a take-it-or-leave-it basis. The effort on the part of the broadcasters to get back some of the control over content that they had frittered away was encouraging. But this device was no substitute for sustaining programming. In New York and perhaps one or two other large cities, listeners could get a degree of balance from a number of specialized stations. FM might expand that kind of balance. The Commission was going to give applicants an opportunity to state whether they "propose a balanced program structure or special emphasis on program service of a particular type or types." But none of these things would take care of the majority of broadcasting communities or of those millions still dependent on secondary service and network service.

What were the facts about performance? Well, it was hard to get at precise figures from station logs, since so many were prepared on the theory that no one would ever look at them. And then the very word "sustaining" seemed to mean all things to all men. Some called participating programs sustaining. "Bonus" stations carrying network programs without direct remuneration from the networks classified all such programs as sustaining. But of 703 stations examined, the Commission could say that the average of sustaining time had been 46.1 per cent. The rub was that (1) the bigger the station, the lower the figure (some of those cited ran as low as 15 per cent), and (2) nearly everybody squeezed them into the worst listening hours (the 6:00–11:00 P.M. average for the 703 stations was only 37.6 per cent; that of some of the stations cited, including rather conspicuously those originating network programs which provided the only fare for 25,000,000 listeners, ran from zero to 5 per cent).

Local live programs.—Regulation 3.104 of the Chain Broadcasting Regulations had failed to achieve the purpose of fostering the development of local programs. An analysis showed that some stations used no non-network programs at all during the evening hours.

How were the broadcasters, whose application forms bristled with glowing words for the local minister or woman's club, the local merchant with honest goods to sell, the budding high-school violinist, doing with local live talent? Here, again, it was hard to arrive at figures. Some broadcasters called phonograph records "live" if a live announcer put in a word for Krausmeier's Delicatessen between records. Everyone classed the reading-off of press association bulletins as "live." But the average for the 703 stations was 15.5 per cent, 4.9 of it sustaining. The figure was lower for the best listening hours, lower still for big stations, on some of which it reached the vanishing-point.

It had been suggested that this situation might be corrected by licensing some stations for non-network broadcasting exclusively. Why penalize every community that had fewer than four stations (the maximum that could affiliate with national chains) by depriving them of good network programs? No, the solution "must be found in terms of a balance of network and non-network programs."

Some broadcasters thought the easiest way to make money was to "plug into the network line in the morning and broadcast network programs throughout the day, interrupting the network output only to insert commercial spot announcements," or to "substitute spot announcements and phonograph records for outstanding network sustaining programs." The average local station employed less than one-third of a full-time musician, less than one-sixth of a full-time actor.

Such figures suggest, particularly at the local station level, that few stations are staffed adequately to meet their responsibilities in serving the community. A positive responsibility rests upon local stations to make articulate the voice of the community. Unless time is earmarked for such a purpose, unless talent is positively sought and given at least some degree of expert assistance, radio stations have abdicated their local responsibilities and have become mere common carriers.

Discussion of public issues.—Here were some of the problems this raised: (1) Shall time for the presentation of one point of view on a public issue be sold? (2) If not, what measures can be taken to insure adequate distribution? (3) If it is to be sold, what precautions should be taken to see that it does not gravitate to those with the most money? (4) Are forums superior to individual presentations at different times? (5) Should such programs be sponsored? (6) How can they be made fair and well-balanced? (7) Should local forums be encouraged, and, if so, how? (8) How insure unbiased presentation of news? (9) Should news be sponsored? (10) How and by whom should commentators be chosen? (11) Should they be forbidden, permitted, or encouraged to express their personal opinions? (12) Is a denial of free speech involved when a commentator is dropped because he has offended (*a*) the sponsor, (*b*) the station, (*c*) a listener minority, or (*d*) a listener majority? (13) What new provisions are necessary or desirable in connection with the operation of the broadcast stations during political campaigns? (14) Does a station operate in the public interest when it charges a higher rate for political broadcasts than for commercial programs? (15) Should a station's right to censor scripts be limited to protection against libel? (16) Should broadcasters be relieved of the responsibility for libel with respect to broadcasts over which they have no control? (17) Should the right to reply be afforded? To whom? How? (18) Should a station be required to submit in writing and file its reasons for refusing time on the air for discussion of controversial issues? (19) What measures can be taken to open broadcasting to types of informational programs which contravene the interests of large advertisers?

The Commission has never laid down, and does not now propose to lay down, any categorical answers to such questions. One matter of primary concern, however, can be met by an over-all statement of policy . . . . the public interest clearly requires that an adequate amount of time be made available for the discussion of public issues; and the Commission, in determining whether a station has served the public interest, will take into consideration the amount of time which has been or will be devoted to the discussion of public issues.

Had it not been enough? At the request of the Senate Interstate Commerce Committee, the Commission had undertaken a study of all programs broadcast from January 1, 1941, through May 31, 1941, relating to the five major questions of foreign policy before the country: Lend-Lease, the convoying of ships to Britain, the acquisition of foreign bases, the acquisition of foreign ships, and maintenance of the British blockade. The four networks had submitted 203 relevant scripts, an average of 1.1 a day. But fewer than half their affiliates carried any of them. And non-network-originated discussions of these issues were in the ratio of 1 to 30. In short, fully 50,000,000 Americans had no opportunity to hear these vital issues discussed on the air during crucial months of decision.

Advertising excesses.—Advertising was essential. It supported American radio. It contributed thereby to the dissemination of useful consumer knowledge and to raising the standard of living. The sponsors had a right to get something for the nearly $400,000,000 they spent annually. Nevertheless, "throughout the history of broadcasting, a limitation on the amount and character of advertising has been one element of 'public interest.' "

What about performance? To begin with, the N.A.B., which in 1929 banned advertising between 7:00 and 11:00 P.M., now permitted up to 4 minutes in less than 2 of those 4 hours. But the six Washington stations, presumed to be superior to stations generally, were thumbing their noses at even these restrictions.

There were other problems. One was the length of commercials. F.C.C. had spotted one that ran 5 minutes. Another was the number, with an exhibit of 16.7 per hour. "Hitchhikers" and "cow-catchers"[7] piled them on, five in a row; and middle commercials; and the phony patriotic tieup, as when B.C. headache powder advised everyone during the war that they could not do their bit without this "remedy"; and bad taste, of the B.O. variety; and propaganda, usually against government ownership or government regulation or government antitrust suits and the like; and intermingling of program material and advertising.

The report then gave comparative earnings tables to indicate that broadcasters can well afford to live up to their promises, including the more detailed ones which the F.C.C. now expected them to make. From 1937 to 1944 gross revenues had risen from $131,205,866 to $316,601,826. More significant, the part of the income dollar which the broadcaster was able to put in his pocket, despite the rising income and corporate tax schedule, had risen from 17 cents in 1938 to 33 cents in 1944.[8]

Coming to Part V: "Summary and Conclusions: Proposals

[7] A few seconds of time frequently are deducted from the commercial periods on a program sponsored by a specific product to "plug" another product manufactured by the same company; if this "free ride" comes at the very beginning, it is called a "cow-catcher," if at the very end, a "hitchhiker."

[8] Before federal income taxes. Net incomes after taxes by no means doubled in five years. The phrase "able to put in his pocket" is, therefore, misleading.

for Future Commission Policy," the report noted that "affirmative improvement of program service must be the result primarily of other (than government) forces." It listed greater self-regulation by the industry as a whole "through its trade associations." It stressed the responsibility of the individual licensee. But its greatest emphasis was on "forces outside the broadcasting industry": professional critics writing in other media, especially the newspapers.

Nevertheless, "the Commission has a statutory responsibility for the public interest." Therefore, "in issuing and in renewing the licenses of broadcast stations, the Commission proposes to give particular consideration to four program service factors relevant to the public interest. These are: (1) the carrying of sustaining programs, including network sustaining programs, with particular reference to the retention by licensees of a proper discretion and responsibility for maintaining a well-balanced program structure; (2) the carrying of local live programs; (3) the carrying of programs devoted to the discussion of public issues; and (4) the elimination of advertising excesses." And in measuring over-all program structure, the Commission would have in mind "balance during the best listening hours."

In the extreme language typical of that paper's comments on the F.C.C., *Broadcasting* announced that democracy was through, the way prepared for a Hitler: "There is at stake the pattern of American life, and you can find that truth in the charred ruins of a chancellory [*sic*] in Berlin."

Poking about in the ashes of Western civilization, *Variety* found quite a different clue:

The first fact radio must face is that broadcasting is made possible only by the use of a public commodity. In the past the industry has only paid lip service to the responsibility inherent in its use of this commodity. To accuse a Commission set up by the government

of assuming undue powers is to completely overlook this basic difference between radio and other private enterprise. . . . . Obviously
the industry has brought upon itself the FCC proposals by its
abuses. . . . . And it's obvious, too, that in the regulations the FCC
now suggests there will be no excessive governmental interference.
. . . . The Constitution requires a broader reading today than it
did a century and a half ago. . . . . The FCC recommendations as
such could well stand as a primer for the operation of a good radio
station.

The Blue Book is celebrating its first anniversary as these
lines are written. What is the net of the Commission's most
courageous move in two decades?

To begin with, no broadcaster has been thrown off the airways for practices cited in the Blue Book as being, in the Commission's view, contrary to "public interest, convenience, or
necessity." This does not mean that the broadcasters successfully ignored the warning. On the contrary, it means that
they altered the practices complained of to a point where the
Commission felt justified in setting down only six stations for
hearings, and in granting the renewals of the first three to be
heard.

It is obvious, therefore, that the broadcasters' concerted
wails that they have been ruined by an unwarranted invasion
of a sacred right vouchsafed to them by the First Amendment
have been, to say the least, somewhat premature. It is equally
obvious that, if it is true that the Commission never really intended to bring the matter to the issue of nonrenewal but
meant only to "throw a good scare into the boys," as one of
the authors of the Blue Book put it, the maneuver was at
least superficially successful.

Not quite so obvious, to the author, are certain other deductions that have been drawn from the Blue Book experience. For example, that the over-all impact of all the radio
programs throughout the country for the past year has been

brought more in line with the five requirements for a free and responsible press outlined by the Commission on Freedom of the Press—or even with the F.C.C.'s expressed ideal. And that compliance indicates that the broadcasters know, deep down in their hearts, that the Blue Book frame of operation is both reasonable and constitutional. And that wherever there is a question as to the theoretical or potential unconstitutionality of a governmental regulation, mere nonenforcement automatically disposes of it. The author proposes to examine these in detail.

1. One of the troubles with labeling "types" of radio programs and reducing the phrase "balanced fare" to even approximate percentages is that the label is likely to look much more impressive in a logbook than the program sounds on the home receiver. Thus it would be possible for a station set down for hearing on charges that it had neglected its considerable rural audience to improve the generous interval of time between citation and hearing by loading up on programs with the word "farm" in their titles; and for a station scolded for too little local programming hastily to summon the high-school band, glee club, and home economics class; and for a station cited for too little controversy to throw half a dozen "forums" into the breach. But it would not be possible to know whether these programs seemed, on the whole, useful without listening to them for a month or so or to know what the audiences thought of them without canvassing those audiences pretty carefully—both tasks for which the Commission has not the time or the men or the money.

The author sincerely believes that he detects a lowering of the program level and a worsening of advertising offenses on the fifteen New York City and New Jersey stations to which he listens almost daily, as compared with a year ago. None of them was cited by call-letters in or by reason of the Blue

Book (although obviously some of the generalized criticisms were meant to apply to them as the shoe fit). Some of the fifteen seem better than the others. The worst occasionally present amazingly satisfying programs, and the best all too frequently present incredibly offensive ones. Two years of diligent listening and script-reading have about convinced the author that the range of excellence in broadcasting lies in a "band" far beyond the reach of the F.C.C. and the Congress, where men do things no one can compel them to do—possibly because they have "social consciences" but more likely because it satisfies their egos or because they feed upon the approbation of those who share their little social islands, or simply because they are artists and, therefore, perfectionists.

This view accords with one deduced from thirty years of working for and observing newspaper and magazine publishers, who are subject to virtually no federal regulation and consequently do pretty much as they please. The broadcasters are very proud of the polls showing that on matters of opinion regarding public affairs the average American feels radio is "more reliable" than newspapers. The same polls show that persons in the higher education brackets do not share this view. It may be that those citizens who want plenty of the red meat of enlightened controversy, and do not mind the relative exertion of chewing on it prefer to get it from men "regulated" only by their own consciences, the pressures of their business and social acquaintances, and the inexorable law of supply and demand.

Perhaps what is wanted is not more answers, but better ones. Blue Books not only cannot produce them; they are likely, by imposing simple "rules" which are easy enough to get around, to retard further that political maturity which the broadcasters have not achieved in a quarter-century of being treated like naughty children.

2. As to the assumption that the broadcasters' apparent compliance in this last of a series of F.C.C. "consent decrees" indicates that they know they have nothing to worry about in the way of governmental encroachment, the author would say that, to the extent that this is so, it is a state of affairs which ought to alarm the rest of us very much. As has been noted in connection with the broadcasters' resignation to the "Mayflower muzzle," only a handful of broadcasters have any background in the tradition of, or deep feeling for, the First Amendment they invoke so freely (as Al Capone once invoked "that Abe's corpse [habeas corpus] thing, it sure is a handy gadget!"). Far more significant than the monotonous chant of *Broadcasting* editorials, it seems to the author, is the growing concern for a free radio as an integral link in a free press manifested by such nonradio champions of the John Peter Zenger tradition as Byron Price of the United Nations secretariat, Ben Hibbs of the *Saturday Evening Post,* and the vast majority of working newspapermen right down through the nonowning, nonmanaging, presumably "exploited" legmen of a thousand city staffs. With the best of reasons for being keenly aware of the shortcomings of the press under virtual laissez faire, its practitioners seem to have weighed the advantages and disadvantages and come to the conclusion that the old way is still the best way. The bewildered silence of the broadcasters may mean nothing more than that the present crop is not competent to speak for an industry which may yet produce a tougher, freer breed.

3. The author, being no part of a lawyer, does not know whether there is anything unconstitutional lurking about the Blue Book or not.[9] He would like to see the Supreme Court

[9] Professor Zechariah Chafee, Jr., in the Commission's special report, *Government and Mass Communications,* takes the view that the Blue Book does not involve the First Amendment. The Commission as a whole, in its

rule on that point at the earliest possible moment. What he does know is that the things the broadcasters do not like about the Blue Book go back much farther than March 7, 1946. In fact, they did not originate with the Commission at all, but with the Congress. In the Radio Act of 1927 (and again in the Communications Act of 1934), the Congress expressly charged the regulatory body to ". . . . prescribe the nature of the services to be rendered . . . . establish the areas to be served by each station . . . . require records of programs . . . . prescribe as to . . . . the purpose for which the station was to be used. . . . ." Then, having dropped the license-based-on-content hot potato (the very issue over which John Peter Zenger risked poverty, prison, and death) in the Commission's lap, the legislators promptly forgot the matter, except for an occasional reminder from individual congressmen looking after the interests of individual broadcasters that the Commission was under no circumstances to "censor" programs.

What was the Commission to do? From the broadcasters' viewpoint, if license-based-on-content is an issue worth fighting for now, it was an issue worth fighting for in 1927. But broadcasting was a struggling infant industry in 1927, and broadcasters were not (and still are not) celebrated for Zenger's kind of all-out devotion to principle. So the broadcasters did not converge on the Capitol. Instead, they worked out with the regulatory body (which did not want to have to look at programs) a sort of little game. According to the rules of this game, broadcasters went through the motions of mak-

---

signed summary statement preceding the present report, and in its general report, *A Free and Responsible Press*, shares this view. The author's position is simply that he does not know whether the Supreme Court of the United States shares it, because the Supreme Court has never formally expressed itself on the subject.

ing promises as to the types of program service they intended offering during the license period—promises which they subsequently ignored and which the regulatory body was also happy to ignore. This farce went on uninterruptedly for eighteen years or so. It went on until coincidence brought into collision the irresistible force and the immovable object. The irresistible force consisted of the vast majority of broadcasters, who, flushed with swollen war profits, threw caution to the winds. The immovable object was a Commission with appreciably more intestinal fortitude than some of its predecessors. Badgered by indignant citizens of mark (and by suddenly interested, self-righteous congressmen), the commissioners told each other, in substance: "All right. The law is there, just the way they wrote it. If they want it enforced now, we'll enforce it." The broadcasters pretended the whole thing was a great surprise. Majority rule changed hands in Washington, and a few congressmen raised the quadrennial tally-ho for an "investigation" of this "Socialist" agency that was daring to carry out the Congress' instructions. The F.C.C. began quietly to give passing marks to the bad boys it had kept after school. By the fall of 1946, the whole matter was right back where it had been.

But not quite where it was. For the Blue Book is still "on the books." If it stays there, it may fall into the hands of commissioners less respectful of our basic freedoms than the present six. Meanwhile, mere nonenforcement in no way disposes of the constitutionality question. And if the court should say that the Blue Book was constitutional, the author would still say that both it and the act of Congress that produced it are, in so far as they touch upon content as a criterion in licensing, unwise, inequitable, and unworkable. Despite certain evidences of arrested mental development, the broadcasting industry is twenty years older than it was when the

Radio Act was passed. A good many broadcasters show the marks of two decades of maturing. Possibly they would all mature more rapidly if they stood on their own feet (which means freedom from the advertising fraternity, as well as from government). The six hundred stations of 1927 have grown to nearly fifteen hundred (as compared with seventeen hundred daily newspapers) and within a few years may reach three thousand. Finally, the F.C.C. is on the point of being pushed, most unwillingly, into the newspaper and motion picture fields (ultimately, one must assume, the magazine and book fields also) through the development of the facsimile press and television. Possibly it is time the Congress had another look at the problem. Among other things, the author would like to have someone explain to him why, if as some say the "trend" is toward license-based-on-content, radio should be singled out for the experiment. Beyond a minimal concern for obscenity and profanity (the bans on which presumably would be retained in any new radio legislation), the Post Office Department does not concern itself with the contents of the books, magazines, and newspapers which the taxpayers help to deliver. Why should the broadcasters' reliance on a publicly owned circulation medium place them in a different category?

Notwithstanding these two reservations—the Mayflower Decision and the Blue Book—the author could not conclude this study of nearly twenty years of federal regulation of radio broadcasting without expressing a feeling of deep respect for the honest job that the F.C.C. has done. It is clear that it would not be possible to grasp the immensity of that task without a careful study of the step-by-step moves. The net of it is worth recapitulating.

The F.R.C. stepped into a situation which seemed so hopeless that many broadcasters were prophesying that radio could not last out the twenties. Even after it had begun to dig out of the mess, industry engineers solemnly predicted that the ether could never be made to support more than 700 stations. In the twelve months between October, 1945, and October, 1946, the Commission authorized 448 new standard stations (only 3 short of the F.C.C.'s previous eleven-year total) to bring the number to 1,335 operating or holding construction permits; more than 500 FM stations to add to the three-score operating in October, 1945; and more than 30 television stations to bring the total having temporary and permanent grants to 36, for a grand total of well over 2,000. Americans had better coverage than any people on earth. Except perhaps in television, they were further along in every technical phase of electronic development. It is quite a record for twenty years. And a large share of the credit for it must go to the Commission. What makes the achievement all the more remarkable is that nearly everyone concerned made the job about as difficult as a job can be made.

THE LOT OF A BUREAUCRAT

The author has referred from time to time to the heavy work-load of the Commission and its continual harassments from the Congress. The subject is worth a special section.

The F.R.C. had found the job cut out for it quite literally killing. One hearing alone required 170,000 affidavits. One out of ten decisions had to be fought through the courts. Congress had allowed the Commission a staff of twenty, including engineers and officeworkers. Two of the five Commissioners were not confirmed for nearly a year, one resigning in disgust after seven months' backbreaking work without pay. Of the remaining three, two were to die with their bureaucratic boots on.

We have seen how the extension of the Commission's jurisdiction to all forms of interstate and international telecommunication added to its burden without adding proportionately to its manpower and funds. The war accentuated this trend. A year before the formal entry of the United States, the President had created the Board of Defense Communications (later the Board of War Communications); had made Fly its chairman; and had assigned the F.C.C. staff to serve as its secretariat. The chairman thus became the central figure during the war in the inevitable struggles between the several branches of the armed forces and a score of private telecommunications users for priorities and sharing in use of facilities and frequencies. Also, before America's entry into the war, the F.C.C. was assigned new and extensive radio monitoring and policing operations dealing with foreign radio broadcasts and code messages within the United States. During the war, these two new units, the Foreign Broadcast Intelligence Service and Radio Intelligence Division, accounted for more than half the total personnel and budget of F.C.C.

Late in 1941 the Commission was obliged to step into the short-wave picture when the seven private licensees[10] were asked to turn their transmitters over to the Coordinator of Information (later the Overseas Branch of the Office of War Information) and the Coordinator of Inter-American Affairs. The subsequent stepping-up by these government agencies of broadcast time twenty fold and of languages employed fourfold involved the construction of four times as many powerful transmitters as the private licensees had operated, the use of relay stations abroad, and new and fluid agreements with foreign powers relating to the sharing of frequencies, including those appropriated from the Axis powers.

Nor was short-wave broadcasting the only form of tele-

[10] N.B.C., C.B.S., G.E., Westinghouse, Crosley, World Wide, and Associated.

communications involved in the kaleidoscope of daily, sometimes hourly, internal and international negotiation. The regulatory power over the domestic telephone and telegraph business, which had received little attention before 1934, when it was located in the Interstate Commerce Commission, had been transferred to the new F.C.C., and the Commission was in the midst of telephone rate studies and the delicate negotiation of a merger of the two domestic telegraph companies when war came. These had to be carried through.

There were corridor rumors that the industry had sworn to "get" Fly and, if possible, the whole Commission, with its "wartime access of authority and confidence." The opportunity seemed to come in an action by the Commission in reporting by unanimous action to the Department of Justice its finding that Representative Eugene Cox had accepted a fee from a Georgia radio station in return for services on its behalf before the F.C.C. (a practice prohibited by federal statute). Cox instituted a year and a half of investigation of F.C.C. by a House Select Committee, of which he himself was chairman until his resignation was forced by newspaper criticism. The license and personnel files and the minutes of Commission meetings were ransacked by the House Committee staff. It was estimated by the F.C.C. general counsel that, in addition to the war load of extra duties, 40–50 per cent of the time of the top administrative and legal staff of the Commission for the eighteen-month period was occupied with the purely defensive task of furnishing materials, evidence, and testimony before the House inquisitors.

There was no way to beat the budget game: if the Commission pared every item to the bone, Congress lopped off a certain percentage as a matter of policy; if the Commission sought to circumvent this by fattening its figures, the Bureau of the Budget cracked down. Thus, instead of the $6,060,000 sought for fiscal 1947, part of it for the hiring of 368 additional persons to speed the processing of a backlog of 1,400 applications, the House scolded the F.C.C. for having a backlog— and pared the figure to $5,560,000.

Loud warnings of doom sounded by lesser Republicans on the morrow of the congressional landslide of November, 1946, were gleefully welcomed by lesser broadcasters. Men who had hounded the F.C.C. for its slowness in handling applications chortled over the prospect that its budget would be slashed indiscriminately. Men who on occasion had praised the Commissioners for standing up to their old congressional masters rubbed their hands in anticipation of their having to grovel before new.[11]

The Commission has weathered such capricious storms before. It must continue to stand up to publicity-seeking, smear-loving, constituent-pandering congressmen. It must continue to resist industry pressures. It must continue to press for adequate funds and staff and for executive care in appointments to its vacancies. If it does these things and suffers reprisals for honest independence, the blame ultimately will fall on a vindictive Congress and an industry that has failed to recognize where its best interests lie.

[11] A classic example of industry inconsistency was the November, 1946, issue of *Broadcasting*, which devoted a page to praising the F.C.C. for having stoutly resisted the efforts of the two Tennessee senators to interfere improperly with its functions, and half a dozen pages to sadistic schoolboy speculation over a hoped-for inquisition by the new Republican majorities.

8

CONCLUSIONS AND PROPOSALS

W HAT remains to be done to make American radio not merely the best in the world but the best it would be possible to achieve? A good deal. Let us examine some of the areas where improvement is indicated. Even in the field of physical distribution and operation, where we are furthest along, there is work to be done.

1. To begin with, although the "blank" sections of the country which do not even get reliable secondary service have been steadily shrinking, we still have a few.

The amount of land area virtually without radio has declined from about 30 per cent in the late 1920's to less than 5; in terms of population from about 10 to less than 2 per cent. But the goal must continue to be 100 per cent.

2. Too many of those who do get reliable secondary service do not have a reasonable choice among stations supplying that sort of service.

No accurate figures appear to be available, but it is known that the percentage figures for those land areas and listeners able to receive only one reliable secondary service are higher than for those which receive none, still higher for those whose choice is limited to two. Here, also, the picture has been slowly improving. But here, also, the goal remains 100 per cent, which might be said to be a choice for everyone among at least four services.

As we have seen, the achievement of these maximum goals

204

has been hampered by two factors: the concentration of powerful clear-channel stations on the seacoasts and the advertising man's lack of interest in the "backward" Great Plains, mountain, and southern areas.

The Federal Communications Commission appears to be on the right track in trying to get around the first of these historic accidents by paving the way for additional clear-channel stations and by indicating to within a few hundred miles the communities in which they must be located to supplement, rather than to duplicate, the services of existing clear-channel stations.

The Commission is also studying alternative and complementary suggestions. Among these are the reported latest plan of the Clear Channel Broadcasting Service, which was said to provide for twenty 750-kilowatt stations divided equally among the national networks, each of which would broadcast four different nation-wide programs simultaneously; the Regional Broadcasters' Committee's elaborate schedule for clear-channel sharing, designed to give most of the country a constant choice among three or more program services; and the Columbia Broadcasting System's proposal for an AM-FM network involving two satellite clear-channel stations in the heart of the hitherto neglected area.

Federal's Pulse-Time principle, Du Mont's photovision beam, Raytheon's microwave experiments, Westinghouse's stratocasting, and Bell Laboratory's wave-guide tube may help to solve both the problem of wider coverage and the problem of wider choice.

3. There are still far too many American communities which, for want of stations of their own, cannot use the medium to ventilate strictly local public issues, develop local talent, or accommodate local merchants.

Possibly the first of these three lacks has more social significance than the other two. If so, it can make the point alone. There are 5,575 communities of 1,000 or more population in this country that have no local radio station. One need not, perhaps, be too concerned for towns of 1,000, or even 10,000, for in small communities local public issues can be, and usually are, ventilated in the newspaper, at business and woman's club, church, lodge, and parent-teacher association meetings, or on the street. But 137 of these 5,575 stationless communities have populations ranging from 20,000 to 300,000. Obviously, in cities of such size the "town-meeting" approach to public issues is out of the question.

It has been said that FM will solve this problem (and numberless others) "automatically." In radio nothing is "automatic." If some of the apparatus used in FM broadcasting is less expensive than that used in AM broadcasting, such items as mechanical upkeep, electric power, heat, rent, staff salaries, talent fees, and line charges are not. FM will do —is doing—a great deal for the larger stationless communities. But, as long as the initiative and most, if not all, the capital to launch a station must come from the community itself, most of those that have done without AM will do without FM—and for precisely the same reasons.

As regards the critical needs of the 137 communities of 20,000 and more population without stations, there is another problem. The bulk of them are, like New Britain, Connecticut (70,000), Meriden, Connecticut (40,000), and Kenosha, Wisconsin (50,000), some distance removed from existing stations. Roughly a third, however, are incorporated suburbs, like Cambridge, Massachusetts (200,000), Evanston, Illinois (65,000), and Jersey City, New Jersey (300,000). Under the F.C.C. FM-allocation practice, these last are treated merely as portions of "metropolitan areas" in which existing stations sometimes get first call, presumably on the assumption that they render adequate "localized" services to all their suburbs because they invariably promise to. Civic leaders of Cambridge, Massachusetts, smarting from the experience of their last municipal elections, which did not seem important to any of the Boston stations, can testify that performance does not always come up to promise.

Finally, the AM broadcasters are still temporizing on FM, pointing to the lack of receiving sets and ready-made audiences. Quite content with the status quo, they boast of what they can do with "a powerful direct signal." A powerful direct signal is no answer to this question. Neither is a cluster of satellite stations merely amplifying the signals of faraway mother-stations; for, while some of what originates in New York or Hollywood is conceivably of reasonably equal interest to all the country, it seems apparent that certain geographical areas and certain segments of the population want things and need things over and above this common fare. As regards communities which cannot support their own stations, this is a matter for the attention of the big stations and networks.

The newspaper press associations recognize this diversity of need and taste. That is why they have "regional" stories and "specials." That is why they offer daily to, say, the *Emporia* (Kansas) *Gazette* stories they do not offer to the *New York Times*, and why they offer to the *Times* stories that they do not offer to the *Gazette*. That is why a third of their Washington and state-capital staffs are employed full time in running down stories which are never seen by the bulk of their clients.

Any one or any combination of the several plans involving simultaneous multiple programming outlined above might help to solve this problem. Synchronized logging and greater use of transcriptions, so that Fred Allen, for example, could be heard at 8:30 P.M., Sunday, by Los Angeles, Denver, and Chicago local time, as well as by New York local time, would help. It does not seem likely, however, that the broadcasters will do much about this problem until they muster the courage to insist on selling between-program spots instead of whole-program periods.

If the F.C.C. paves the way for some new clear-channel stations, it might consider laying down stipulations other than just where they must be located. The Commission might, for example, say that anyone applying for one of them would have to be prepared to devote reasonable proportions of his time to each of the various geographical areas and each of the important listener groups within range of his signal. Doubtless it will be said that this suggestion brings the F.C.C. into the zone of "program control." Of course, this is nonsense. One might as well say (as, to be sure, Colonel McCormick of the *Chicago Tribune* did) that, when a city council or a court compels a newsstand proprietor to display all the newspapers available in a community, it is violating the First Amendment.

Under the free-enterprise system, as the author understands it, a broadcaster has a perfect right to say: "The hell with the farmers, small-town people, suburbanites, and long-haired music and drama lovers," and no right whatever to say it if he is using something that belongs to the farmers, small-town people, suburbanites and "long-hairs" to prevent a more public spirited broadcaster from serving them.

On the other hand, it seems clear that, if the F.C.C. were going to ask the big broadcasters to provide more extensive (and expensive) service, it might wish to be in a position to offer certain inducements. It might, without disturbing the one-station-to-an-owner-in-any-area rule, wish to relax the "gentlemen's agreement" limiting over-all ownership. It might even wish to avoid an inflexible one-to-an-area AM-FM rule where circumstances would seem to argue for common ownership of an FM station (to serve the urban center) and an AM station (to serve outlying areas with wholly or largely nonduplicative programs), utilizing the one transmitter site, studio building, staff, etc. Finally, the Commission might consider not only permitting but actively encouraging the adoption of country-wide time and the wider employment of transcribed programs which this would, in any case, make necessary.

Educational institutions, state and municipal governments, foundations, eleemosynary groups, and wealthy citizens of public spirit generally could, of course, do something about creating stations where none exist. The time may well have come for all these to ask themselves whether projects in which they are investing far larger sums than would be required to launch an FM station are any more significant and far-reaching.

On a more humble scale, there is much, perhaps, that plain citizens in stationless communities might do. For example, a canvass of local merchants to obtain pledges of advertising, much in the fashion in which advertising pledges are solicited by prospective newspapers, might eventuate in an offer of profitable affiliation from at least two of the national networks. Certainly, there could be no valid objection to the citizens of a stationless community sending an emissary to the F.C.C. to say that, although no prospective broadcaster had come forward, the community was hopeful of producing one within a reasonable time and therefore felt justified in praying the Commission to earmark a frequency for it.

4. Cheaper, better, more quickly installed alternative systems for interconnecting stations in networks are moving from the laboratory at a pace which does not reflect the actual priority of need.

As regards the new FM stations, and particularly the non-commercial ones, the industry and the F.C.C. must do much more than merely dot the country with them. Radio's chief asset is that it is the only medium which can bring to all the people, simultaneously and within a matter of seconds, an important message, announcement, or news item. Except as stations are in, or on short notice can be linked into, a nation-wide network, it is a meaningless paper asset.

It has been remarked that the noncommercial and "marginal" (i.e., of no interest to national advertisers) stations at least could achieve the effect of network broadcasting by exchanging transcribed programs. Certainly, they could handle the bulk of their programs in that way. So, by the same token, could the commercial broadcasters. *Par contre*, when transcriptions would not do for commercial broadcasters, they would not do for noncommercial broadcasters either.

The author suggests:

To the F.C.C., that it:

Place the realization of the maximum goal of a choice among at least four clearly and consistently received stations for all Americans above all other factors in pressing for an early and continuing solution of the problems involved;

Stipulate that anyone desiring to operate a new clear-channel station must undertake to devote reasonable proportions of his time to each of the various geographical areas and each of the important listener groups within range of his signal;

Relax its over-all ownership rules, subject to the above conditions and any others, and refrain from imposing the one-to-an-area rule inflexibly in all AM-FM situations;

Actively foster the adoption of country-wide time and the wider use of transcriptions;

210

Earmark, wherever possible, at least one FM channel for each stationless community of 20,000 or more population for a reasonable time, regardless of whether any applicant has applied for it;

Do everything possible to realize a practical wireless relay system in 1947;

Explore all possible means of reducing artificial barriers which may prevent new groups from acquiring stations, such as inflated purchase prices and network policies which may restrict affiliation with them.

To the broadcasters, that they:

Subordinate short-term personal interest in co-operating with the F.C.C. to the fullest in realizing the maximum goal of a choice among at least four clearly and consistently received stations for all Americans;

Put the horse before the cart with FM by producing the stations and programs and by letting the sets and audiences come along in natural sequence, as they did in AM radio;

Adopt a country-wide time system;

Abandon their traditional aversion to transcribed programs in favor of a more realistic attitude;

Explore to the fullest the whole field of multiple programming, with a view to serving more adequately the constituent areas and groups within range of their signals.

To educational institutions, state and municipal governments, foundations, eleemosynary groups, and wealthy citizens seeking an outlet for a social conscience, and to plain citizens in stationless or badly served communities, that they:

Explore thoroughly their opportunities to create more (and better) AM, FM, or television stations and networks.

THE CONTENT

So much for physical distribution and operation. There are also weak spots under the general heading of program quality, balance, and adequacy.

211

1. The total national product of news, organized and processed by radiomen for radio audiences, is not adequate.

To be sure, the ether crackles with news. Having outdone itself (and now and then the press) during the war, radio at the start of 1947 was coasting along on the war's momentum. Probably as much as 80 per cent of the country was getting press-association bulletins at intervals of not less than every hour.

But 80 per cent is not enough. Nor is the mere reading-off of news bulletins enough. The average radio listener is no more able to evaluate the news which is hurled at him from every direction than is the average newspaper headline-scanner. Indeed, a diet of nothing but unrelated headlines may confuse more than it enlightens him. It may even, on the radio, give him subconscious ear-hardening, or ennui, if the newscasters do not soon stop approaching everything, from tomorrow's weather to today's political climate in Moscow, with the same impartially breathless urgency.

News requires to be integrated with other news and with history. Newspapers employ large staffs of trained, well-paid (in relation to other newsmen, at least) editors to give this treatment to press-association stories. Most big broadcasting stations also employ news staffs. But what some of these news staffs do has always been a mystery to working newspapermen. They do not appear to do much with or to the bulletins that come off the press-association teleprinters, except to boil them down a bit and read them off. True, the press associations prepare "special" files for radio clients. These are presumably peculiarly adapted to the needs of radio, and International News Service at least has made an honest effort of late to overcome the suspicion that they are nothing more than dressed-up by-products. But, just as the reports which for fifty years have been "specially" prepared for the press have not rendered the telegraph and cable desks[1] obsolete, so the "special" radio reports do not relieve the radio news departments of a further refining and processing job.

News needs to be related to the significance-evaluations of qualified experts. That is where the commentator comes in. The author estimates that about 40 per cent of the people of America got, in 1946, what was described as commentary at the rate of about 2 hours a week, half of it outside the best listening periods, 90 per cent of it supplied by "commentators" who lacked even the minimal qualifications for such work.[2]

2. Statistically "good" individual performance in the news and commentary field too often is marred by wholly unnecessary flaws and inhibitions.

Among examples may be listed the superficiality noted above, the broadcasters' reluctance to assume vigorous editorial leadership (which surely cannot be laid entirely to the Mayflower Decision); their corollary insistence on getting a sponsor to shoulder the responsibility (and the cost) of "opinionated" news (i.e., anything that departs from the text of the by no means always unopinionated press-association dispatches); and the failure, ever since the one brave gesture in

[1] Newspaper telegraph and cable desks on the better newspapers do much more than paste up press-association stories and indicate to the copy desk the styles of headlines to be put on them. These telegraph and cable editors are the people who skilfully weave the stories of one or more special correspondents and two or three press associations together, frequently adding to them office-written "supplementers" (called "shirttails" if they follow the main story under a dash, "side-bars" if they appear alongside under separate headings) to achieve the maximum of instant intelligence under the pressure of deadlines. Later, of course, and with more leisure for research, the editorial and Sunday writers will achieve even more fulness of context and perspective.

[2] Say, either a sound college education or its equivalent in experience as a highly trained writer-observer of, or practitioner in, the specialized fields of political science, economics, government, etc.

the early 1930's, to train or recruit enough good news-evaluators and to support them, against courts, congressmen, and other witch-burners, in their honest convictions.

3. The total national product of useful public discussion is inadequate.

Not more than 15 per cent of the people of America were exposed to so-called "forum" programs in 1946 at the rate of about 1 hour a week, again with half of it outside the best listening periods. In terms of tangible results, the picture is even more disheartening, for, after nearly a quarter-century of radio news, commentary, and discussion, during which time several billion words were aired under these headings and several thousand waterproof wrist watches and pencils were given to several thousand persons for answering several tens of thousands of presumably topical questions correctly, a Public Opinion Research poll revealed (in 1945) that 75 per cent of the people did not know what a price subsidy was, 70 per cent did not know how a peace treaty was approved by the United States, 60 per cent had never heard of the Atlantic Charter, and 63 per cent did not know that this country had been receiving reverse Lend-Lease to the value of hundreds of millions of dollars.

It is possible that the manner in which most of the forum programs were staged had something to do with the disappointing results. Why do the broadcasters insist on bringing to the microphone unrehearsed amateurs who usually turn out to be deadly serious bores? Good newspapers, more concerned for the reader's right to be informed than for the right of a few readers to get their names in print, do not confine their attention to antagonistic and minority views to the letters columns. In the author's view, one of radio's most serious mistakes has been the avoidance of a responsibility which the press long ago assumed: to mirror the views of conflicting groups by hiring trained men and women to canvass these groups and translate their views into terse, professional, attention-rousing language rather than by throwing their columns open to the untrained "spokesmen" of the groups themselves.

The broadcasters' failure to adopt this method leaves room for the suspicion that some of them may have hoped that the very dulness and clumsiness of the forum type of program would soon eliminate it. The technique has become alarmingly common in radio: one does the sort of thing he does not understand but feels compelled to do in order to mollify the F.C.C. (or his more literate critics); he does it as badly as possible, and the Hooper ratings are low; so he turns to his critics with a triumphant "You see, the people just don't want it." (This comment would not, of course, apply to those broadcasters who honestly felt that they were choosing the least of several possible evils when they wrote the ban on selling time for the discussion of controversial public issues into the 1929 National Association of Broadcasters Code. But even they ignored the significant question of whether the broadcasters had any moral right either to give or to sell time for the discharge of a function which they themselves ought to discharge.)

4. Statistically "good" individual performance in the discussion field too often is marred by wholly unnecessary flaws and inhibitions.

These would include the tendency to stage them at times when few can listen conveniently, superficial handling, a grim determination to stick to one-sided "issues" like juvenile delinquency and avoid equally vital problems confronting democracy, the familiar reluctance to assume vigorous editorial leadership, and the fact that "good" performance tends to be concentrated in a few urban areas served by independ-

215

ent (here the word is used in its literal, as well as its broadcasting, sense) stations.

*5. Taking the country as a whole, one finds that minorities do
not have sufficient opportunity to be heard on controversial issues.*

*6. Individual stations that honestly try to solve the problem are
more often than not frustrated by the advertising men and their
inexorable time schedules.*

Too often the "answer" does not reach as large an audience
as heard the "charge," either because an equally good day and
hour cannot be found or because, in the case of the networks,
fewer affiliates carry the "answer."

The author is persuaded that both the industry and the
F.C.C. worry unduly about the fairness of selling time for the
presentation of minority views. The observation that those
with the most money would get all the best of it applies equally to all the other media, including handbills, posters, direct-
mail matter, sound trucks, propaganda books, propaganda
"documentary" films, and newspaper and magazine advertising. The sums involved are not of an order calculated to exclude any important minority (especially when, as is usually
the case, the local unit involved can draw on others throughout the country for financial assistance). Yet they are large
enough (particularly in the instance of political parties, which
pay a premium rate) to give the broadcaster a certain amount
of financial independence in dealing with sponsors and advertising men.

*7. Taking the country as a whole, one finds that minority lis-
tener tastes are not adequately served.*

Here, again, the reasons are not elusive. The advertising
man whose only test of a gag or a song or a show is how it went
over on the rival station or network week before last will
never permit those broadcasters who live in mortal terror of
him to experiment.

It is a truism in all the media (and especially in the theater) that new techniques rarely "pay off" immediately and sometimes never do. Yet the more imaginative play and movie producers, book publishers, and newspaper and magazine editors are constantly gambling. Why should the broadcaster play it safe? The fact that he does is all the more ironical because he alone is dependent on something that the people own. There may be, numerically, more "bobby-soxers" than lovers of good drama, good music, sprightly conversation, and stimulating discussion. However, the latter pay the larger share of taxes, and it is just possible that they have a larger voice in shaping the future of our society.

8. Statistically "good" individual performance too often is marred by wholly unnecessary flaws and inhibitions.

Toward the end of 1946, C.B.S., stung by what it apparently regarded as an unfair critical evaluation of its overall effort based on ignorance of what it included, began a series of advertisements which reproached the critics for "not knowing *how* to listen." What C.B.S. ignored or overlooked, in the advertisements as in its general practice, was the fact that the critics knew well enough where to find C.B.S.'s "good" things for minority tastes but were not always able to adjust their working, sleeping, and recreation schedules so as to hear them conveniently. To say to these critical minorities that you intend to take care of them at times which are not "required for serving the larger mass audience" (a broadcasting euphemism for taking care of the advertising man first) is rather as if a restaurateur told discriminating diners that he could serve them only out of regular hours.

Besides, the broadcaster who sincerely wishes to serve minority tastes is likely to find (as many of them have found) that this requires more than a look-around at the other media for talent. Taking broadcasting at its own estimate as an enter-

217

tainment medium, one would probably be fair in saying that no other entertainment medium ever leaned so heavily on its fellows or developed so little talent peculiarly its own. The networks have amply demonstrated that not every successful playwright can write for the radio and that not every Broadway or Hollywood actor can bring his talent undiminished to the microphone.

9. *Taking the country as a whole, one finds that the over-all quality of the "entertainment" fare in radio leaves something to be desired.*

The coincidence that radio came along just as vaudeville was perishing was perhaps happier for the vaudevillians than for the rest of us. Broadway (and even Hollywood, which is hardly celebrated for "star" turnover) has run through four "generations" of comedians during the radio lifetimes of "Amos 'n' Andy," "Fibber McGee and Molly," "Burns and Allen," "Lum and Abner," Jack Benny, Fred Allen, Edgar Bergen, and Eddie Cantor, all of whom are still going strong. In radio, a Red Skelton or a Bob Hope is still "new" after half-a-dozen years of precisely the same routines.

The effect on these veterans has been rather marked, for even the most loyal Hope or Allen or Bergen fan can tire (say, after the second or third year) of Crosby's horses, Senator Claghorn's loathing for Damyankees, and Charlie McCarthy's allowance difficulties. (To the credit of Allen and Bergen be it said that they know when enough is too much and would like to get off the merry-go-round.)

Except for the work of three or four pioneers like Corwin, Welles, Oboler, and MacLeish, there has been literally no radio drama worthy of the name that has not been lifted bodily from the theater. The sum of it has been piddling. Time, money, facilities, and encouragement have been begrudged the aforementioned pioneers to a point where only Corwin remains hopefully in the wings, so to speak.

218

The author is no psychologist and therefore approaches the land-mine-sown battlegrounds of women's and children's shows with some trepidation. It seems fairly obvious to him, however, that, if the majority of American women really are "helped" by vicarious excursions into divorce, adultery, and incurable disease, the psychologists who are engaged from time to time to swear to this "fact" might find better employment looking into what may be happening to the human race. And it seems equally obvious that children's shows in which unpleasant brats go unpunished by doltish parents or in which the one mistake in an otherwise perfect crime is explained with such painstaking care as to encourage the most cautious nascent delinquent to try it with the improvements do not clarify the goals and values of society which the Commission on Freedom of the Press had in mind in assigning as the fourth task for the media of mass communication the "presenting and clarifying" of "the goals and values of the society." It is just possible that the true impact of the broadcasters on these goals and values eludes the Hooper telephone girls and that it cannot even be accurately measured in box-tops or soap-chip sales.

Audience-participation shows, the newest craze in radio (because the formula is only five or six years old), deserve a paragraph. So far as the author knows, the first audience-participation show ever submitted to a broadcaster was a 1927 effort approved by a superintendent of schools and a college president as "a positive contribution to adult education." The broadcaster to whom it was first shown thought it was sufficiently entertaining to try on the public; but, as he did not feel able to finance it on a sustaining basis and could find no advertising agency that did not think him utterly mad to suggest such a thing, nothing came of it. A decade and more later, the idea bobbed up again, but with the by now familiar new wrinkles: the questions and answers must under no circumstances add to the sum total of useful knowledge, they must be asked and answered in a setting reminiscent of the oldtime vaudeville stage on amateurs' night, and the whole proceeding must be managed in such a way as to screen out the more intelligent citizens with their silly inhibitions about vulgar exhibitionism. Once again, as always, the advertising man had turned a remarkable opportunity into a cheap sideshow.

The argument that the people get what they want in radio entertainment may be open to a few challenges. Women's magazines which stress thoughtful articles and stories in which competent, recognized writers probe deeply into typical human problems outsell the lurid pulp "love" variety, magazine for magazine. Wholesome children's books outsell the newsbutcher's product, and *Parent's Magazine* has even demonstrated that constructive comic books can hold their own with the trashier brand. Motion pictures like *National Velvet*, *Boy's Town*, *Our Vines Have Tender Grapes*, *Pinocchio*, and *Journey for Margaret* have outbox-officed gangster and "wayward-youth" fare with the young. The number of those Americans who every year pay good money to college bursars for the privilege of amassing useful information may not be much under that for those who troop weekly into studios in the hope of being rewarded with a pair of Nylons (and a lusty cheer from the studio audience if they're from Brooklyn) for their ability to identify a few strains of "popular" music. It seems almost unbelievable that the hundreds of thousands of soldiers, sailors, and marines returning from death with a consuming passion to improve their minds found radio ready with little more than a calfskin traveling bag and some small talk about the relative merits of American and European girls.

It is possible that the fact that the broadcasters do not

build their own entertainment shows has something to do with all this. The advertising agencies have turned the writing of women's and children's shows in particular into a sweatshop assembly-line operation reminiscent of pulp-magazine production, in an understandable effort to pare to the minimum the running costs of formulas which they feel no longer need to be "sold" to the public. The advertising agencies likewise have resisted every effort to replace shopworn comedians, singers, and bands with new talent, so long as the oldtimers could keep their Hooper ratings above 15. The agencies know that mere lack of competition will tend to keep the ratings up, just as a man who runs a 100-yard dash against himself invariably wins. But, as long as the public keeps on buying tea-bags, toothpaste, and coffee, the agencies do not care.

The broadcasters have assumed many curious and untenable positions during their quarter-century in business, but probably none is more insecure (and insincere) than the bland contention, so often reiterated, that the listener does not want anything he is not now getting and that any time he does he has only to ask for it. The public cannot ask for something it does not know exists or could exist. It did not ask for the novel (Fielding gave it to us). It did not ask for the printing press. It did not ask for Shakespeare or Walt Disney or news magazines. It did not ask for football or movies or the 25-cent pocket book. It did not even ask for radio.

The first task of the purveyors of entertainment and intelligence is to anticipate, gamble on, whet, stimulate, elevate, and/or broaden the public taste. There has always been an element of risk in it. If the advertising men are not willing to share the risk in radio, perhaps the broadcasters had better place themselves in a position to assume the whole of it. The best of them will find, as the best of the publishers, producers, and creators in the other media have found, that giving the people more than they demand is sometimes profitable.

10. The broadcasters have not yet provided a means for listeners to hear at a more convenient later time programs which circumstances have caused them to miss when first broadcast, or to hear over and over programs that are good enough to be heard over and over.

A combination of the adoption of country-wide time, the wider employment of transcriptions, and the development of one or more of the several methods for multiple program broadcasting should go far toward solving this defect, which places radio at a distinct and quite unnecessary disadvantage compared to the other media.

11. As even the broadcasters at their 1946 N.A.B. convention agreed, there is far too much "commercialism" in radio.

The statement customarily is made in terms of the ratio of commercial to sustaining programs on the air. The author never has felt that the distinction is very real. If the advertising men had demonstrated, over a period of more than twenty years, that they could produce the best radio fare, the author would be willing to let them produce all radio fare, provided that the Communications Act were amended to bring them under F.C.C. license. Since they have demonstrated what he regards as quite the opposite, the author would like to see them produce none at all. It is not a question of there being certain types of programs that the advertiser is peculiarly well fitted to do and certain other types that the broadcasters are peculiarly well fitted to do. The advertisers do not even display much knowledge of psychology or public taste or public need in their commercial "plugs."

The reasons why the broadcasters got off on the wrong foot with the advertisers are understandable. However, a twenty-year test of so drastic a variation from the accepted practice in the press seems both fair and adequate. The results simply do not indicate that the variation is as acceptable as the accepted practice, for all the latter's faults. The inference seems obvious.

All these shortcomings of the radio fare suggest many possible remedies or fruitful lines of exploration. The author suggests:

To the broadcasters, that they:

Assume a position of vigorous editorial leadership in public affairs;

Reject the role of parasite feeding on the older media and set about training their own producers, directors, actors, writers, editors, commentators, and entertainers;

Develop more plausible discussion techniques;

Assume the responsibility for adequately treating all important controversial public issues, substituting the criterion of public need for the criterion of acceptability to sponsors, advertising men, or overly sensitive public officials;

Improve their machinery for letting important minorities be heard and, with this in view, abandon their preoccupation with the theoretically admirable but practically unreal and unworkable distinction between bought time and free time for the discussion of controversial public issues;

Develop more memorable radio drama;

Make it a rule that no one who is not professionally qualified to help people with their problems will be allowed to use the airways to perpetrate palpable fraud;

Create an adequate clearing house for praiseworthy and especially successful new program ventures, so that those broadcasters who are honestly seeking to improve their service will have the benefit of all the brains and imagination in the industry;

Explore the possibilities for multiple programming from a

single station, with a view to serving neglected areas and minority tastes more adequately;

With the same aim in view, juggle their programs so as to place more of those designed for general public education and for minority tastes in the better listening periods;

Experiment, experiment, experiment; the public is expected to gamble two or three billion dollars on new AM, FM, and television receiving sets within the next five years; surely, the broadcasters should do some gambling on better, fresher, more varied fare.

Now improvement of physical distribution and operation, of competitive opportunity, and of program quality, balance, and adequacy may be sufficiently all-embracing as goals. But the suggestions thus far offered would be superficial and unrealistic, were they not to be accompanied by suggestions in the field of basic human relationships. Indeed, some of these relationships, if not corrected, might in themselves frustrate attainment of the goals.

BASIC RELATIONS

The author has indicated that he does not believe that the broadcasters could make much progress along the lines of program improvement which he has suggested unless and until they first radically changed their relationship with the advertising men. It is possible that they would also have to change their relationships toward one another, toward the government, toward the other media of mass communication, and toward the public. This, in turn, suggests improved relationships toward the broadcasters on the part of the government, of the other media, and of the public. Finally, it suggests a clarification of the proper functions of the various interested agencies of government in their relations with the broadcasters, with the public, and with one another.

224

1. The broadcasters need to achieve, immediately, that degree of arm's-length relationship with the advertisers which fairly characterizes all but a submarginal handful of newspapers and magazines.

The author has set forth to the best of his ability the reasons why he believes this step is of the first order of priority for the broadcasters. The broadcasters have given him a dozen reasons why they profess to believe that such a step should not or could not be taken. Let us examine some of them.

It has been said that advertisers dictate policy in the print media, also. The studies of the Commission on Freedom of the Press indicate that the Commission does not believe this to be the fact in the vast majority of instances. Certain facts, however, seem too obvious to permit of debate. One is that the advertisers do not actually prepare the reading matter in the print media or weave their sales messages into the reading matter. Another is that the bulk of newspaper and magazine publishers do not regard the sale of goods and services as their only, or even their primary, reason for being.

It has been said that it makes no difference whether A, who writes radio shows, B, who produces them, C, who directs them, and D, E, and F, who act them, are on the pay roll of a broadcasting station or on the pay roll of an advertising agency. They would be the same people, the broadcasters say, and so they would be bound to write, produce, direct, and act in precisely the same way. To say this is, it seems to the author, to miss completely the point made above.

It is hard to rationalize the statement. One invariably asks himself: Are they ignorant of the basic human desire to please whatever bosses man has, or is this a tacit admission that the broadcasters' goals are, in fact, the same as the advertisers': to sell goods and services? It is like saying that Frederick Lewis Allen, Ben Hibbs, and Virginius Dabney would be just as satisfactory editors for *Harper's*, the *Saturday Evening Post*, and the *Richmond* (Virginia) *Times-Dispatch*, respectively, if they were employed by a national advertising agency. It discounts, perhaps through ignorance, the classic "war" between editorial people and the "front office." Indeed, it skims over the constant struggle between the creative people in radio, both those who work for the broadcasters and those who work for the advertisers, pay roll–wise, and their masters—the advertiser and the advertiser-cowed broadcaster.

The truth is, as hundreds who have done it can testify, that a newspaperman *does* express himself differently when he becomes an advertising man. He even thinks differently. Or perhaps it would be more correct to say that, if he finds he cannot think differently, he goes back to newspaper work, breathing imprecations and maledictions against the whole advertising fraternity.

To change from one to the other is rather like changing goals in a football game. It does not involve the question of whether the men in the blue jerseys are any better than the men in crimson. The fact is that the two teams are facing in opposite directions, aiming for goalposts separated by the length of the playing field, each determined to reach one set and frustrate every attempt of its rival to reach the other. A man who ran first this way and then that or who hesitated uncertainly in midfield would not be regarded as a very useful football player. For precisely the same reasons an advertising man who subordinated the selling of goods and services to other interests would not be a very effective advertising man, from his employer's standpoint. And a broadcaster who subordinated other interests (presumably, in his case, informing and entertaining the public) to the selling of goods and services would not be a very good broadcaster, from the public's standpoint. In the circumstances, therefore, it might be useful to number the players and give them different-colored jerseys.

It has been said that if any attempt were made to exclude advertising men from the preparation of radio's "reading matter," the advertising men (including the sponsors) would simply abandon radio to economic starvation. Here we are asked to believe either that radio is not really so effective as an advertising medium as the broadcasters have been telling us and that the sponsors who have been using it were prompted solely by charitable motives; or that their advertising messages could not stand on their own merits, as they are obliged to do in the other media, but must be slipped over on a public which otherwise would reject them; or that people do not listen to the commercials at the beginning and end of programs but only to middle commercials.

It is difficult for the author to reconcile these things with the broadcasters' repeated claims that radio is far and away the most effective medium for the advertisement of certain types of goods and services, that listeners actually "like" the commercials, and that the majority of them do not turn their sets off or down during the commercials between programs, even when these commercials are what are known as "local station-break spots" and are therefore wholly unrelated to the programs preceding or following them.[3]

2. The broadcasters need to produce a set of standards for service to the public which reflects the best practices and the highest aims within the industry, and they need to devise effective means of penalizing those broadcasters who consistently flout it.

Under Judge Miller, the N.A.B. appears to be making an honest, if somewhat belated, effort to achieve a "highest common denominator" Code rather than merely one agreeable to

[3] It is interesting to note that this type of advertising is growing in dollar volume faster than any other and in 1946 accounted for just over a third of all gross revenue in radio.

all broadcasters and advertising men. Such a Code might well include a ringing declaration of independence from the advertiser. It might well include those points in the F.C.C.'s Blue Book which the better broadcasters know to be sound. It might put the emphasis on more discussion of controversial public issues rather than on the precise manner in which this is to be achieved. It certainly should give more than passing attention to the need for a purely broadcasting approach to the problem of presenting more useful information of all sorts.

To be at all effective in improving American radio, such a Code would have to carry with it certain sanctions for non-observance. Since the newspaper publishers and editors apparently have concluded that the boycott, and even such a mild sanction as expulsion from membership in a trade-association, are not consonant with the First Amendment, this approach does not appear to be too promising in radio. There remains the not inconsiderable power of disclosure. The fear that flagrant violations of the N.A.B. Code would be paraded before other broadcasters, the F.C.C., and the listening public would exercise a restraining influence on all but the most defiant.

From the standpoint of the N.A.B., even this much would be easier said than done. It may surprise the layman to learn that recent interpretations of the antitrust laws by the Department of Justice make it far from certain that the N.A.B. would not be prosecuted for imposing even the "sanction" of publicity. In co-operation with F.C.C. Chairman Denny, Judge Miller took steps in 1946 to iron out this difficulty. It is to be hoped that he will continue to enjoy the full co-operation of all the government officials involved.

3. The broadcasters need to improve their relationship with the government.

The author purposes suggesting, in the following pages,

how the relationships of the various branches and agencies of government toward the broadcasters might be clarified. On the assumption that they will be, eventually, as a result of natural pressures which are being exerted, the broadcasters need to clarify some of their own attitudes toward government.

Some broadcasters appear to regard the F.C.C. and the Communications Act as temporary annoyances. They would conserve energy for more useful pursuits if they reconciled themselves now, after twenty-five years, to the fact that a very large degree of government regulation of radio will always be their lot, just as it will always be the lot of the railroads and the airlines. It is a curious paradox that the very broadcasters who are forever abusing the F.C.C. for its slowness are invariably the ones who constantly needle the Congress to initiate sweeping inquiries, on the flimsiest of pretexts (or on no pretext at all), into the F.C.C.'s conduct. Such inquiries as eventuate as often as not turn out to be time-consuming and unfruitful "witch-hunts." And even when the Congress ignores the broadcasters' clamor for them, the net effect of the clamor is usually a drastic cut in F.C.C. appropriations, with a consequent loss of manpower and an equally inevitable further slowing-down of the F.C.C. tempo. It is difficult to imagine how any but those broadcasters with the minds of immature children at Halloween could gloat over the prospect of a punitive expedition by the new Republican Congress against the F.C.C. The first and worst sufferers from any such grandstanding would surely be the broadcasters.

4. On the other hand, the government needs to do some clarifying in the interest of improved relationships.

It seems to the author that the issues raised by the Mayflower Decision and the issuance of the Blue Book need to be clarified without further delay, if they are to be clarified in an atmosphere of reason. Commercial television is an accomplished fact, though on so modest a scale that it has had no great impact either upon the public or upon the motion picture industry. A facsimile newspaper is being distributed regularly in Miami, Florida, and half a dozen others are promised by 1948. If the Mayflower and Blue Book issues are allowed to drift along until they become entangled in cross-media licensing problems, forcing an angry showdown in the Congress, the end-result is likely to be a vindictive crippling of the F.C.C., which would leave that agency unable properly to discharge even its "traffic policeman" function.

This might indicate a concerted effort on the part of the industry and the Commission to secure an early Supreme Court ruling as to the constitutionality of both measures. Whatever the outcome, however, the issues involved appear to raise problems which the Supreme Court could not settle. Even supposing both the Mayflower Decision and the Blue Book licensing procedure are said by the nine men comprising the present court to be unquestionably constitutional, there remains the question whether they are workable, equitable, or wise.

And since the Blue Book at least stems from the Communications Act, any logical routing would seem to indicate Capitol Hill as the first stop. Indeed, since so many members of the Congress appear to be chafing for appointment to a committee to investigate the F.C.C., the new Republican steering committees might wish to divert their energies to a thorough re-examination of broadcasting legislation in the light of conditions quite different from those that obtained when such legislation was last enacted.

Does the Congress still wish the F.C.C. to weigh over-all program adequacy as one of several factors in considering original license applications, applications for renewal, and revocations? If so, it must stand behind the Blue Book, insist that the Commission enforce it rigidly, give the regulatory body the money and authority required to enforce it rigidly, and be prepared to amend the Constitution if the court finds any of these steps unconstitutional. The legislators cannot have it both ways. The Communications Act without the Blue Book is, in so far as it touches on program adequacy, a farce. A Blue Book unenforced soon becomes a farce, for the "scare" technique will work only about once. A regulatory body that cannot know from day to day where it stands with the legislature and that lives in constant fear of capricious legislative reprisal for doing the legislature's bidding is a farce.

Would the Congress prefer to transfer to the communities the task of measuring over-all program adequacy against the broadcasters' promises and some simple standard of judgment, leaving with the Commission the power to deny or revoke on the ground of poor program performance, but only upon certification from the communities?

Does the Congress wish to strip the F.C.C. of all but its powers to police the ethereal traffic, leaving program adequacy entirely to the law of supply and demand?

Does the Congress wish to abolish the F.C.C. altogether?

The Congress must do something. For the hour is late, and the Commission has exhausted its original mandate without achieving a result wholly satisfactory to anyone—least of all to the listeners who elect Congressmen.

5. The other media of mass communication, and especially the newspaper and magazine press, need to recognize radio as a coequal partner, entitled to both support and honest criticism.

6. The listening public needs to be more constructively critical of its radio fare, and it needs to develop techniques for bringing its constructive criticism to the attention of the broadcasters.

231

The need for a larger community voice in the choice of radio programs has been apparent throughout the brief history of the industry. Hoover, it will be recalled, spelled out a division of critical responsibilities in 1924: ". . . . leaving to each community a large voice in determining who are to occupy the wave lengths assigned to that community." Recognition of the soundness of that principle is inherent in the rules and regulations of the regulatory body since 1927. It is inherent in the support (by no means consistent or unanimous) of the existing listener groups by the broadcasters.

Notwithstanding, Hoover's suggestion has never been adopted, for it cannot be said that fifty thousand unsolicited letters a year to the F.C.C. represent an honest attempt to implement Hoover's proposal; or that a hearing and licensing procedure which leaves 999 out of every 1,000 citizens blissfully unaware of the identity of their station-owners does; or that halfhearted industry support of three-score organized listener groups does.

The first step might be to extend the pattern of organized listener groups to more communities. How could this be accomplished? For the answer, one may look to the factors that contributed to the setting-up of the two or three score that exist: some were organized by aggressive individuals in the communities without outside aid, others were incubated by the broadcasters; in every instance, someone supplied initiative. It would seem, therefore, that the fact that there are some eight hundred communities with radio stations and several thousand communities that get secondary service, none of which has a listener council, indicates lack of initiative rather than a complacent attitude toward radio. The N.A.B.'s N.O.R.C. survey underlined the need for some national agency to fire the imaginations of more potential community catalysts in more communities. The Commission on Freedom of the Press recommends the creation of such a body—"a new and independent agency to appraise and report annually upon the performance of the press." It prefers an agency unrelated to, and unsupported by, the press. The radio councils here proposed would, in the author's view, be better off without direct support from the broadcasters.

The second step might be to insure that organized listener groups will be truly representative of the communities for which they undertake to speak. As the Wisconsin group and others have demonstrated, it is possible for a relatively small group to ascertain the wishes of an entire state, given enough volunteers willing to lick stamps and ring doorbells, without an enormous outlay of capital.

The third step might be to make certain that all community councils use substantially the same general standards of judgment and the same survey techniques.

The fourth step might be to integrate the work of the community councils with that of the national council and also with that of the F.C.C.

It has been suggested that the community councils should be set up as public administrative agencies, somewhat after the fashion of draft and ration boards, the members to be appointed by the mayor and subject to law, the expenses to be borne by local governments. The author prefers a voluntary basis. Removing something from the jurisdiction of a federal agency and placing it under the legal jurisdictions of hundreds of local agencies would be rather like leaping from the frying pan into the fire.

How could such community councils integrate their work with that of the F.C.C.? Certainly in the same way that existing councils assist the F.C.C.: by supplying qualified, on-the-spot testimony on the service that a broadcaster is rendering in a given community. The day might even come (provided the courts did not find the practice unconstitutional) when the F.C.C. could accept almost automatically the judgments of bona fide listener councils on program quality, balance, and adequacy, as one of many factors governing licensing policy.

Such a plan has many obvious defects: politics, inertia, uneven performance, prejudice, danger of domination by "crackpots" and reformers, and prostitution by the broadcasters (as with some of the early film review boards). The author has been fully aware of them. All are present in every detail of the democratic process. To say that such a plan would be bound to fail is to say that democracy has failed. The author is skeptical of the skeptics.

The author suggests:

To the broadcasters, that they:

Stop trying to rationalize an accidental and unnatural relationship, steel themselves against the reflex cries of anguish from those who habitually cry before they are hurt, and take the first long step toward that "freedom of the press" for which they clamor: adoption of the practice of offering time for the advertising of commercial goods and services only on the basis of time-periods limited to 120 consecutive seconds between programs, the programs to be developed entirely by the broadcasters and to have no topical or other connection, except for the coincidence of time sequence, with any advertising matter;

Take the initiative in co-operating with the F.C.C. to bring about an early court test of the constitutionality of the Mayflower Decision and the Blue Book;

Stop dreaming of a day when there will be no government regulation of radio;

Stop cheapening the First Amendment by invoking it every time the F.C.C. issues a routine ruling;

Follow the lead of F.C.C. Chairman Denny and N.A.B.

President Miller toward harmonious co-operation between the industry and the F.C.C.

To the F.C.C., that it:

Either amend the Mayflower Decision to permit broadcasters to air their partisan views, on condition that they provide equal time for an answer, or enforce it in an instance which will insure its speedy review by the courts as to constitutionality;

Enforce the procedures outlined in the Blue Book in an instance which will insure its speedy review by the courts as to constitutionality.

To the N.A.B., that it:

Draft a "Code of Standards" calling for the immediate establishment of an arm's-length relationship between broadcasters and advertisers, indorsing such portions and basic principles of the F.C.C. Blue Book as appear to the better broadcasters to be reasonable and workable, and pointing the way toward improving techniques in the handling of discussion of controversial public issues and in the presentation of useful information generally;

Prepare to publicize, thoroughly and impartially, flagrant individual departures from the Code.

To the Department of Justice, the F.C.C., and the Congress, that they:

Take whatever steps are necessary to insure that the N.A.B. has the proper legal sanction under the antitrust and other laws for the above.

To the Congress, that it:

Recognize that the recent congressional election results in no wise constituted a popular mandate to make punitive expeditions against executive agencies where no evidence of inefficiency or wilful wrongdoing exists;

Re-examine the Communications Act of 1934 as amended, with a view to giving the F.C.C. a more explicit charter, particularly in the field of over-all program evaluation, and to providing adequate authority and funds for the effective operation of such a charter.

To the newspaper and magazine press, that it:

Support the broadcasters in their quest for equal constitutional freedom, provided that the broadcasters meanwhile qualify themselves for such guaranties by securing their freedom from advertisers;

Devote at least as much emphasis to honest, constructive criticism of radio as a medium for entertainment and public information as they now devote to honest, constructive criticism of the theater, books, and motion pictures.

To all who may be interested in the improvement of radio, that they:

Explore the possibilities of greater listener participation in the evaluation of radio fare.

APPENDIX I

REGIONAL NETWORKS

NOTE.—Many of the following networks are organized very loosely, many stations are affiliated with more than one network, and some of the networks are used infrequently.

NETWORK	NUMBER OF STATIONS (Power in Watts)			TO-TAL	STATES OR REGIONS
	100–500	1,000–5,000	10,000–50,000		
Arizona Broadcasting System...	4	2	....	6	Ariz.
Arizona Network.............	2	1	....	3	Ariz.
Arkansas Network............	6	3	1	10	Ark., Tenn.
Arrowhead Network...........	3	2	....	5	Minn., Wis.
Connecticut State Network....	4	2	....	6	Conn.
Dairyland Network...........	3	1	....	4	Minn.
Don Lee Broadcasting System*.	28	11	....	39	West Coast, Calif., Ore., Wash., Idaho
Georgia Major Market Trio....	.....	3	....	3	Ga.
Intercollegiate Broadcasting System......................	17 campus and university noncommercial stations				
Intermountain Network*......	4	3	....	7	Utah, Idaho, Wyo.
Iowa Tall Corn Network.......	7	2	....	9	Iowa
Kansas State Network.........	3	3	....	6	Kan.
Lone Star Chain..............	1	6	....	7	Texas
Mason Dixon Radio Group.....	4	2	....	6	Del., Pa.
Michigan Radio Network*.....	6	3	....	9	Mich.
Mid-states Group.............	.....	3	....	3	Iowa, S.D.
Minnesota Radio Network.....	3	....	1	4	Minn.
Mississippi Valley Network....	63	14	1	78	12 states from Mo. to Minn.
New England Regional Network*	1	3	3	7	New England
Northwest Network...........	5	4	1	10	Minn., Wis., N.D.
Oklahoma Network*...........	6	1	....	7	Okla.
Quaker Network..............	14	4	....	18	Pa.
South Central Quality Network.	.....	4	1	5	Tenn., Ark., Miss., La.
Southern Minnesota Network...	3	....	....	3	Minn.
Sunshine Trio................	3	....	....	3	Fla.
Tennessee Valley Network.....	2	1	....	3	Tenn.
Texas Quality Network........	.....	1	3	4	Texas
Texas State Network..........	10	5	1	16	Texas
Tobacco Network, Inc.........	7	....	....	7	N.C.
Tri-city Stations.............	3	....	....	3	Va.
West Virginia Network........	2	2	....	4	W. Va.
Wisconsin Network...........	16	4	....	20	Wis. and Mich.
Wolverine Network...........	14	....	1	15	Mich., Wis., Ill.
Yankee Network..............	9	14	....	23	New England
Z-Net.......................	2	1	....	3	Mont.

* Affiliated as groups with a national network.

GROUP OWNERSHIP OF UNITED STATES
BROADCASTING STATIONS

The national networks:

A.B.C.	C.B.S.	N.B.C.
WJZ	WABC	WEAF
WENR	WTOP	WRC
KGO	KMOX	WMAQ
KECA	KNX	WTAM
	WBBM	KPO
	WCCO	KOA
	WEEI	

The regional networks:

Don Lee Broadcasting System—KHJ, KFRC, KGB, KDB.

Newspaper interests:

Cleveland Plain Dealer—WHK, WHKK, WHKC, WKBN.

Gannett newspapers—WHEC, WENY, WHDL, WTHT, WDAN, WOKO, WABY.

Hearst Radio, Inc.—WBAL, WISN, WCAE.

Cowles Stations—KRNT, WNAZ, WOL, WHOM, WCOP.

Gene Howe–T. E. Snowden Group (80 per cent of stock owned by *Amarillo Globe* and *News*)—KGNC, KFYO, KTSA, KRGV.

McClatchy Broadcasting Company—KFBK, KMJ, KWG, KERN, KOH.

Morgan Murphy–Walter Bridges Group (32 per cent of stock owned by publisher of *Superior Telegram*)—WEBC, WMFG, WHLB, WEAU. Murphy also has interest in KVOL and Bridges in WJMC.

Oklahoma Publishing Company—WKY, KIZ, KVOR.

John H. Perry—WCOA, WJHP, WTMC, WDLP.

Scripps-Howard Group—WCPO, WNOX, WMC.

Lancaster newspapers—WGAL, WORK, WKBO, WEST, WAZL, WDEL; minority interest in WILM.

Other groups:

Westinghouse Radio Stations—WBZ, WBZA, KDKA, KYW, WOWO, KEX.

Fort Industry Company—WSPD, WWVA, WMMN, WLOK, WHIZ, WAGA, WGBS; minority in KIRO.

General Tire & Rubber Company—WNAC, WAAB, WEAN, WICC, WONS.

Georgia Broadcasting System—WRBL, WATL, WGPC.

John A. Kennedy—WCHS, WBLK, WPAR; minority in WSAZ.

Pierce E. Lackey—WPAD, WHOP, WSON.

Clarence and Martin Leich—WEOA, WGBF, WBOW.

John J. Louis—KTAR, KVOA, KYUM, KYCA.

McClung Stations—KHSL, KYOS, KVCV.

The Nunn Stations—WLAP, WCMI, KFDA, WBIR.

George A. Richards-Leo Fitzpatrick Group—WJR, WGAR, KMPC.

Adeline B. Rines—WCSH, WRDO, WLBZ.

Symons-Craney Group—KGIR, KXL, KFPY, KPFA, KRBM.

Harry C. Wilder—WSYR, WTRY, WKNE, WELI.

The Friendly Group—WSTV, WFPG, WJPA, WKNY.

APPENDIX II

EXCERPTS FROM 1929 CODE

1. Recognizing that the radio audience includes persons of all ages and all types of political, social and religious belief, every broadcaster will endeavor to prevent the broadcasting of any matter which would commonly be regarded as offensive.
2. When the facilities of a broadcaster are used by others than the owner, the broadcaster shall ascertain the financial responsibility and character of such client, that no dishonest, fraudulent or dangerous person, firm or organization may gain access to the radio audience.
3. Matter which is barred from the mails as fraudulent, deceptive or obscene shall not be broadcast.
4. Every broadcaster shall exercise great caution in accepting any advertising matter regarding products or service which may be injurious to health.
5. No broadcaster shall permit the broadcasting of advertising statements or claims which he knows or believes to be false, deceptive or grossly exaggerated.
6. Every broadcaster shall strictly follow the provisions of the Radio Act of 1927 regarding the clear identification of sponsored or paid-for material.
7. Care shall be taken to prevent the broadcasting of statements derogatory to other stations, to individuals, or to competing products or services, except where the law specifically provides that the station has no right of censorship.
8. Where charges of violation of any article of the Code of Ethics of the National Association of Broadcasters are filed in writing with the managing director, the Board of Directors shall investigate such charges and notify the station of its findings.
    a) There should be a "decided difference" between what might be broadcast before 6:00 P.M. and what might be broadcast

240

after that hour. The time before 6:00 P.M. was declared to be included in the "business day," and it was decided that "part at least" of it might be devoted to "programs of a business nature." After 6:00, "time is for recreation and relaxation; therefore commercial programs should be of the good-will type."

b) Commercial announcements, "as the term is generally understood," should not be broadcast between 7:00 and 11:00 P.M.

c) "The client's business and product should be mentioned sufficiently to insure an adequate return on his investment, but never to the extent that it loses listeners to the station."

APPENDIX III

1939 "STANDARDS OF PRACTICE"

Children's programs.—Programs designed specifically for children reach impressionable minds and influence social attitudes, aptitudes and approaches and, therefore, they require the closest supervision of broadcasters in the selection and control of material, characterization and plot. This does not mean that the vigor and vitality common to a child's imagination and love of adventure should be removed. It does mean that programs should be based upon sound social concepts and presented with a superior degree of craftsmanship; that these programs should reflect respect for parents, adult authority, law and order, clean living, high morals, fair play and honorable behavior. Such programs must not contain sequences involving horror or torture or use of the supernatural or superstitious or any other material which might reasonably be regarded as likely to over-stimulate the child listener, or be prejudicial to sound character development. No advertising appeal which would encourage activities of a dangerous social nature will be permitted. To establish acceptable and improving standards for children's programs, the National Association of Broadcasters will continuously engage in studies and consultations with parent and child study groups. The results of these studies will be made available for application to all children's programs.

Controversial public issues.—As part of their public service, networks and stations shall provide time for the presentation of public questions including those of controversial nature. Such time shall be allotted with due regard to all the other elements of balanced program schedules and to the degree of public interest in the questions to be presented. Broadcasters shall use their best efforts to allot such time with fairness to all elements in a given controversy. Time for the presentation of controversial issues shall not be sold, except for political broadcasts. There are three fundamental reasons for this refusal to sell time for public discussion and, in its stead, providing time for it without charge. First, it is a public duty of broadcasters to bring such discussion to the radio audience regardless of the willingness of others to pay for it. Second, should time be sold for the discussion of controversial issues, it would have to be sold, in fairness, to all with the ability and desire to buy at any given time. Consequently, all possibility of regulating the amount of discussion on the air in proportion to other elements of properly balanced programming or of allotting the available periods with due regard to listener interest in topics to be discussed would be surrendered. Third, and by far the most important, should time be sold for the discussion of controversial public issues and for the propagation of the views of individuals or groups, a powerful public forum would inevitably gravitate almost wholly into the hands of those with the greater means to buy it. The political broadcasts excepted above are any broadcasts in connection with a political campaign in behalf of or against the candidacy of a legally qualified candidate for nomination or election to public office, or in behalf of or against a public proposal which is subject to ballot. This exception is made because at certain times the contending parties want to use and are entitled to use more time than broadcasters could possibly afford to give away. Nothing in the prohibition against selling time for the presentation of controversial public issues shall be interpreted as barring sponsorship of the public forum type of program when such a program is regularly presented as a series of fair-sided discussions of public issues and when control of the fairness of the program rests wholly with the broadcasting station or network.

Educational broadcasting.—While all radio programs possess some educative values, broadcasters nevertheless desire to be of assistance in helping toward more specific educational efforts, and will continue to use their time and facilities to that end, and, in cooperation with appropriate groups, will continue their search for improving applications of radio as an educational adjunct.

News.—News shall be presented with fairness and accuracy and the broadcasting station or network shall satisfy itself that the arrangements made for obtaining news insure this result. Since the number of broadcasting channels is limited, news broadcasts shall not be editorial. This means that news shall not be selected for the purpose of furthering or hindering either side of any controversial public

243

issue, nor shall it be colored by the opinions or desires of the station or network management, the editor or others engaged in its preparation or the person actually delivering it over the air, or, in the case of sponsored news broadcasts, the advertiser. The fundamental purpose of news dissemination in a democracy is to enable people to know what is happening and to understand the meaning of events so that they may form their own conclusions, and therefore, nothing in the foregoing shall be understood as preventing news broadcasters from analyzing and elucidating news so long as such analysis and elucidation are free of bias. News commentators as well as all other newscasters shall be governed by these provisions.

Religious broadcasts.—Radio, which reaches men of all creeds and races simultaneously, may not be used to convey attacks upon another's race or religion. Rather it should be the purpose of the religious broadcast to promote the spiritual harmony and understanding of mankind and to administer broadly to the varied religious needs of the community.

Commercial programs and length of commercial copy.—Acceptance of programs and announcements shall be limited to products and services offered by individuals and firms engaged in legitimate commerce; whose products, services, radio advertising, testimonials and other statements comply with pertinent legal requirements, fair trade practices and accepted standards of good taste. Brief handling of commercial copy is recommended procedure at all times. Member stations shall hold the length of commercial copy, including that devoted to contests and offers, to the following number of minutes and seconds: daytime: 15-minute programs 3 minutes 15 seconds, 30-minute programs $4\frac{1}{2}$ minutes, 1-hour programs 9 minutes; nighttime: $2\frac{1}{2}$, 3 and 6 minutes respectively. Exceptions: the above limitations do not apply to participation programs, announcement programs "musical clocks," shoppers' guides and local programs falling within these general classifications. Because of the varying economic and social conditions throughout the United States, members of the N.A.B. shall have the right to present to the N.A.B. for special ruling local situations which in the opinion of the member may justify exceptions to the above prescribed limitations.

Resolution adopted by the seventeenth annual convention of N.A.B.—To clarify the phrase "accepted standards of good taste" and the canons of good practice set forth in the N.A.B. Code, therefore be it *Resolved:* That member stations shall not accept for advertising: (1) any spiritous or "hard" liquor, (2) any remedy or other product the sale of which or the method of sale of which constitutes a violation of law, (3) any fortune-telling, mind-reading, or character-reading, by hand-writing, numerology, palm-reading, or astrology, or advertising related thereto, (4) schools that offer questionable or untrue promises of employment as inducements for enrollment, (5) matrimonial agencies, (6) offers of "homework" except by firms of unquestioned responsibility, (7) any "dopester," tip-sheet or race track publications, (8) all forms of speculative finance; before member stations may accept any financial advertising, it shall be fully ascertained that such advertising and such advertised services comply with all pertinent federal, state and local laws, (9) cures and products claiming to cure, (10) advertising statements or claims member stations know to be false, deceptive or grossly exaggerated, (11) continuity which describes, repellently, any functions or symptomatic results of disturbances, or relief granted such disturbances through the use of any product, (12) unfair attacks upon competitors, competing products, or upon other industries, professions or institutions, (13) misleading statements of price or value, or misleading companies of price or value.

COMMITTEE VERSION OF CONTROVERSIAL-ISSUES SECTION

Carrying out their mission as instruments of democracy in providing avenues for the discussion of public matters, member stations shall at all times hold their facilities in readiness, consistent with proper program questions of general interest.

Because listeners possibly in no other way would be assured of the opportunity to hear the opposing views on any controversial subject discussed, time will not be sold for such discussions, nor will such discussions be permitted on sponsored advertising programs unless representative spokesmen from at least two clearly defined and different sectors of public opinion participate in the same program at the same time.

The right of a speaker to express his opinion shall be modified only by conformity with existing laws, including the laws of libel and slander and the standards of good taste.

Throughout the country, there has grown up, of late, the practice of restoring something akin to the Colonial "town hall" meeting, wherein the clash of opinions and ideas are broadcast in a radio-forum debate so that the greatest number of citizens may hear the issues, evaluate the different opinions advanced, and act upon them. Such forum practice is recommended.

Fair consideration to all.—1. Without prejudice, radio stations will consider, fairly, the request for time of every responsible individual or organization. Should time be secured for a speaker or program through the request of some group or organization, the identification of such group or organization shall be clearly stated before and after the broadcast period.

Different points of view.—2. In presenting discussions of a controversial public question, stations will make every effort to provide fair and equal opportunity for each responsible point of view to be heard. However, the failure of an opposition viewpoint to avail itself of this opportunity should not, in itself, preclude any discussion of a given question.

Handling of discussions during strikes.—3. No time may be sold for the discussion of issues arising from a strike. If time is given for such discussions, it will be given on a fair and equal basis to all interested parties. If time is denied, the broadcaster will determine in his own mind that he has attempted faithfully to serve the public interest in such action.

APPENDIX IV

EXCERPTS FROM 1939 *CODE MANUAL*

FOREWORD

Few businesses are confronted with such a complex intermingling of social, public and economic interests as is the business of broadcasting. Of necessity, then, the NAB Code must be a continuous evolution of interpretation and policy to meet changing conditions of taste and circumstances. Moreover, in an industry which may be revolutionized overnight by new technical discoveries from the laboratory, a social-minded vigilance is needed at all times, and in all directions. . . . . The work of the Committee is advisory and interpretive. It has not been—nor will it ever be—dictatorial or arbitrary. . . . .

CONTROVERSIAL PUBLIC ISSUES

The Code Committee realizes that whether a matter is a public controversial issue or not is one sometimes difficult to determine, particularly in national or statewide affairs. At the same time, the Committee feels that controversial public issues in the United States . . . . have a way of rising swiftly to the surface. . . . . In the majority of cases, therefore, the broadcaster finds that the public controversial issue and the spokesmen, for and against, may be ascertained and identified fairly well in advance. . . . . The broadcaster can render no greater public service than to set aside ample allotments of time for full discussions of public matters, both controversial and non-controversial. Such broadcasts not only permit him to discharge his public service duty, but they build new listener interest and new audience, valuable to the station. . . . . If a speaker, in discussing what is thought to be non-controversial, finds himself receiving sustained and substantial opposition from a representative section of the audience, he has himself uncovered a "public con-

247

troversial issue" and has set in motion the mechanics of the Code to provide a hearing for those taking a different public point of view. . . . . If the opposing view refuses to debate or to use time offered for the purpose of presenting its views through their [*sic*] spokesmen, this should not prevent the one side from being heard, for, obviously if such a policy existed, the continued refusal of an opposition to use time offered would bar any discussion of the matter over the air. . . . .

What is the "public interest, convenience or necessity" of our 130,000,000 fellow citizens? Certainly it differs as between those who live in rural areas and those who live in urban America. . . . . How, then, can the broadcaster carry out the obligations imposed by his franchise and be in a position to serve this complex "public interest"? He has but *one* means: through the acceptance or through the rejection of matter offered for broadcasting. . . . . Radio is not a common carrier, forced to sell time to all with the means to buy, first come, first served. . . . . Let it be remembered that *American radio is predicated upon the right of the listener to hear, not upon the right of an individual to be heard*. . . . . The Code has evoked some misconceptions about free speech . . . . is it possible for 130,000,000 individuals to exercise their right of free speech on but 800 radio stations? Of course not. . . . . Radio can accommodate only the spokesman, not every follower. Our requirement is that if one side of a controversial issue is presented, the listener has the right to hear the opposing viewpoint under similar conditions. . . . .

On October 2, 1939, Congress was called into special session to consider the position of the country with reference to the European War. It was quite evident from all sources of public expression that Americans desired to stay out of the war. It was equally evident that the methods through which our neutrality might best be obtained was a matter in which there was a "*discernible divided public opinion*." The Code Compliance Committee issued the following statement at the conclusion of its meeting in Washington October 2, and 3, 1939:

"Following careful survey of the members of the Committee drawn from different sections of the country, and the issues itself as resolved yesterday in Congress, the Committee feels that while all Americans desire to stay out of the war and to preserve neutrality, the methods of achieving and maintaining the same are matters automatically falling within the sphere of 'public controversial issues' and as such should be presented on free time and not on paid time." . . . .

Matters pending before a legislative body are not regarded as "public proposals subject to ballot." . . . .

. . . . There is nothing in the Code which *would bar nor which would encourage birth control discourses on the air*, this being one of those matters which must be left to the discretion of the individual station or network management. . . . .

Were manufacturers or merchants permitted to divert the purpose of their radio programs from that of advertising their products to one of furthering the cause of their particular brand of political, social or religious beliefs, then the entire structure of commercial broadcasting in this country would be undermined and the confidence of listeners destroyed. . . . .

Discussion (or dramatization) of labor problems on the air is almost always of a controversial nature. Even the so-called facts about labor, such as the American Federation of Labor's audited membership figures, are usually challenged. Therefore, the presentation of a labor program usually calls for "at least one other program" because of the division in the ranks of organized labor. It is not always possible to balance a labor program with an employers' program. . . . . The situation is further complicated by the fact that employers, as a rule, won't discuss their labor problems on the air, and are inclined to frown on those stations, especially in smaller communities, which open their facilities to labor leaders. And yet the broadcasting industry cannot ignore the fact that a good share of its audience is interested in labor problems. . . . .

As in all other cases, the public interest must be the test for scheduling labor programs. . . . . A station probably would be justified in rejecting a request for discussion of a strike by six waitresses in a side street restaurant. . . . . On the other hand, a strike by six employees of a power plant which threw a city into darkness would be of prime public interest. Similarly, a labor leader's discussion of unemployment in the steel industry would be of little interest in an Iowa agricultural community. . . . . The *forum type* of program is recommended for labor programs. . . . .

.... Not all stations, independent or affiliated, can afford a talent reservoir adequate to compete with metropolitan-produced educational programs. *Nor is such needed or desirable.* Given adequı te and intelligent cooperation from local school and civic groups, the average station may produce a character of educational and civic broadcasting, tailored to the needs of the listening area, which no outside operation may hope to fill. . . . .

The background of the Federal Radio Education Committee is of extreme importance to the broadcasting industry. Educators of our country have been interested in radio since the inception of broadcasting. . . . . By 1927, the interest of educators had broadened and the Carnegie and Rockefeller Foundations had become interested. . . . . With the formation of the Adult Education Association, the Carnegie Foundation approached the industry and the government in the hope that something significant might be done in realizing the social possibilities of radio broadcasting. . . . . However, in 1929 small groups of educators began a campaign of agitation. . . . . These small groups availed themselves of financial backing and were successful in muddying the waters of possible cooperation. A series of incidents, including the Fess Bill which proposed that 15 per cent of available broadcasting facilities be set aside for education, and later the movement that in America we adopt the British system of broadcasting, were incited by these groups. . . . .

The authors of the *Code Manual* then accuse "these small groups" of fostering Section 307-C of the Communications Act of 1934, which provided that "the Commission shall study the proposal that Congress by statute allocate fixed percentages of radio broadcasting facilities to particular types or kinds of non-profit activities," and applaud the F.C.C. for recommending that this not be done. The *Manual* notes that a "conference was held in May 1935 in Washington under the auspices of the Commission. As a result, the Commission created the Federal Radio Education Committee. .... A preliminary budget of $27,000 to finance necessary basic planning work was underwritten jointly by the educators and the broadcasters. The Carnegie Foundation contributed the educators' half of this amount and made their funds available immediately. The broadcasting industry, however, made the regrettable mistake of allowing more than six months to pass before its share of the money was made available. . . . . The FREC established nine projects of research and experimentation . . . . the Rockefeller and Carnegie Foundations agreed to contribute two-thirds of the cost amounting to $167,500. . . . . The broadcasters were committed . . . . to raise the remainder. . . . . Because some stations have not as yet paid in, their exists an industry deficit of around $35,000. . . . ."

NOTE ON SOURCES

BOOKS

The author has found the literature on radio singularly meager and, with the exception of those volumes dealing with the technical development of electronics or with research techniques initiated by the industry, disappointingly unrewarding. Of perhaps two-score books turned up in a search of the nation's libraries, three-fourths are limited to certain narrow phases of the problem, and a good half of the remainder suffer from superficiality or obvious bias or both.

Particularly helpful in tracing the technical history of broadcasting in relation to federal regulation was *Telecommunications*, by James M. Herring and Gerald C. Gross, a simple, concise account which, unfortunately, ends with the year 1936. Some material on the early growth of the great national networks was drawn from *History of Radio to 1926* and *Big Business and Radio*, by Gleason L. Archer, and *Radio Networks and the Federal Government*, by Thomas P. Robinson, although all three show the marks of having been written from the library of the National Broadcasting Company.

Valuable data on the relationships of broadcasting with education were found in *American Universities and Colleges That Have Held Broadcast License*, *Development of Radio Education Policies in American School Systems*, and *Radio Network Contributions to Education*, by Carroll Atkinson, and *Education's Own Stations*, by S. E. Frost. Useful in the study of audience research techniques were *Radio Research: 1941–1942–1943* and other volumes by Dr. Paul F. Lazarsfeld and Dr. Frank Stanton, and *Radio Audience Measurement*, by Mathew Chappell and C. E. Hooper. Measurably helpful in assessing the role of the advertising agencies and sponsors were *A Decade of Radio Advertising*, by Herman S. Hettinger, and *The History of An Advertising Agency* (N. W. Ayer), by Ralph M. Hower.

In a quite different category were two books which made an honest effort to evaluate the whole problem: *Radio's Second Chance*, by Charles A. Siepman, and *Broadcasting and the Public*, a report of the Federal Council of the Churches of Christ in America. The former, while hortatory in style and given rather more to pietism than to specificity, succeeds in capturing the mood of dissatisfaction prevailing in 1946; the latter, an admirable little book full of wise counsel, deserves, in the author's opinion, more attention than it received at the time of its publication in 1938.

Also studied, though with more fragmentary results, were *Sound and Fury*, by Francis Chase, Jr.; *Radio in Wartime*, by Sherman H. Dryer; *Television*, by W. C. Eddy; *Modern Radio*, by Kingdon S. Tyler; *National Policy for Radio Broadcasting*, by C. B. Rose, Jr.; and *The Rape of Radio*, by Robert West.

NEWSPAPERS, MAGAZINES, AND PAMPHLETS

In the circumstances it was thought advisable to turn to the current and back files of newspapers and magazines and to the voluminous publicity material issued over a period of twenty years by the broadcasters.

Among the newspapers consulted were the *New York Times* (1919–46), the *New York Evening Post* (1919–28), the *New York Herald* (1919–24), the *New York Herald Tribune* (1945–46), the *Cleveland Plain Dealer* (1938–46), and the *St. Louis Post-Dispatch* (1943).

Other periodical publications checked included the *Atlantic Monthly*, *Advertising Age*, *Billboard*, *Broadcasting*, *Variety*, *Broadcasting Yearbook*, *Fortune*, *American Mercury*, *McLean's Magazine*, *Harper's*, *Saturday Evening Post*, *Time*, *Public Opinion Quarterly*, *Annals of the American Academy of Political and Social Science*, *Radio Broadcast*, *FM and Television Digest*, and *Tide*.

In addition, some hundreds of brochures, pamphlets, and publicity releases of thirty or forty stations and networks were scanned for relevant data.

PUBLIC DOCUMENTS

Having discovered early in the game that no one person had ever plowed through the *Annual Reports*, *Rules and Regulations*, transcripts of hearings, statements, memoranda, and publicity releases of the Radio Bureau of the Department of Commerce, the Federal Radio Commission, and the Federal Communications Commission, the author assigned a research analyst to this task in July, 1945. On completing it, she proceeded to read and card-index all pertinent passages in the *Congressional Record* (1919–46).

The Federal Communications commissioners and their staff, particularly Edward Brecher of the Legal Department, were especially helpful in making this material available.

PROGRAM MONITORING

The author and his research assistants reviewed more than 200 scripts and monitored more than 800 local programs on thirty-eight stations and 400 network programs on nine stations.

PREPUBLICATION CHECK

The first, second, and third working drafts of this report were circulated among some forty representatives of government and the industry and a dozen independent critics. Criticisms, corrections, and suggestions were subsequently discussed orally with approximately a third of these. The majority of changes suggested were made.

INTERVIEWS

By far the most rewarding source of information, however, was tapped through the interview method, for the richest lore of radio lies in the minds of the men who have helped to shape it—men who, for the most part, have never had the time to commit their recollections to paper.

The author is extremely grateful for the opportunity to spend several hours each with Paul W. Kesten, vice-chairman of the board, Frank Stanton, president, and William C. Ackerman, reference director, of the Columbia Broadcasting System; William S. Hedges, vice-president, Horton Heath, director of information, and Henry Ladner, assistant general counsel, of the National Broadcasting Company; Robert D. Swezey, executive vice-president and general manager, Robert Schmid, vice-president in charge of advertising and promotion, Esterly Page, vice-president in charge of engineering, and Carl Haverlin, vice-president in charge of station relations, of the Mutual Broadcasting System; Robert Saudek, director of public service programs, of the American Broadcasting Company; Justin Miller, president of the National Association of Broadcasters; Julius Seebach, former program director of C.B.S. and vice-president in charge of program operations for WOR (New York); Nathan Strauss, president of WMCA (New York); Oscar Turner, western manager of the R.C.A.–Victor Division; Bruce Robertson, associate editor of *Broadcasting;* James O. Weldon, consulting engineer and former chief of the Telecommunications Bureau of the

Office of War Information; Dwight Norris, assistant director of public relations of the New York, New Haven and Hartford Railroad and former top time salesman of N.B.C.; Jack Gould, radio editor of the *New York Times;* Edward Klauber, former executive vice-president of C.B.S. and associate director of the Office of War Information; Elmer Davis, outstanding commentator and former director of the Office of War Information; Mrs. Dorothy Lewis, co-ordinator of listener activity, National Association of Broadcasters; Don Francisco, vice-president of J. Walter Thompson; Thurman L. Barnard, vice-president of Compton Advertising, Inc.; William B. Benton, assistant secretary of state and founder and former chairman of the board of Benton and Bowles; F.C.C. Chairman Charles R. Denny and Commissioners Clifford J. Durr, E. K. Jett, Paul A. Walker, Ray C. Wakefield, and Rosel Hyde; Price Administrator Paul Porter, former F.C.C. chairman; Harry M. Plotkin, assistant general counsel; Edward Brecher, former special assistant to the chairman; Charles Clift, special assistant to Commissioner Durr; and Dallas W. Smythe, chief of the economics division of the F.C.C.

Also helpful to the author and his staff were Theodore C. Streibert, president of the Bamberger Broadcasting Corporation; George Biderman, associate editor of *Advertising Age*, and Robert Stephan, radio editor of the *Cleveland Plain Dealer*, who wrote detailed criticisms; Oscar Katz, associate director of research, Mae Dowell, director of general information, reference department, and Agnes Law, librarian, C.B.S.; Miriam Hoffmeir, program analyst, N.B.C.; Richard Puff, manager of research, M.B.S.; Edward F. Evans, research director, A.B.C.; J. R. Poppele, vice-president and chief engineer, WOR (New York), and Alberta Curtis, research director, WNEW (New York).

The author is particularly grateful to Dr. Robert D. Leigh, Director of the Commission on Freedom of the Press, for many hours of helpful criticism, suggestion, and discussion during the year and a half's labor of preparing the present report.

Finally, the author wishes to express his grateful appreciation to Miss Emilie Rashevsky and Mrs. Elizabeth Arnason of the Commission staff for their loyal and invaluable assistance in assembling the material for the report.

LLEWELLYN WHITE

NEW YORK CITY
February 15, 1947

HISTORY OF BROADCASTING:
Radio To Television
An Arno Press/New York Times Collection

Archer, Gleason L.
Big Business and Radio. 1939.

Archer, Gleason L.
History of Radio to 1926. 1938.

Arnheim, Rudolf.
Radio. 1936.

Blacklisting: Two Key Documents. 1952–1956.

Cantril, Hadley and Gordon W. Allport.
The Psychology of Radio. 1935.

Codel, Martin, editor.
Radio and Its Future. 1930.

Cooper, Isabella M.
Bibliography on Educational Broadcasting. 1942.

Dinsdale, Alfred.
First Principles of Television. 1932.

Dunlap, Orrin E., Jr.
Marconi: The Man and His Wireless. 1938.

Dunlap, Orrin E., Jr.
The Outlook for Television. 1932.

Fahie, J. J.
A History of Wireless Telegraphy. 1901.

Federal Communications Commission.
Annual Reports of the Federal Communications Commission.
1934/1935–1955.

Federal Radio Commission.
Annual Reports of the Federal Radio Commission. 1927–1933.

Frost, S. E., Jr.
Education's Own Stations. 1937.

Grandin, Thomas.
The Political Use of the Radio. 1939.

Harlow, Alvin.
Old Wires and New Waves. 1936.

Hettinger, Herman S.
A Decade of Radio Advertising. 1933.

Huth, Arno.
Radio Today: The Present State of Broadcasting. 1942.

Jome, Hiram L.
Economics of the Radio Industry. 1925.

Lazarsfeld, Paul F.
Radio and the Printed Page. 1940.

Lumley, Frederick H.
Measurement in Radio. 1934.

Maclaurin, W. Rupert.
Invention and Innovation in the Radio Industry. 1949.

Radio: Selected A.A.P.S.S. Surveys. 1929–1941.

Rose, Cornelia B., Jr.
National Policy for Radio Broadcasting. 1940.

Rothafel, Samuel L. and Raymond Francis Yates.
Broadcasting: Its New Day. 1925.

Schubert, Paul.
The Electric Word: The Rise of Radio. 1928.

Studies in the Control of Radio: Nos. 1–6. 1940–1948.

Summers, Harrison B., editor.
Radio Censorship. 1939.

Summers, Harrison B., editor.
A Thirty-Year History of Programs Carried on National Radio Networks in the United States, 1926–1956. 1958.

Waldrop, Frank C. and Joseph Borkin.
Television: A Struggle for Power. 1938.

White, Llewellyn.
The American Radio. 1947.

World Broadcast Advertising: Four Reports. 1930–1932.